Cooperative Teaching

Cooperative Teaching
Rebuilding and Sharing the Schoolhouse

SECOND EDITION

Jack J. Hourcade
Jeanne Bauwens

pro·ed
An International Publisher
8700 Shoal Creek Boulevard
Austin, Texas 78757-6897
800/897-3202   Fax 800/397-7633
www.proedinc.com

© 1995, 2003 by PRO-ED, Inc.
8700 Shoal Creek Boulevard
Austin, Texas 78757-6897
800/897-3202   Fax 800/397-7633
www.proedinc.com

Library of Congress Cataloging-in-Publication Data
Hourcade, Jack J.
   Cooperative teaching : rebuilding and sharing the schoolhouse / Jack J. Hourcade,
Jeanne Bauwens.—2nd ed.
      p.   cm.
   Prev. ed. main entry under Jeanne Bauwens.
   Includes bibliographical references and index.
   ISBN 0-89079-887-7
   1. Teaching teams.   2. Interpersonal relations.   3. Classroom management.
   I. Bauwens, Jeanne.   II. Title

LB1029.T4 B38   2003
371.14'8—dc21

                                                           2002069866

This book is designed in Goudy and Utopia.

Printed in the United States of America

1   2   3   4   5   6   7   8   9   10   06   05   04   03   02

Contents

Chapter 7   Moving In:
Resolving Issues in Cooperative Teaching ◆ 161

Chapter 8   Rearranging the Furniture:
Adjusting to Cooperative Teaching ◆ 183

Chapter 9 Reflecting on the Changes:
Considering Administrative Implications of Cooperative Teaching ◆ 219

Chapter 10 Having the Open House:
Sharing Cooperative Teaching ◆ 235

Foreword to the Second Edition

When Jeanne Bauwens and Jack Hourcade published their first edition of *Cooperative Teaching: Rebuilding the Schoolhouse for All Students*, the schools they sought to rebuild still had (in spite of legislative and social initiatives) an "us"/"them" mentality. "Us" referred to the teachers and students who most reflected middle-class America, while "them" referred to students coming from single-parent homes, living in poverty, or whose special academic, linguistic, or behavioral needs differentiated them from their peers. For the most part, teacher preparation programs focused on the type of students and curricula the teachers expected to teach (e.g., elementary education, special education, secondary education with content-specific emphasis).

In this second edition of their popular, widely used textbook, Hourcade and Bauwens have brought their prescient book up to date by addressing a much broader audience. Today's teachers see themselves in new ways. Their boundaries have expanded far beyond the student- and discipline-specific norms that were common a decade ago. The timely new chapter about electronic collaboration that Hourcade and Bauwens have added to the second edition helps teachers find like-minded peers with whom to collaborate. New networks of teachers, many of whom may never meet face-to-face, can rebuild schoolhouses together, transcending the boundaries of space, time—and pessimists in the classrooms next door.

To be effective, many teachers must revisit and revise core assumptions for teaching students in their classes whose life experiences have not been, nor ever will be, typical. Hourcade and Bauwens have provided an excellent resource for such rethinking. It is a text that will be a valuable, well-organized push-off point for beginners, and an accessible, thought-provoking book for teachers who have been in the field for decades. For school administrators, this book can be a blueprint for reexamining the fundamental assumptions that shape their schools.

If the goals of this book became commonplace, you could imagine the comfortable, clean, teachers' lounge of the future. In that airy, inviting room, conversation (over fresh coffee, doughnuts, and an ever-present assortment of juicy fruit) would include teachers talking constructively about all their students. The language of "yours" and "mine" would never be heard as teachers discuss the students they share. The worn school copy of *Cooperative Teaching*, part of the up-to-date teachers' library in the lounge would be read regularly. A seasoned teacher could be heard to say, "You know, last night I used the guidelines in that chapter on electronic collaboration to join a new electronic mailing list, and I got some great ideas!" Such an ideal is not beyond the reach of dedicated teachers and school administrators.

Many experienced educators remember the altruistic instincts that first brought them into the field of education: "To make a difference," "To encourage and inspire," and "To prepare the next generation." Connecting these goals to practices that will address student needs outside of the experience (and comfort zone) of many teachers requires rethinking. This book can help structure that rethinking.

Enjoy the journey Hourcade and Bauwens have provided for you in this new edition. Combine this book with your enthusiasm, your talent, and your skills to transform our schools to benefit *all* students.

— Sharon F. Cramer, PhD
Professor, Exceptional Education Department,
Buffalo State College, New York
Author of *Collaboration: A Success Strategy
for Special Educators*, Allyn & Bacon, 1998

Foreword to the First Edition

The world of remedial and special education is changing. In special education, the long march from isolation to integration that began before the passage of P.L. 94-142 (Education for All Handicapped Children Act) has placed ever-increasing numbers of students with disabilities in general education classes for most or all of their academic day. There is increasing emphasis on full inclusion, which extends mainstreaming to students who in the past would not have been seen in general education classes, including students with the most severe disabilities. On a parallel track, Chapter 1/ Title 1 programs increasingly have moved away from pull-out models toward the use of in-class models and other innovative methods to meet students' needs within the heterogeneous class.

Each of these trends creates opportunities for at-risk children to take their rightful place in the inclusive school and community of their peers. At the same time, each presents teachers and administrators with challenges. How can the needs of all students be met in very heterogeneous classes?

One answer to this is cooperative teaching, a teaming approach between general educators and special educators or other support services providers. Cooperative teaching lets educators work flexibly to enable all students to receive the instruction they need to succeed in a high-expectations curriculum. Cooperative teaching solves many problems in the integration of efforts between general education teachers and support services providers, and it allows each educator to contribute unique skills to facilitate the education of all.

Yet cooperative teaching has its own difficulties. How can partners in cooperative teaching coordinate their efforts? How can they build supportive relationships? How can they deal with scheduling? How can they find time for planning? How can teachers and administrators evaluate the success of their cooperative teaching?

These and many other questions are answered in these pages. Jeanne Bauwens and Jack Hourcade have worked for many years helping schools implement cooperative teaching, and they have assisted many educators in developing and refining collaborative skills. They have seen the problems as well as the potential of cooperative teaching and offer educators moving toward cooperative teaching a practical, thoughtful, and down-to-earth guide to planning, implementation, and self-evaluation. This book provides a wealth of information, experience, and wisdom for schools undertaking reform of their programs for at-risk students. The journey toward cooperative teaching is not one educators should take alone. With this book as a companion, they should experience success in building schools in which all students can achieve their full potential.

—*Robert E. Slavin*
Johns Hopkins University

Preface

At the beginning of the 21st century the nation's schools are the topic of intense national debate. At the core of this discussion are such basic issues as the effectiveness with which the schools are responding to the needs of the great student diversity that characterizes contemporary classrooms.

It is perhaps more accurate to speak of "diverse diversities," because students are multidimensional. Student diversities include linguistic diversity, ethnic and cultural diversity, academic diversity, socioeconomic diversity, and behavioral diversity. The nation's schools have never experienced greater student diversity in typical classrooms. For the schools, the primary question emerging from this student diversity is this: "How can educators best respond to the variety of needs these very different students bring to the classroom?"

Answers to this question are as diverse as the students themselves. Some argue that the nation should in effect abandon its public schools, moving to a voucher system where students attend private schools. Others suggest that technology will save education because computers and the Internet will be best able to respond to the diverse needs of students today. Our position is that the answer lies in changing the ways in which teachers work, moving teachers from isolation to collaboration. Teachers can do their best work for students when they work together, not by themselves.

Given the substantial attention that student diversity in general education classrooms has received, surprisingly little attention has been given to diversity of the educators working in those same classrooms. Although students with very different characteristics and needs are learning the value of working together in cooperative learning groups, in too many schools educators continue to work as detached and solitary individuals. In a world characterized by collaboration, the model of one educator teaching in one classroom for the entirety of the day is no longer appropriate. In more and more effective schools, professional collaboration is surfacing as a new paradigm for education. Cooperative teaching is at the forefront of this emergence of professional collaboration.

In cooperative teaching, two educators combine their complementary sets of professional knowledge and skills and work simultaneously in general education classrooms. In this second edition of our book, we hope to continue to support educators who are looking for a more effective way to better serve *all* students in their classrooms, while also reinvigorating and revitalizing themselves personally and professionally.

As in the first edition, in this second edition we continue our previous organizational analogy of a home remodeling project. In doing so we certainly hope to provide the basic theoretical and factual information underlying cooperative teaching. However, our emphasis remains on providing practical, field-tested ideas and strategies to help practitioners effectively incorporate cooperative teaching into their professional lives.

ABOUT THE SECOND EDITION: NEW FEATURES AND COVERAGE

Since we first began writing about cooperative teaching in the late 1980s, we have seen an upsurge of interest in the topic. When we first prepared this book in the early 1990s, it was a bit unusual for us to come across educators who had implemented cooperative teaching. Since that time, it has become increasingly commonplace at more and more schools. In fact, professional collaboration has become a required competency for teachers in many districts.

Each chapter in the book has been substantially updated to incorporate new and emerging knowledge and skills for even more effective cooperative teaching. One of the most dramatic changes in education since the first edition has been the rapid growth of technology in the schools, and indeed throughout society. To respond to this development, we have included an entirely new chapter, Chapter 5, "Installing the Wiring: Electronic Collaboration." This chapter explains how educators can collaborate with each other electronically even when physically separated. Specific coverage in this new chapter includes audio- and videoconferencing, e-mail, bulletin boards, electronic mailing lists, and the Internet, as well as an activity in which the reader can take a self-examination quiz to determine readiness for electronic collaboration.

ORGANIZATION OF THE SECOND EDITION

Chapter 1, "Surveying the Situation: An Overview of Collaboration," reviews the great changes that have occurred in the nation's schools in the last decade, and the need for equivalent change in how teachers go about their work. This chapter also includes an overview of collaboration, explaining the growing necessity for such an approach in the contemporary educational system.

Chapter 2, "Reviewing the Options: Types of School Collaboration," explains the many different approaches to collaboration in the schools, distinguishes between indirect and direct collaboration, and notes advantages and disadvantages of each approach to collaboration.

Chapter 3, "Developing the Blueprints: Planning for Cooperative Teaching," explains one especially promising approach to collaboration, cooperative teaching, and outlines the necessary elements for successful cooperative teaching. This chapter also contains new coverage of universal design for learning (UDL) principles, and how they can be effectively incorporated into cooperative teaching.

Chapter 4, "Getting Construction Under Way: Implementing Cooperative Teaching," discusses the issues of time, scheduling, and administrative support, and offers a number of suggestions on how to handle these concerns. A new section titled "Pictures of Possibilities" provides 24 verbal and graphic descriptions of cooperative teaching situations that focus on general educators, special educators, and paraeducators working in cooperative teaching arrangements in both elementary and secondary settings.

Chapter 5, "Installing the Wiring: Electronic Collaboration," is a new chapter that describes professional communication and collaboration through the use of technology.

Chapter 6, "Inspecting the Job: Evaluating Cooperative Teaching," includes new content explaining the difference between evaluating and coaching, provides an overview of program evaluation, outlines practical procedures for identifying potential areas of impact of cooperative teaching, and explains how each might be evaluated to determine program effectiveness. The chapter also includes a new rubric to evaluate the effectiveness of a cooperative teaching program.

Chapter 7, "Moving In: Resolving Issues in Cooperative Teaching," identifies the interpersonal skills and issues critical to successful implementation of cooperative teaching, including the concept of the Emotional Bank Account, and offers ways to minimize problems emerging from these new professional relationships.

Chapter 8, "Rearranging the Furniture: Adjusting to Cooperative Teaching," gives an overview of change and how people respond to change, identifies possible conflicts as school professionals begin cooperative teaching, and supplies a variety of practical strategies for conflict resolution.

Chapter 9, "Reflecting on the Changes: Considering Administrative Implications of Cooperative Teaching," notes how the "nature of change" is changing today, and identifies the critical roles that principals and other change facilitators play in bringing about substantive change in the schools. The chapter also discusses leadership, and offers practical ways in which administrative support for change can be elicited and demonstrated.

Finally, Chapter 10, "Having the Open House: Sharing Cooperative Teaching," explains why it is so important that the results of cooperative teaching be shared with others, and includes a number of ways in which this might be done, including a new and substantial discussion of electronic dissemination.

In each chapter a variety of practical examples are included to illustrate fundamental concepts. In addition, field-tested reader activities are included at the end of each chapter. These activities enable the reader to engage in self-analysis in preparation for moving into cooperative teaching.

ACKNOWLEDGMENTS

The main theme of this book is that there is more power in professionals working together than separately. Thus it is only fitting that we acknowledge the many individuals who have helped us prepare this book. In particular we would like to thank the literally thousands of educators with whom we have worked throughout the world who have developed and implemented cooperative teaching in their schools. The courage to take a chance and change in a most fundamental way is the single most important quality we admire and respect in these professionals.

We also would like to acknowledge the encouragement and support of our colleagues at Boise State University and elsewhere. Their willingness to listen to and provide feedback on new ideas exemplifies the collaborative spirit.

As always, the staff at PRO-ED have maintained an optimal mix of professionalism and friendliness throughout the book's development. The help and encouragement from Jim Patton and Chris Ann Worsham are especially appreciated. The wonderful illustrations by Jason Crosier are a great addition to this second edition.

The Council for Exceptional Children has long been an advocate for collaboration, especially through cooperative teaching. Their encouragement and support for cooperative teaching has served to bring this approach to collaboration to the attention of thousands of educators.

On a more personal note, Jeanne would like to thank her husband, Laurence, for his constant and powerful support in all areas of life. Jack would like to thank his companion, Holly Anderson, for sharing her unique spark of life with him, and also thank his son, Michael, for helping him to understand the power that relationships have to mold the soul.

Surveying the Situation:
An Overview of Collaboration

*Imagination is the means to make images and to move
them about inside one's head in new arrangements.*
—Jacob Bronowski

Throughout the 1990s the thriving American economy was good finan-
cially for many businesses, individuals, and families. Some people and
businesses used their financial prosperity to remodel old buildings, transforming
them to better meet present and future needs. Like old buildings in need of remodeling, America's schools are hearing cries for structural and systemic "remodeling,"
"reform," "restructuring," or "renewal," so that they, too, better meet present and
future needs.

More and more educators, as well as laypersons, are concluding that the present
structure of the educational system is unable to meet the present and future needs of
its users. The high profile of education in the 2000 presidential election, and the

questions raised by both sides about the function of the nation's schools, summarized the sense of many that the educational status quo is inadequate. The widespread calls for dramatic and fundamental changes in the way the educational system is structured are attributable in large part to a variety of substantial developments in society, developments that are reflected in the schools.

In terms of cultural and linguistic diversity of students, the state of California may be the best example of what America is likely to look and sound like in the future. In California in 1997, students with limited English proficiency comprised 25% of the total school population, up from 15% less than 10 years earlier (California Department of Education, 1997). In fact, the majority of California's schoolchildren are members of a minority group. Nationally, demographers project that all but two states (Arkansas and Mississippi) will see an increase in their minority enrollments between now and 2015 ("Minority Groups," 2000).

Such growth in minority group populations is becoming more common throughout the nation's schools. By the mid-1990s, enrollment of White students in the nation's 10 largest central city school districts ranged from a high of 31% in San Diego to a low of 6% in Detroit (Orfield, Bachmeier, James, & Eitle, 1997). In several states, including California, Hawaii, New Mexico, Texas, and Mississippi, students in minority groups actually constitute a majority of the school population (U.S. Department of Education, 1996). The nation's fifth largest district, Broward County in Florida, reported in the year 2000 that its students spoke a total of 52 different languages. The number of students there identified as having limited fluency in English has doubled in the 6-year period from 1993–1994 to 2000 ("Mixed Needs," 2000). The growth of racial and cultural diversity in the nation's schools is likely to continue for the foreseeable future.

Children living in one-parent homes or in poverty also present significant challenges to educators. These two conditions often coexist. In 1997, 59.1% of children in households headed by a single female lived in poverty (U.S. Census Bureau, 1998). Poverty and its correlates of malnourishment and substance abuse predispose children to the development of a variety of behavior and learning problems (T. E. C. Smith, Polloway, Patton, & Dowdy, 2001, pp. 355–356). During the 1990s, the number of children living in families of the working poor (families in which one parent is working but the household income is still below the poverty line) grew dramatically ("High Poverty," 2000). By the late 1990s, almost 20% of America's schoolchildren lived in poverty (U.S. Census Bureau, 1998).

The number of schoolchildren in poverty increases dramatically for students from cultural minority backgrounds, with 36.8% of children from Hispanic backgrounds and 37.2% of children from African American backgrounds living in such circumstances (U.S. Census Bureau, 1998). Concentrated poverty in schools is associated with lower achievement for both poor and nonpoor students who attend such schools. In addition, teachers in such schools tend to be the least prepared to teach ("High

Poverty," 2000). As a result, the ongoing rise in the nation's schools in the number of students on Individualized Education Programs (IEPs) in special education is far from surprising, though no less challenging.

The challenges presented to the schools are further complicated as inclusive placements of students with disabilities into general education classrooms becomes the norm. This results in even greater diversity in student ability and achievement levels in the nation's classrooms. During the 1995–1996 academic year, 45% of the nation's elementary school students on IEPs received the entirety of their educational programs in regular classrooms, while another 29% were pulled out into separate programs for a small portion of their school day. Thus nearly three fourths of students with disabilities received most or all of their educational programs in general education classrooms. This trend is likely to continue to grow in the foreseeable future (U.S. Department of Education, 1998). The roles for both general and special educators who work with students who have disabilities are changing, and little is being done systemically to address these changing roles (Sack, 2000).

The tremendous explosion in student heterogeneity is causing educators to confront one basic issue: the increasing mismatch between the ways that schools historically have taught students, and what these diverse students require from the schools in order to be successful. The training and experience that veteran teachers possess often are outdated for today's classrooms (Sack, 2000).

Traditionally, such programs as special education and related services, bilingual education, and programs for economically disadvantaged students targeted specific subgroups of the student population. These students then received segregated support outside of the general education classroom. This educational structure, however, has come under considerable criticism (e.g., Meese, 2001, pp. 44–46).

The rapid increase in student diversity in many classrooms and schools has reached the point where it is simply no longer practical to pull out students of varied ability levels, cultural groups, and linguistic backgrounds. In addition, the fundamental efficacy of pullout programs has come into question (e.g., Vaughn, Moody, & Schumm, 1998; Walther-Thomas, Korinek, McLaughlin, & Williams, 2000). Finally, such segregatory practices are being criticized in terms of ethical considerations (e.g., Stainback, Stainback, & Ayres, 1996, p. 33). Indeed, the 1997 federal reauthorization of the Individuals with Disabilities Education Act (IDEA) explicitly required that students be given access to the general education curriculum within the context of age-appropriate general education settings as the first phase of their Individualized Educational Program. In addition, under Section 504 of the Rehabilitation Act of 1973, public schools are expected to make "reasonable accommodations" in curriculum and instructional procedures for the many students who manifest significant disabling conditions but are not eligible for special education services under IDEA.

Today, the question is not whether students with diverse backgrounds *should* be included in the general education classroom. It is *how* inclusive instruction might be provided most effectively for all students, including those with diverse backgrounds and learning aptitude. Rather than describing some students as "at risk," it may be more useful to instead conceptualize some *educators* as "at risk" because of the difficulties many teachers face as they try to provide appropriate educational programs to diverse students. For example, a 1998 survey by the U.S. Department of Education found that only one in five public school teachers said they felt prepared to address the needs of diverse students ("Minority Groups," 2000).

One way to conceptualize the traditional role of support services in the educational system is to consider the nation's schools as a house where students and educators live. Traditionally, some students did not seem to fit well in the schoolhouse (for example, they were too big or too small, or they behaved in ways that disturbed the efficient and quiet functioning of the household). In these cases the education system constructed a variety of makeshift add-on arrangements to avoid a massive remodeling of the schoolhouse itself.

To continue with this analogy, the people in charge of the schoolhouse initially refused even basic entry to many of these students (e.g., T. E. C. Smith et al., 2001). Even when they were admitted, often these students were placed in the equivalent of a garage attached to the main schoolhouse or in a small house built just for these students that was separate from the main schoolhouse. (Actually, in some cases this analogy comes quite close to the literal reality.)

In any case, these segregated arrangements allowed educators to leave the main schoolhouse unchanged. Students who did not fit perfectly into the preexisting schoolhouse simply were taken out of that structure and placed in one of these separate structures.

As student populations become more culturally, linguistically, academically, and behaviorally diverse, the inadequacies of these makeshift detached school arrangements have become more and more obvious. The traditional practice of providing stopgap separate arrangements for the growing numbers of diverse students who do not fit the traditional schoolhouse cannot respond effectively to their needs (T. E. C. Smith et al., 2001).

When homeowners find that their home no longer meets their needs, they have two options: to search for a new home that does fit those needs, or to remodel their old home so that it fits these new needs. The old schoolhouse that may have served well in the past simply does not meet the present needs of the more diverse educational family that lives there today. Although the education family and its needs have changed dramatically over the last few decades, the schoolhouse has remained largely unchanged. However, unlike homeowners, educators do not have the option of finding another educational house into which to move. Their only choice is to remodel the schoolhouse.

> Schools are part of the larger national fabric of institutions. There has been a general erosion of faith in government institutions, period. So maybe there's been some loss of faith [in the public schools], but I think that core faith that Americans have about education is still there. People believe deeply in the ability of schools to solve societal problems and to help children reach their potential. (O'Neil, 2000, p. 9)

Perhaps one way to think about improving schools is for educators to see themselves as educational architects and remodelers. Before beginning a remodeling project, an architect surveys the construction site and analyzes the present structures, including their current capabilities and the emerging functions the structure must support in the future. The results of this analysis then guide the subsequent remodeling efforts.

Similarly, educators must begin their rebuilding of the schoolhouse by first surveying the existing requirements, functions, and structures of the schoolhouse. This includes a comprehensive identification of the needs of the various members of the educational family, an examination of the structures presently in place, and a review of their present and future use. Once this information is known, a determination of how best to remodel the schoolhouse then can be made.

OVERVIEW OF COLLABORATION

Historically, teachers and other school professionals have worked isolated from each other. The traditional organizational structure of one teacher per one class of students prohibited educators from participating in the sort of collaboration that characterizes the productive and efficient contemporary workplace (Fullan & Hargreaves, 1991). Thus it is not surprising that much of the present-day effort to remodel the educational schoolhouse centers on the establishment of structures that facilitate greater professional collaboration.

During a home remodeling project, a variety of craftsmen arrive on the scene with different sets of skills, tools, and equipment. If workers present on any given day do not have the specific skills, materials, or tools necessary to do a particular job, then a specialist must be called.

Alternatively, the various jobs that are required in a remodeling project may be seen by many of the workers as being someone else's responsibility. In fact, at times union or governmental regulations require one worker to stand aside while a specialist is called in to do a task that the already present workers could have done easily.

Similarly, whenever a job in the schools (e.g., educating a particular student) was out of a narrow range of "normalcy," the general educator traditionally surrendered much responsibility for teaching the student to a specialist (i.e., the educator referred the student to a specialized support services provider). This approach is based upon several presumptions. The first of these presumptions is that there are two distinct types or groups of students: typical and atypical (e.g., disabled, non–English speaking, or similarly atypical). The second presumption holds that school professionals can reliably distinguish between the two groups. The last presumption is that there are two qualitatively distinct sets of instructional procedures, curricula, and materials, each of which is appropriate for one group and inappropriate for the other (e.g., Lovitt, 1993).

However, each of these presumptions is at best questionable. At worst, they are simply wrong (Friend & Bursuck, 1996). In addition, the simple inefficiency of such an approach is causing educators to look for an alternative way to go about their work of educating the nation's schoolchildren.

In short, what is required for many educators to be successful in their work is a higher degree of professional sharing (e.g., Pugach & Johnson, 2002). This includes sharing educational tools and techniques, sharing professional knowledge and skills, and, most important, sharing responsibility for all students. The best way to achieve this sharing is through collaboration.

COLLABORATION

Collaboration is an ongoing style of professional interaction in which people voluntarily engage in shared

- program planning,
- program implementation,
- program evaluation, and
- overall program accountability.

Most fundamental, collaboration is a way for people to interact. It is not a process, or an end in and of itself. Collaboration is a way to think about and structure shared planning and working relationships.

The potential of collaboration to enhance professional productivity can be ascertained by reviewing significant inventions of the 20th century. Modern aviation technology, personal computers, and feature-length films all were produced by collaborative efforts. This work occurred in environments that not only respected such initiatives but fostered an ethic of sharing (Bennis & Biederman, 1997). In the schools, collaboration is based on the shared and ongoing commitment of two or more professionals to joint ownership of, and joint obligation to, a larger part of a school's educational responsibilities than either professional individually had assumed in the past.

There is not a single unique approach called "collaboration." Instead, there are a number of ways in which collaborative efforts might be structured. In the remodeling of the schoolhouse, collaboration can be thought of as the basic organizing theme of a large set of possible blueprints for the project. The particular blueprint or approach to collaboration that is finally selected depends on the unique needs and requirements of that particular schoolhouse and its residents. However, all effective approaches to professional collaboration share several basic features.

BASIC FEATURES OF COLLABORATION

Self-Examination and Commitment to Change

A fundamental feature of collaboration is the willingness of the involved educators to, in essence, start from scratch. Educational collaborators must

- be ready to comprehensively evaluate themselves and the present system;
- be prepared to discard many of their old practices and procedures that are nonfunctional or irrelevant for contemporary educational programs; and
- be active in seeking out or developing, implementing, and evaluating new and more effective procedures.

For example, assume that a home remodeling project has resulted in a completely redone and modernized kitchen. Before the remodeling project began, the people in the house probably had developed well-established and habitual roles over the years in joint tasks such as cooking and cleanup. After the remodeling, they may find that the changed physical arrangement of the kitchen makes their old routines inefficient and inappropriate. But they also find it difficult to give up their old roles and practices. The resulting problems could have been lessened if the homeowners had discussed beforehand the inevitable need to make changes in their routines.

Similarly, as school personnel move into collaborative arrangements, they must make similar adaptations to the new structures and features of the remodeled schoolhouse. The process of self-examination and commitment to change involves a three-phase sequence of adjustment. These phases are as follows:

1. willingness to change
2. identification of current practices and needed procedures
3. implementation of necessary changes

The roles and requirements inherent in collaboration demand that educators make fundamental changes in the way they work. People are generally reluctant to accept changes in the professional status quo because they are comfortable. For most people change is frustrating and uncomfortable (Brant, 1993). Initially, some school professionals may refuse to recognize that changes in the way schools function might even be useful, much less necessary. The willingness to accept the changes needed to improve schools' abilities to meet the needs of all students is the first stage in this process of self-examination and adjustment. Professionals unwilling to recognize that substantive changes are necessary are unlikely to be successful collaborators.

People don't resist change. People resist being changed.
—O'Neil (2000, p. 7)

After accepting that fundamental changes are needed, the involved personnel must then identify the established practices and beliefs that are no longer appropriate. This involves facing the fact that old and dear methods that have become second nature may need to be discarded. For example, educators only recently have begun to accept that pullout programs (in which students with even mild disabilities are taken from the general education classroom to a special education resource room) may not be the most efficacious way to develop academic skills in these students (e.g., Walther-Thomas et al., 2000, p. 18).

Finally, the changes must be translated into actual practice. School professionals may be willing to go through abstract intellectual exercises to identify the possible changes that collaboration will require. However, in the absence of personal and systemic commitments to implementation of these changes in practical settings, success is unlikely.

Sharing

One of the most critical features of collaboration is sharing. Traditionally, educators have worked as self-contained instructional units. That is, within their individual classrooms, educators historically have had great autonomy (Lortie, 1975). The quality of education provided was determined largely by each individual educator. Each educator had almost complete responsibility for the students in his or her class, and almost no responsibility for any other students. The collaborative structures that are evolving in schools throughout the world require school professionals to adopt a very different philosophy, one in which all educators are responsible for all students.

In collaboration, sharing occurs in a number of ways. The involved professionals must share a similar set of attitudes, beliefs, and values about schools, teaching and learning, and students. Walther-Thomas et al. (2000) suggested that collaborative partners must share a common view of what "should be" for their school. In the absence of a high degree of agreement concerning such questions as the fundamental role of schools, what, how, and where students should be taught, and the desired outcomes of the educational process, collaboration will not be as effective as it might be.

The collaborators also must share responsibility for the decisions that must be made and their outcomes. All activities are owned jointly. Similarly, accountability for the outcomes of those activities is shared. Problems that occur also are shared. Such sharing is inherent in the belief that all students in the school are the responsibility of all educators.

In truly collaborative efforts, resources also are shared, including time, money, materials, and, especially, the skills and ideas of the involved professionals. The belief that all aspects of the educational system (including students, responsibilities, and resources) are "ours" instead of "mine" or "yours" is fundamental to the development of true collaboration.

It is important to make a clear distinction between sharing and equality. Although sharing is ongoing through any sort of collaboration, it does not imply that the educational tasks and responsibilities always are equal. Indeed, at any given time there likely will be some imbalance, with one school professional assuming a relatively greater proportion of these responsibilities than the other. The differentiation and identification of roles should be guided by specific program and student needs and by the unique competencies and strengths each professional brings to his or her work, not by the need for a superficial appearance of equality.

Volunteering

Administrative mandates play an important role in establishing direction for organizations. Given the power that collaboration has to dramatically improve teaching and learning in the schools, there is a danger that administrators arbitrarily may impose a collaborative structure upon a school. Although such an administrative temptation is understandable, the nature of collaboration requires voluntary commitment of the involved educators. Without voluntary commitment, any resulting collaboration will be collaborative in name only.

As noted by futurist Michael Fullan (1997, p. 35), one cannot mandate what truly matters. The more complex a change is, the less it can brought about through force. If collaboration is arbitrarily imposed without voluntary commitment, the educational status quo is likely to remain largely unchanged beneath a thin veneer. Such superficial change is unlikely to be long lasting.

Valuing

One limitation of traditional educational programs is that educators historically have worked in isolation, largely unaware of their colleagues' knowledge and skills. As collaboration becomes more common, educators will be working together more intimately than ever before. In so doing they will likely see the contributions of their colleagues as valuable, even if different from their own. Educators will likely see that the varying sets of skills and competencies contributed by all school professionals gain greater educational power in combination.

The valuing of one's partner grows over time, as each participant gains experience with the other. Each must feel comfortable giving the other feedback and suggestions, including the disclosure of thoughts and feelings that normally one does not share. Each partner must trust that the other will appreciate this openness, and will reciprocate. If an educator does not or cannot value suggestions and input from a collaborator, then any collaboration will occur at best on only a surface level.

THE NATURE OF CHANGE: A FORCE-FIELD ANALYSIS

Almost any individual or group periodically encounters suggestions or proposals for change. Sometimes these changes happen; sometimes they do not. Why does change occur in some cases and not in others?

As educators ponder changing the way they go about their work, and specifically consider the changes inherent in moving into collaboration, they may want to consider a force-field analysis of the acceptance of collaboration ("Force-Field Analysis," 2000). Specifically, there are "facilitating forces" that move educators toward collaboration, and "restraining forces" that inhibit movement (see Figure 1.1).

Facilitating Forces

Legal Pressures

The 1997 revisions of the Individuals with Disabilities Education Act (IDEA) require that students with disabilities have access to the general education curriculum (D. D. Smith, 2001). This mandate weakens the traditional separate and segregated self-contained structure of traditional special education programs. The Individualized Education Program for each student with a disability must now address access to and participation in the general education curriculum, and must note why a student cannot participate in the general curriculum at a particular point in time (Project Forum, 1999). These new legal requirements are compelling special and general educators to work together more closely than ever before.

Parent Pressures

Many parents of students with disabilities are requesting more inclusive placements while maintaining special education services. In these situations general and special educators must coordinate their educational services.

Growing Societal Concerns

In 1983, the release of *A Nation at Risk* (National Commission on Excellence in Education) served to remind many professionals and laypersons alike of the large and

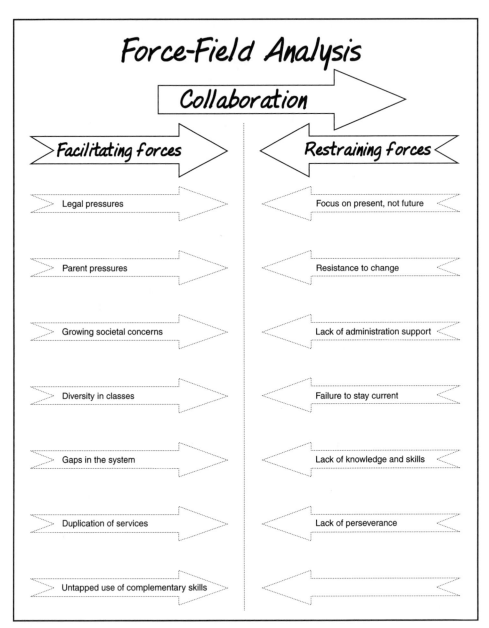

Figure 1.1 A force-field analysis of educational collaboration.

growing numbers of America's schoolchildren who increasingly were being ill-served by the traditional educational structures of the schools. These concerns continued through the 1990s and led many politicians to implement such policies as (a) high-stakes testing for students in order to move from grade to grade and ultimately to graduate, and (b) teacher accountability standards. In the 2000 presidential election, arguably the single issue that received the greatest attention from the candidates and the electorate was education, despite the historic reluctance of the federal government to become involved in what traditionally has been a state issue, and is evidence of society's growing concerns about the effectiveness of the nation's schools.

Diversity in Classes

As noted in the opening pages of this chapter, student diversity (language, ethnicity and cultural background, behavior, academic and intellectual aptitude) has been growing rapidly in the nation's classrooms. Increasingly, classrooms where minority groups are the majority are becoming the norm. The additional demands that this tremendous student diversity places on teachers is making it harder for the one classroom–one teacher model to be successful.

Gaps in the System

For much of the past 30 years students with disabilities were provided specialized services in pullout programs. General education teachers were responsible for typical students, and special education teachers had equivalent responsibility for students with disabilities. However, growing evidence suggests that most students do not benefit from this out-of-class support model (e.g., Walther-Thomas et al., 2000, p. 18). The disjointed nature of this model results in gaps in curriculum and instruction, making learning even more difficult for these struggling students. In fact, this approach has been suggested to be a "Solomon-like compromise by educators which cleaves in twain the educational life of children" (Bunch, 1997, p. 16).

Duplication of Services

A related problem inherent in this disjointed approach is that whereas some educational services may be overlooked, others may be duplicated. Unbeknownst to each other, a general educator, a special educator, and perhaps even another specialist may all be attempting to use the same materials and instructional techniques to teach the same content to the same student.

Untapped Use of Complementary Skills

The traditional separation of general educators from special educators and other specialized school professionals means that students never experience the power inherent in the combined skill sets that these professionals might bring to the general education classroom. When school professionals are separated, there is no chance for them to learn from each other. Each type of educator often possesses specialized skills that are complementary to other types of educators. However, unless given the opportunity to work together, they will be unable to share these skills with their colleagues (Bauwens & Hourcade, 1997).

As powerful as these facilitating forces are in moving educators toward collaborative models, other powerful factors serve as restraining forces, inhibiting the adoption of change.

Restraining Forces

Focus on Present, Not Future

President John F. Kennedy once said, "Some men see things as they are and ask, 'Why?' I see things that never were, and ask, 'Why not?'" Unfortunately, many educators fail to even see things as they are and ask, "Why?" The often-overwhelming practical difficulties in simply keeping up with the day-to-day demands of teaching prevent many from thinking very far beyond, "What will I do tomorrow?" It is impossible for many educators to think how they might move into collaboration when such a simple task as, for example, ensuring that there are enough classroom materials for all students seems impossible.

Resistance to Change

As is the case with almost any group of people, school professionals often resist change, even when the need to change appears obvious. Change represents more work (at least initially), and is characterized by uncertainty. Many prefer the "devil one knows" of working alone to the "devil one doesn't know" of collaboration. In addition, the physical and professional isolation of most educators within their own classrooms seems to facilitate resistance to educational innovation (Lortie, 1975).

Lack of Administration Support

One powerful factor consistently associated with the success or failure of such proposed school changes as moving toward greater collaboration is the support, or lack thereof, of school administrators. Arguably the most influential individual here is the school principal, who is in a unique position to articulate the school mission, promote a particular instructional climate, and monitor and influence instruction (Krug, 1992).

Most staff members within an organization lack time to deal with planning for the future, because their time is consumed with taking care of day-to-day demands. It is the responsibility of a leader to take care of tomorrow (Barker, 1999). Without substantial administrative leadership and support for systems transformation, few substantial changes toward collaboration can be expected to last or to succeed.

Failure To Stay Current with Professional Developments

An ongoing issue in education is the professional isolation of teachers. The physical isolation of teachers in the "egg crate" structure of schooling (Lortie, 1975) prevents teachers from working together, from learning from each other, and from improving their collective expertise as an educational community (Fullan & Hargreaves, 1991). Although school districts should spend 10% of their budgets on professional development for teachers, they typically spend only about 1% (National Staff Development Council, 2000). Combined with the negligible support most districts offer teachers for professional development, many school professionals are unaware of the magnitude of change toward increased collaboration in the nation's schools.

Lack of Knowledge and Skills

According to a long-standing educational truism, most teachers teach essentially as they were taught. A recent survey of 2,000 special and general educators found that veteran teachers' training and experience often are outdated for the new collaborative roles they are expected to assume in the contemporary American school. In addition, new teachers also reported little training in these skills (Sack, 2000). Few teacher preparation programs provide coursework specific to collaboration. As a result, most school professionals do not begin their careers prepared for collaboration. They lack knowledge about both the benefits that collaboration offers, as well as effective implementation strategies. Even if educators are interested in collaboration and understand its advantages, they do not know how to begin.

Lack of Perseverance

Put bluntly, being an agent of change is hard work. It takes much more energy to bring about such substantial school change as collaboration than it does to inhibit such development. Thus, even when change agents begin with initially large reserves of excitement and energy about their task, over time they become worn down. Without ongoing administrative support, the change effort withers and dies.

The restraining factors that inhibit the widespread adoption and implementation of collaborative structures in the nation's schools can be collapsed into three general types of barriers. These are (1) attitudinal barriers, (2) structural barriers, and (3) competency barriers (National Board of Employment, Education and Training Schools Council, 1992). Each of these may be subdivided further as shown in Table 1.1.

TABLE 1.1
Types of Barriers to Collaboration

Attitudinal	Structural	Competency
• Power	• Administrative	• Knowledge and skills
• Tradition	• Legal	
• Cynicism	• Paperwork	
	• Time, scheduling, and workload	

Attitudinal Barriers

The first significant potential general barrier is the attitudes of the involved parties concerning change, especially change toward collaboration. Attitudinal barriers include such issues as power, tradition, and cynicism.

Historically, educators have had great autonomy and personal power in their individual instructional programs. Collaboration, however, asks educators to give up some degree of this professional autonomy and independence.

For example, support services providers may fear that, as they move into collaboration in the general classroom, they will lose professional status, with their role becoming the equivalent of an instructional aide. It is not unusual to hear educators say that they agree with collaboration in principle but disagree with it in actual practice in their own programs. The underlying reason may be an unwillingness to share educational responsibilities and duties, accompanied by an unstated but deeply felt fear of losing power. The reluctance of educators to share power presents a formidable barrier to the implementation of collaboration.

Tradition also carries great weight in the schools. To acknowledge that things should be changed is also to acknowledge that things at present are less than perfect. Proposed changes require educators to abandon familiar and comfortable routines, and, at least initially, usually results in disruption, discomfort, and possibly more work. Because each school essentially develops its own blueprints for collaboration as it evolves, it is not possible to predict exactly what the final structure will look like. A fear of the unknown and the comfort of tradition are powerful inhibitors of change.

Over the years many experienced school professionals have seen educational proposals discussed with great excitement, implemented with much fanfare in the schools, and then result in unfavorable outcomes before finally coming to premature and ignominious ends. After a history of such experiences, many educators develop great cynicism regarding subsequent proposed innovations.

Structural Barriers

Structural barriers include obstacles such as administrative systems, legal considerations, paperwork, and time, scheduling, and workload. Most schools are built around the concept of one educator having primary (if not sole) responsibility for some 25 to 30 students, either for an entire school day at the elementary level, or for 1-hour blocks at the secondary level. Schools were not designed to accommodate programs in which two (or more) school professionals maintain shared responsibility for students.

Over the years, the educational system has become encumbered with various laws and regulations concerning the delivery and documentation of specialized educational services, especially to students with disabilities. These regulations were developed to ensure that students with disabilities and other special needs actually received the services to which they were entitled. However, these laws have resulted in the untenable position of some educators being allowed to teach only those students who have been found to be legally eligible for specialized services. Other students with equivalent educational needs who fail to meet eligibility criteria guidelines are denied this assistance.

The present administrative structure guiding special education policies and procedures in essence says that only some students are entitled to additional assistance to meet their needs. This position is incompatible with fundamental educational ethics, and conflicts with a central philosophy of collaboration, which is that all educators are responsible for all students.

Another structural barrier to collaboration is that of paperwork, especially in the area of educational support services. Most educators identify the quantity of paperwork required in these programs under present administrative requirements as a substantial obstacle to the implementation of more flexible service-delivery strategies, including collaboration. About two thirds of special education teachers spend between 10% and 30% of their time on special education paperwork, whereas 12% of special educators spend more than half their time on IEP paperwork alone (Sack, 2000).

This amount of time is understandable given that the paperwork required in most support services programs typically results in the use of a bewildering number of forms. For example, for a student with a disability to receive special education throughout most of the United States, the following documentation is either encouraged or required:

- Child find form
- Prereferral form
- Referral form
- Activity tracking form
- Parental notice form
- Parental rights form
- Parental consent for initial evaluation form
- Parental consent for obtaining information form

- Noneducation agencies form
- Individual evaluation report form
- Multidisciplinary team report form
- Individualized education program form
- Parental consent for periodic re-evaluation form
- Program exit form

With so many forms, most multiple pages, it is not surprising that paperwork can be considered an obstacle to the implementation of widespread collaboration between general educators and support services providers. Many general educators understandably are concerned about the potential workload associated with students with IEPs being added to their already heavy loads and busy schedules.

In addition, general educators see themselves as being asked to take on even greater overall workload if students with special needs remain in their rooms and are not pulled out to receive their education elsewhere with specialists. A common concern among many general educators is that they already are overburdened with job responsibilities and have inadequate time to complete their work. In implementing collaboration, when professionals in the schools are faced with the prospect of still more responsibilities and the likelihood of (at least initially) a still heavier workload, many understandably are reluctant.

As far as the specialized services providers, at present many go about their work largely through a pullout, segregated system. That is, students with speech and language needs leave the general education classroom to go to the speech therapy room to work with the speech therapist, students with learning disabilities leave the general education classroom to go to the resource room to work with the special educator, and so on. Professionals providing traditional support services through this rigidly structured approach often are unable to see how they might additionally assume collaborative roles and responsibilities over and above their already full work loads.

Competency Barriers

Educators and their administrators frequently report that lack of knowledge and lack of skills impede the widespread implementation of collaboration. Significant numbers of general educators have reported that teaching students with a wide range of different learning needs is an area of major difficulty for them (e.g., Batten, 1991; Scruggs & Mastropieri, 1996; Zionts, 1997, p. 9). Preservice teacher education programs traditionally have not given educators the necessary knowledge or skills to assume instructional roles based on collaboration (T. E. C. Smith et al., 2001, p. 49).

Historically, educators have worked in professional isolation. Although school professionals may be knowledgeable about what their positions required in the past, they often have not been prepared in either the planning skills or the interpersonal skills required to move into the more collaborative educational system of the future (Friend, 2000). Although perhaps skilled in working with students, they may have little experience in working with other professionals. The absence of a well-defined blueprint for collaboration is unsettling for many.

The difficulties inherent in remodeling the schoolhouse should not be underestimated. Restructuring the schools while simultaneously continuing to provide educational programs has been compared to trying to repair the wing of a 747 jet while it is in flight (Donaldson, 1993). However, failure to identify, acknowledge, and resolve these obstacles to collaboration at the onset almost inevitably will lead to yet another educational innovation failing to deliver on its promise.

Misunderstandings About Collaboration

Many homeowners remodeling their home have found themselves disappointed with the end result. These disappointments often originated in misunderstandings between the homeowners and the professional remodelers. The homeowners' request for "larger windows" or "lighter cabinets" may not mean the same thing to the contractor as it does to the homeowners. Similarly, the contractor's suggestion for "more contemporary light fixtures" or "moderately priced" carpeting may have another meaning for the homeowners than the one the contractor intended. These misunderstandings can cause significant problems.

Misunderstandings about collaboration can cause distress and even failure as educators attempt to implement collaboration. From her perspective as a long-time advocate for collaboration, Friend (2000) has identified the following four significant myths and misinterpretations concerning collaboration.

Myth #1: Everyone Is Doing It

A perusal of contemporary school mission statements quickly reveals that almost every school purports that its staff functions collaboratively. However, saying that one collaborates can be very different than actually collaborating. The truth is that although many school professionals engage in some sort of shared efforts, often these efforts fall short of true collaboration. Their work together may be essentially directive, in which a leader defines tasks, and members assume them. Alternatively, colleagues may simply be meeting to report findings or to share information. These efforts, although perhaps commendable, do not represent true collaborative work.

Myth #2: More Is Better

In many aspects of life people assume that if something is good, then more of it is even better. However, in reality more is not necessarily better, and often is worse. Collaboration demands time, and time is a limited resource. More and possibly unnecessary collaboration does not mean that schools will function better; it may even impair the overall efficient functioning of the school.

Myth #3: It's About Feeling Good and Liking Others

Although there are pleasant interpersonal benefits of school professionals collaborating, one must not assume that these benefits are the primary rationale underlying the adoption of collaboration. Collaboration is simply a means to more successfully provide quality education to an increasingly heterogeneous student population. Even if it is more fun, it should not be adopted if it does not accomplish this primary educational task better than traditional approaches.

Myth #4: It Comes Naturally

Many educators assume that because they have experience in social settings with other adults, and because they have professional experience in working effectively with children, that they have the interpersonal skills required for effective collaboration. Whereas one might lack some specific skills in collaboration and still be able to work with a colleague, in most circumstances successful collaboration requires a specific set of skills. Although this may come naturally for some, most educators require professional preparation.

CONCLUSIONS

As owners and residents of the schoolhouse, many educators are concluding that an extensive remodeling job is in order. As one teacher commented (Sack, 2000), "My frustration is trying to be 'all things to all people.' I am supposed to keep perfect paperwork, collaborate with other teachers, train and grade peer tutors, keep in constant touch with parents, and still find time to teach my students!"

As appropriate as the current school structure may have been for the functions and demands of schools in the past, changes in the educational family's roles and needs are making it clear that the present schoolhouse cannot accommodate the educational family of the future. There is little disagreement that this school remodeling project will require moving from professional isolation to professional collaboration (Friend, 2000). Schools that are successful in providing effective educational programs to diverse students are finding collaboration central to that process (Kugelmass, 2000). The primary question for schools today is how this collaboration might best be structured (e.g., Goodlad & Lovitt, 1993).

As anyone who has lived in a home during a remodeling project will attest, the traumatic disruptions during the construction period create great levels of stress and frustration. The experience often is so unsettling that the decision to remodel is questioned frequently. After the project is complete, however, and the occupants have become accustomed to the new environment, the homeowners often wonder how they managed to live in the home before the changes.

With the completion of this chapter's survey of the educational construction site and the identification of facilitating forces and restraining forces impacting the remodeling project, the next step is to begin studying and evaluating the possible structural features that might be incorporated in the blueprints for the remodeling of the schoolhouse. Chapter 2 reviews the major collaboration options available, noting the advantages and disadvantages of each.

CHAPTER 1 ACTIVITY

Collaboration Readiness Scale

For most educators, moving into extensive collaboration is a substantial departure from the old ways. Rather than blindly leaping into the unknown, it is useful to begin by determining how ready one is to move into collaboration.

The following Collaboration Readiness Scale was adapted from a scale prepared by Conner (1989) to determine the readiness of business professionals to move from traditional ways of conducting business to innovative approaches. The Collaboration Readiness Scale allows educators to assess their overall readiness to move into collaborative ventures in the schools and to identify any especially significant aspects of concern about such a move.

Some schools have found it useful to have all educators who are beginning collaborative efforts take the Collaboration Readiness Scale prior to starting any staff development efforts. In this way the training can be specifically targeted to respond to specific concerns. In addition, the scale may be readministered as a posttest to determine the effectiveness with which pretraining concerns were resolved. Additional administrations of the scale over time can help document educators' growing levels of comfort with collaboration.

Please respond to each of the following items with your truthful personal reaction. The results will be most useful to you if your responses are as honest as possible.

_____ 1. The basic purpose of collaboration
    a. is clear to me.
    b. is unclear to me.

_____ 2. I believe that within the schools there is
    a. a high need for collaboration.
    b. a low need for collaboration.

_____ 3. In terms of my school's or district's planning for collaboration, I personally feel
    a. very involved.
    b. not very involved.

_____ 4. As information about collaboration is disseminated in my school or district, I believe
    a. little or no miscommunication has taken or will take place.
    b. a great deal of miscommunication has taken or will take place.

_____ 5. Overall I believe collaboration offers
   a. relatively low cost and high rewards.
   b. relatively high cost and low rewards.

_____ 6. As I consider how the philosophies and ideas of collaboration mesh
with my school's or district's existing values and beliefs, I see that
   a. a good fit exists.
   b. direct conflicts exist.

_____ 7. As I consider key people in my school or district, I believe that
there is
   a. good support for collaboration.
   b. weak or mixed support for collaboration.

_____ 8. As I consider the implementation of collaboration in my school or
district, I believe that social relationships will
   a. remain positive or be further improved.
   b. remain negative or be adversely affected.

_____ 9. As collaboration is implemented in my school or district, I believe
that
   a. the necessary supports will be provided.
   b. the necessary supports will not be provided.

_____ 10. As collaboration is implemented in my school or district, I believe
that there will be
   a. minimal negative impact on budgets.
   b. a significant negative impact on budgets.

_____ 11. As collaboration is implemented in my school or district, I believe
that
   a. an appropriate amount of time has been allowed between
awareness and implementation.
   b. not enough time has been allowed between awareness and
implementation.

_____ 12. In terms of planning for my participation in collaboration efforts
in my school or district, I feel
   a. my habit patterns are being respected.
   b. my habit patterns are being ignored.

_____ 13. In terms of the basic characteristics of my job, I think that implementing collaboration will have
   a. positive effects (or at least no negative effects).
   b. primarily negative effects.

____14. I think that the move toward increased collaboration is
   a. a meaningful event warranting my attention.
   b. just another change for the sake of change to be ignored or tolerated.

____15. In terms of my personal wishes, I
   a. feel the freedom to fail while learning to collaborate.
   b. would rather avoid failing by staying with things I already know.

____16. There is a certain security in doing things the way they have always been done in the past. This security in doing things the way I've always done them is
   a. not important to me.
   b. important to me.

____17. In terms of my own capability and competence, in general I have a
   a. high level of confidence in myself and my skills.
   b. low level of confidence in myself and my skills.

____18. As I consider those who are promoting collaboration in my school or district, in general I have
   a. a high degree of respect for and trust in them.
   b. a low degree of respect for and trust in them.

____19. In terms of participating in the efforts of my school or district to implement collaboration, in general I
   a. do not feel great pressure for results.
   b. feel great pressure for results.

____20. As I consider the present system of my school or district, I find that I
   a. do not have a strong vested interest in the present system.
   b. do have a strong vested interest in the present system.

____21. As I consider the efforts of my school or district to implement collaboration, I perceive
   a. high congruence between collaborative objectives and my own personal and professional goals.
   b. low congruence between collaborative objectives and my own personal and professional goals.

____22. As I consider the efforts of my school or district to implement collaboration, I believe that

a. it should be relatively easy to reverse any consequences if collaborative efforts are not fully successful.
b. if collaborative efforts do not work, it will be difficult or impossible to reverse the consequences.

SCORING

Score 3 points for each *a* response you recorded and 1 point for each *b* response. Your total score is the sum of all these points.

Number of *a* responses × 3 = _____
Number of *b* responses × 1 = _____
Total = _____

Place a mark on the continuum below to indicate your total score.

Collaboration Readiness Scale

66	55	44	33	22
High	Moderately High	Caution	Moderately Low	Low

INTERPRETATION

There are a number of ways the scale might be analyzed. Rather than using the scales only on an individual basis, some school personnel have found it useful to group the respondents by their professional training and discipline (e.g., general educators, support services providers, administrators). It is not unusual for these subgroups to have specific unique patterns in their concerns. This data can then form the basis for further individualized training.

High Readiness (scores of 61–66)
Scores in this range suggest strong readiness for collaboration, with very little resistance in evidence. An extremely positive prognosis for success is indicated.

Moderate Readiness (scores of 50–60)
Scores in this range indicate moderate readiness, though some resistance may exist. Overall the prognosis for effective implementation of collaboration is positive if the strategies designed to implement the collaboration can effectively address and resolve the existing concerns.

Caution (scores of 39–49)
Successful implementation of collaboration is likely to occur only when readiness factors outweigh hesitation factors. When the forces are equal, as they are in this category, there exists the risk of investing a great deal of effort to

accomplish very little. Each positive move may be countered by an equally negative reaction. This may result in the appearance of movement when, in fact, real change (i.e., collaboration) is not occurring.

Moderate Hesitation (scores of 28–38)

Scores in this range suggest a low level of readiness for collaboration, with considerable overt resistance. The prognosis for collaborative success is low unless the involved parties design and implement effective strategies to modify the negative climate concerning collaboration.

High Hesitation (scores of 22–27)

Scores at this level indicate virtually no readiness for collaboration and extremely high levels of resistance. The implementation strategy must totally reverse the resistant atmosphere or the prognosis for success is most negative.

ITEM COMMENTS

In addition to the above overall score, the following individual item comments can be of use to you as you engage in this self-analysis concerning your readiness for collaboration. By reading the explanations of those items to which you responded *b*, you may be able to more clearly determine the underlying reasons for hesitation in moving forward with changes toward collaboration. This determination is a first step in the process of adapting to such fundamental change as collaboration in the schools.

1. The purpose of collaboration sometimes is not made completely clear. When educators lack full understanding of why collaboration is being implemented, anxiety and suspicion can fill the information vacuum.

2. Educators may not see a need for collaboration. Even if educators fully understand the rationale for collaboration, they may disagree that it is needed.

3. Educators may not be involved in the planning. Generally people most fully support that which they helped create. If educators do not believe they have a sufficient degree of input into the planning of collaboration, there will be hesitation or even active resistance.

4. There may be poor communication regarding collaboration. Even if collaboration affects only one other person, communication can be easily distorted.

5. For some educators the perceived cost of implementing collaboration is too high, or the rewards inadequate. For educators to be motivated toward collaboration, a reward for accomplishment must be provided in the form of something they truly value. It must compensate for any physical, intellectual, or emotional price they perceive they will have to pay.

6. The compatibility of collaboration may be perceived to be low. Compatibility refers to the degree to which educators view the basic philosophies underlying collaboration as aligning with the existing values of their school or district, and with their own personal beliefs. Resistance may be at its highest when collaboration appears to conflict with concerns and issues that educators hold as fundamental or consider to be sacred.

7. At times key people in the school or district may not be seen as advocates for collaboration. If educators perceive that their principal or other important individuals or groups are not genuinely supportive of collaboration, educator acceptance is difficult to secure.

8. If educators view collaboration as adversely affecting the way they relate to people who are significant to them, acceptance is reduced.

9. Sometimes educators sense that there will not be adequate school or district administrative support for collaboration. If collaboration requires school or district resources that educators think are inaccessible (e.g., money, time commitments, new equipment or facilities, specialized training), they are likely to become disenchanted with the idea and withdraw.

10. Educators may believe that collaboration will have a negative impact on their operating budgets. Due to poor planning or unexpected drops in revenues, operating budgets can be overburdened with the initial training costs involved in planning and implementing collaboration.

11. At times educators and others most impacted by collaboration sense that it is being introduced either too quickly or too slowly, in either case causing difficulties. When planning how fast collaboration is to be introduced, it is necessary to think in terms of optimal timing. The most appropriate speed may not be the maximum speed possible.

12. Sometimes educators feel that in the effort to implement collaboration their well-established habit patterns are ignored. Promoters of

collaboration who lack knowledge about change and sensitivity concerning educators' behavior patterns instead find themselves inadvertently promoting distrust and alienation.

13. Some educators perceive that collaboration will negatively impact key job characteristics. Educators will be more resistant to collaboration if they perceive that it generates a decrease in (a) their autonomy, (b) the level of challenge the job offers, (c) the type of feedback they receive, or (d) the degree of importance the school or district places on their job.

14. A common problem in implementing collaboration is that educators have been exposed to a long history of meaningless or poorly executed changes. If educators see collaboration as simply another in a series of ill-planned events, their enthusiasm for collaboration will be greatly diminished.

15. A fear of failure is not unique to educators. Collaboration involves learning, and learning usually involves initially higher levels of mistakes. When people are not given the freedom to make mistakes while learning, they become afraid and easily discouraged.

16. Educators, like most human beings, tend to seek security in the past. If collaboration produces frustration or anxiety, educators may long for an earlier time when their jobs were not so complicated.

17. Some educators lack confidence in their abilities. Educators must perceive that they already possess the skills and knowledge required for implementing collaboration or that the necessary training will be provided. In the absence of this support they are unlikely to welcome change.

18. Educators may not respect or trust those promoting collaboration. In this case, a lack of acceptance and enthusiasm for collaboration will quickly become evident. Trust and respect typically emerge over time, as professionals work with each other and come to recognize the contributions each makes.

19. At times educators will sense excessive pressure to accept the proposed change. When educators are already busy and under stress, the additional pressure brought on by the changes inherent in collaboration may be too much for them to assimilate.

20. For some educators collaboration represents a threat to their vested interests. A major source of resistance is the perception of collaboration

as threatening to educators' economic interests or to their professional prestige.

21. At times there may be a perceived incompatibility between school or district objectives for collaboration and the personal goals of educators. Resistance is increased if educators believe collaboration will block or significantly restrict the achievement of their personal ambitions.

22. Educators may worry that the status quo cannot be reestablished if collaboration proves unacceptable. The fewer permanent negative consequences that result from having tried collaboration, and the easier it is to reverse collaborative relations, the more likely it is that educators will not resist implementation.

Reviewing the Options:
Types of School Collaboration

Choice is the strongest principle of growth.
—George Eliot

Once homeowners decide to remodel their home, their next task is to check with architects or professional home remodelers to determine the possible features and structures they might want in their new home. Their decisions are based on a number of considerations, including cost, practicality, size of the area, functionality, materials, and family size. Similarly, once the decision has been made to remodel the schoolhouse by making education more collaborative, the next step for educators is to determine the exact structures and specifications of their collaboration remodeling project. As is the case with homeowners, educators first must be aware of the various structural possibilities that are available. Then, by considering their own unique needs, they can effectively identify the specific blueprints that will best meet their needs.

Understandably, most educators would prefer to see answers offered in simple, concise packages. But what would happen to a remodeling business that offered only one standard set of "off-the-shelf" remodeling plans to any client who came in the door, regardless of his or her individual needs and situations? That business would quickly fail, because no one-size-fits-all set of remodeling plans can meet the diverse needs of all homeowners. Similarly, the heterogeneity of schools makes it difficult to identify one approach to collaboration that will be equally applicable and successful in all educational situations. As Albert Shanker (1989), past president of the American Federation of Teachers, noted, "There is no one blueprint for schools." Instead, a wide variety of collaborative structures are available to professionals in education.

One should keep in mind two fundamental considerations in collaboration. First, the particular approach or approaches selected should be chosen based on both educator and student needs. Both sets of need must be understood clearly before changes are implemented. A homeowner who says, "I want a remodeled kitchen," will be presented with hundreds of possibilities. Before the homeowner can narrow the choices down, he or she must analyze what is not working in the current kitchen, and what is needed to meet those needs. In addition, the homeowner should note those aspects of the current kitchen that are working well, so that they can be retained. Similarly, educators must first identify the needs of both themselves and their students that presently are unmet in their schools, while noting the existing educational arrangements that are working effectively.

Second (and perhaps needless to say), by its very definition collaboration requires knowledge about and skills in the development of interpersonal relationships. Without these prerequisites, collaboration will not reach its potential.

OPTIONS IN COLLABORATION

Educational collaboration is an educator-based support structure. Many schools already have teams of educators working together for a variety of purposes. These include grade-level teams in elementary schools, in which educators discuss issues of curriculum and instruction; departmental teams at the secondary level, which plan directions for their individual content areas; and support services teams, which make determinations about programs and instructional procedures for individual students with special needs.

One way to think about collaborative efforts in education is to categorize them as *indirect collaboration* or *direct collaboration*. These two categories are further explained below.

In *indirect collaboration*, two (or more) educators work together outside the classroom, meeting and developing educational plans and strategies. Only one educator, however, the general education teacher assigned to that class, then directly provides educational services to students in the general education classroom. In *direct collaboration*, two (or more) school professionals not only meet and plan beforehand but also then work together in the classroom, providing instruction to the whole group, small groups, or individual students.

Indirect Collaboration

A typical indirect collaborative structure begins with the general educator requesting assistance. He or she might meet with one or more "experts" to explain areas of concern and to ask for suggestions. Following this meeting, one of these expert colleagues may come into the general education classroom. This visit is for observation and information gathering, not to directly teach students or assume educational responsibilities for that classroom. Following a subsequent analysis and discussion with the members of the collaboration group, the general educator then returns alone to the classroom with one or more suggestions, and attempts to implement them for the targeted student(s). This indirect collaborative approach, with ultimate instructional responsibility remaining solely with the classroom teacher, has been the traditional format for most collaborative efforts.

For example, a teacher might approach the school's speech therapist for suggestions of what might be done for a student who is responding to questions with only one-word answers. After discussing the situation with the student's teacher, and perhaps visiting the classroom and observing, the therapist might suggest to the teacher ways he or she might phrase questions during classes to elicit more elaborate responses from the student. The teacher would then return to the classroom, try those suggestions, and perhaps report back later.

Over the past 20 years, a variety of consulting models based on this indirect collaboration model have been proposed. These include collaborative consultation, peer collaboration, coaching, and teacher assistance teams.

Collaborative Consultation

In the 1980s many general educators were faced with new challenges, as students with disabilities increasingly were returning to the general education classroom from their formerly segregated special education pullout programs. The collaborative consultation model emerged to help general educators develop and deliver instruction to these students (Idol, Paolucci-Whitcomb, & Nevin, 1986).

Described as "an interactive process that enables people with diverse expertise to generate creative solutions to mutually defined problems" (Idol et al., 1986, p. 1), the collaborative consultation approach structures interactions between the general education teacher who is responsible for teaching students who are presenting instructional challenges, and the consultant, a person who has unique knowledge or skills (e.g., a facilitator for gifted and talented students, a speech therapist, or a special educator).

In collaborative consultation, when an educational problem or concern exists in the general education classroom, the general education teacher seeks out the expert consultant. The two meet outside the classroom, and the general educator describes the problem to the expert, who then suggests possible solutions. The general educator takes those proposed solutions back to the classroom for implementation, usually reporting back to the specialist about the effectiveness (or lack thereof) of the suggestions.

Peer Collaboration

Another indirect form of collaboration, peer collaboration (Pugach & Johnson, 1988) evolved in part from concerns about the special education referral process. When faced with the challenges of teaching academically and behaviorally diverse students, general educators too often simply referred them for special education evaluation.

In peer collaboration, two general educators collaborate by working through a four-step process to identify effective classroom interventions. In the first step, problem description and clarifying questions, the general educator requesting assistance writes out and reads to the peer a short description of the problem, who then asks clarifying questions. Once the problem has been clarified to the satisfaction of both, the initiator then summarizes the problem. The initiating teacher then generates at least three practical and minimally disruptive intervention options, and after discussion, the two educators select the intervention strategy that seems most likely to succeed. The final step in peer collaboration is to plan an evaluation procedure for the selected intervention strategy. The two peer collaborators agree to meet again in 2 weeks to assess progress or begin the peer collaboration process over again.

Coaching

More recently, newer indirect collaborative models have emerged. In coaching, school colleagues are paired as support for each other (Walther-Thomas, Korinek, McLaughlin, & Williams, 2000, p. 79).

Coaching has been defined as

> . . . a form of mediation that may be applied to interactions in a variety of patterns, situations, and settings with the intention of enhancing self-directed learning in self and others. (Costa & Garmston, 1999, p. 4)

One purpose of coaching is to implement innovations that benefit students (Ray, 1998). Coached teachers practice new strategies more frequently and more appropriately, exhibit greater long-term retention of knowledge and skill, and exhibit clearer understanding of the purposes and uses of new strategies (Joyce, 1988). Effective coaching is built on the incorporation of two fundamental communication skills, questioning and paraphrasing, into ongoing exchanges between the partners. This dialogue generates higher and more effective levels of self-analysis and metacognition in the participants.

The fundamental nature of teaching has been described as a constant stream of decisions. In that conceptual framework, teacher behaviors are seen as the result of decisions, either conscious or unconscious (Shulman, 1986). The ultimate purpose of coaching, then, is to help participants make better decisions about instruction.

In the cognitive coaching model proposed by Costa and Garmston (1999, p. 24), there are four phases of coaching. In the first, "Planning," the coach mediates by helping the colleague clarify goals, identify indicators of success, and anticipate approaches, strategies, and decisions. In the second phase, "Monitoring," the coach helps the colleague review the indicators. In the third phase, "Analyzing," the coach guides the colleague through reflections of the colleague's overall impressions of his or her instruction, any supporting information contributing to those impressions, and any cause-and-effect relationships that have emerged. In the fourth and final phase, "Applying," the coach guides the colleague to construct for himself or herself new learnings about his or her teaching to be used in future instruction.

When the two partners share similar professional roles, responsibilities, and professional status, the support structure is referred to as peer coaching. When the collaborators are equals, it may be easier to establish an atmosphere of trust and collegiality (Robbins, 1991). In peer coaching, one colleague observes the partner's lesson, and later reviews that lesson with the partner. Each would then share observations and insights, and ultimately collaboratively identify ways in which the instruction could be made even better (Joyce & Showers, 1995).

Part of the value in this approach is that as teachers help one another in this questioning fashion, they gain additional skills in asking themselves appropriate questions and ultimately solving problems on their own. This is based on metacognition theory; that is, one's increasing knowledge of one's own learning strategies (e.g., Weinstein & Mayer, 1986, p. 323).

Coaching differs significantly from a related approach, mentoring. In mentoring, one partner typically has considerably more knowledge and professional experience than the other. For example, Feiler, Heritage, and Gallimore (2000) described a mentoring model in which "teacher–leaders" are selected by their principals for their curricular expertise and leadership skills. These teacher–leaders assist their colleagues by planning with them, demonstrating lessons, sharing assessment strategies, and providing feedback on observed lessons. In such approaches the relationship between the partners clearly takes on a senior versus junior perspective. The more experienced partner is clearly the leader in identifying problems and generating solutions.

Neither peer coaching nor mentoring is inherently superior to the other. One easily can envision scenarios in which both participants are more comfortable when one partner has a level of professional expertise that is clearly superior to the other's. If so, then a mentoring structure may be more effective than peer coaching, where the coach may lack sufficient professional background or experiences to guide the partner most effectively. The choice between mentoring and peer coaching should be made according to both partners' comfort.

It should be noted that imbalance in professional status, experience, and power between the participants in professional collaborative relationships may cause significant issues. Theoretically both participants should share responsibility for the education of all students, and also share accountability for the success or failure of any developed programs. However, in actual practice the less experienced educator may quite accurately sense that he or she lacks the skills to handle the situation. Otherwise, why would there have been a need to seek assistance from an expert? In such situations, this teacher may simply present a problem to the specialist and then wait passively for a solution.

Conversely, great pressure to solve the problem lies with the specialist. If the proposed solution is not successful, it is perceived to be the expert's fault. The unstated implication in this situation is that the less experienced educator is automatically absolved of ongoing responsibilities for students who are failing to progress after being referred to the expert.

For many teachers, having another professional observe and subsequently discuss teachers' work is typically associated with another process, that of evaluation. There are significant differences, however, between coaching and evaluation, in terms of structure, function, and purpose (Costa & Garmston, 1999).

In evaluation, the partner is usually a school administrator who observes a teacher during instruction and makes a judgment concerning his or her overall level of competence, using a predetermined set of criteria. Often this process is legally or bureaucratically mandated. The criteria that the administrator uses in evaluation may include factors correlated with student success, such as planning effectiveness, but often includes other criteria, such as grooming and participation on school committees. Many teachers approach this situation with significant trepidation, and likely would opt out of it if possible.

In coaching, the partner instead is a colleague or peer whose purpose is to help the teacher become more reflective, analytical, and, ultimately, more effective. Coaching is a purposefully designed collegial relationship where teachers support one another in reflecting critically on their cognitive processes when developing and conducting lessons (Costa & Garmston, 1985). The entire process is more balanced and collaborative than is the case in evaluation, and is more likely to generate higher levels of trust and self-revelation (Costa & Garmston, 1999).

Teacher Assistance Teams (TAT)

All of the above models of indirect collaboration are essentially ways in which only two educators interact together. However, approaches involving multiple indirect collaborators also have been developed.

One of the earliest approaches suggested to facilitate collaboration among educators was the teacher assistance team (TAT; Chalfant, Pysh, & Moultrie, 1979). The TAT was designed as a means of supporting general educators so they could more effectively teach students with learning or behavior problems in general education classrooms.

The TAT is a four-member team. Each team has three relatively permanent core members who are experienced master teachers elected to participate on the TAT by their colleagues. The fourth and changing member is the educator seeking help. Parents, students, and relevant others also may participate, though it is not required.

In the TAT approach to collaboration, a referring educator brings to the TAT a student problem and describes to team members the student's strengths and needs, as

well as interventions that have been attempted. If possible, at least one team member observes the student in the classroom prior to the meeting. The team then conducts a problem-solving meeting to help the referring educator clearly define the problem. In this meeting all involved parties brainstorm and then refine possible solutions to the problem. The educator then takes those ideas back to the classroom. Several weeks later a follow-up meeting is held to review the effectiveness of the selected strategies.

In all of these indirect collaboration models—collaborative consultation, peer collaboration, coaching, and TAT—the teacher receives advice, suggestions, and recommendations from others, but ultimately he or she returns to the classroom alone. Instructional responsibility and accountability remain solely with the single teacher. Despite the resources that are provided outside the classroom, indirect collaboration does not change the essential nature of the one teacher–one classroom structure of traditional instruction in the schools.

Direct Collaboration

The key to direct collaboration is the simultaneous presence of two or more educators in the general education classroom, jointly planning for, instructing, and evaluating heterogeneous groups of students. This is in stark contrast to most indirect models of collaboration, in which, after meeting with one or more other school professionals, the teacher returns to the classroom alone.

Direct collaboration differs from indirect collaboration in several other critical dimensions. For instance, indirect collaboration often occurs episodically in response to a difficult situation that has emerged. When that situation has been resolved, the collaborative structure disappears. In direct collaboration, on the other hand, the relationship between the educators is ongoing and sustained over time. Indirect collaboration is often characterized by professional asymmetry, wherein one partner is the expert and the other in need of assistance. In direct collaboration, the participants function as equals. Finally, and most significantly, in indirect collaboration the teacher returns to the classroom alone, maintaining all instructional responsibility for the students in that classroom. In direct collaboration, two or more educators are in the classroom together, sharing responsibility for all students.

For example, in engaging in direct collaboration a speech therapist and a general educator might regularly work together in the general classroom where one or more students have language needs. The two professionals together plan and implement language-enrichment exercises for the entire class, or collaboratively teach specific language skills to carefully structured subgroups of students within the class.

Over the past decade, one approach to direct collaboration, *cooperative teaching*, has gained great acceptance. A number of other terms have been used to refer to similar arrangements, including coteaching, collaborative teaching, or team teaching.

Similarly, programs that are described as class-within-a-class or in-class supports are functionally cooperative teaching structures. However, in this book we will use the term cooperative teaching to refer to a specific approach to collaboration.

COOPERATIVE TEACHING

In its early development Bauwens, Hourcade, and Friend (1989) initially described cooperative teaching as

> an educational approach in which general and special educators work in a co-active and coordinated fashion to jointly teach heterogeneous groups of students in educationally integrated settings (i.e., general classrooms). . . . In cooperative teaching both general and special educators are simultaneously present in the general classroom, maintaining joint responsibilities for specified education instruction that is to occur within that setting. (p. 18)

Cooperative teaching evolved from analyses of the weaknesses of indirect approaches to collaboration. Specifically, educators using indirect collaboration reported that, although they did receive assistance, ultimately they still returned to their classrooms to "sink or swim" alone. In cooperative teaching, the support services provider who is collaborating with the general educator is actually working simultaneously with the general educator in the classroom for at least some part of the instructional day. The most distinctive feature of cooperative teaching, and the one that most differentiates it from indirect approaches to collaboration, is this joint and simultaneous direct provision of instruction.

In cooperative teaching, the participants jointly determine who teaches what, when, how, and whom through a shared analysis of the needs of the students in the class at any given time, and the specific sets of skills and knowledge each professional brings to the classroom. For example, traditionally general educators are knowledgeable about curricular sequencing in academic areas and are skilled in large group instruction. Many support services providers are especially skilled in areas such as curricular and instructional adaptations and in the development and provision of individualized instruction. The combination of these previously separate sets of skills provides a powerful instructional package.

Because both professionals are simultaneously present in the classroom, they share the responsibility for the education of all students in that classroom. The relative roles of expert and help-seeker vary constantly throughout the day, as each professional takes on those functions in which he or she has greater competence.

The social interactions and support system of the involved educators evolve naturally as they continue their work together. The fact that both are present in the classroom simultaneously means that each will see any student difficulties in the actual situations in which the problems occur. Thus both educators can work together to generate practical educational interventions that are likely to be effective.

Since its introduction in the late 1980s cooperative teaching has been creatively implemented in a variety of ways and environments that were unimagined at that time. Bauwens and Hourcade (1997) noted that cooperative teaching had evolved substantially beyond simply general and special educators working together. Because of the ever-increasing diversities in general education classrooms, diverse approaches have emerged in which educators from a seemingly endless variety of professional backgrounds work together, sharing instructional responsibility for all students. The authors have observed such successful expansions of the original concept of cooperative teaching as the following groupings:

- general educator and bilingual/ESL educator
- general educator and adaptive physical educator
- general educator and speech–language therapist
- general educator and gifted and talented facilitator
- general educator and Title 1 teacher
- general educator and occupational or physical therapist
- general educator and school counselor or school psychologist
- general educator and paraprofessional
- general educator, paraeducator, and special educator

Reflecting the advances in cooperative teaching developed since the original definition was proposed in 1989, the following definition more accurately reflects contemporary conceptualizations of cooperative teaching.

▶ Cooperative teaching refers to direct collaboration in which a general educator and one or more support services providers voluntarily agree to work together in a coactive and coordinated fashion in the general education classroom. These educators, who possess distinct and complementary sets of skills, share roles, resources, and responsibilities in a sustained effort while working toward the common goal of school success for all students.

This definition is elaborated below.

As noted earlier, the primary distinguishing characteristic of direct collaboration is the simultaneous presence of two or more educators actively delivering instruction in general education settings. Rather than the general educator seeking suggestions outside the classroom, and then returning to the classroom alone, in cooperative teaching the specialist is there in the classroom. This approach offers two distinct advantages over indirect collaboration. First, students in need of support can receive specialized support in a powerful way in the least restrictive environment. Second, each educator can observe, and begin to acquire and use, those unique strategies and skills the partner brings to the classroom.

For cooperative teaching to be successful, it is critical that it be voluntary for all participants. More than one cooperative teaching attempt has failed when it was arbitrarily imposed by administrators upon unwilling partners. Such "arranged marriages" are nearly always doomed to failure. When change is demanded, people feel threatened and defensive. Pressure to change seldom results in experiences of joy and excitement in learning (Morimoto, 1973, p. 255).

Any educational program is more likely to be successful when carefully planned beforehand. In cooperative teaching, this planning is complex in that the needs and contributions of at least two separate individuals must be coordinated and interwoven. This is necessary if students are to acquire skills and then use them in the general education classroom. This coordinated planning contrasts traditional approaches in which the general educator and the support services provider proceeded separately and largely independently, providing different kinds of services in physically different locations.

Perhaps the greatest power of cooperative teaching is the combination of two distinctive sets of professional skills. These skills provide an instructional package more responsive to the diversity of student needs than either educator can provide in isolation.

Cooperative teaching also inspires a spirit of sharing. In traditional educational approaches, each educator has theoretical ownership of his or her own set of materials, lesson plans, schedules, and students. In cooperative teaching, educators must share materials, planning and instructional responsibilities, and, most important, responsibility for the educational success of all the students in the classroom. Because this effort is sustained over time, unlike the sporadic efforts that characterize indirect collaboration, this sense of sharing is more likely to be nurtured, and to grow.

Although cooperative teaching is effective in solving problems that are inherent in other approaches to collaboration, it does present its own set of challenges. An especially significant challenge is that professionals in the schools must make significant changes in their well-established professional identities.

For example, special educators have long administered programs in which students with special needs were removed from their classrooms into pullout programs (e.g., resource rooms or self-contained special classes). Now those special educators are being asked to work in the general education classroom with larger groups of students with great diversity. The potential exists for these special educators to lose professional identity and autonomy.

Nevertheless, cooperative teaching is becoming increasingly popular as the approach to collaboration that responds most effectively to the need for school professionals to work together to teach educationally diverse groups of students (Friend, Reising, & Cook, 1993). Though requiring an initially significant commitment of time and resources, cooperative teaching offers benefits in both the short term and the long term.

In the short term, all students receive the powerful instruction required for educational success in the classroom (Harris et al., 1987; White & White, 1992). In the long term, cooperative teaching builds schoolwide collaborative problem-solving skills, and a school culture that supports the ongoing learning of both students and teachers. These outcomes help break the cycle of dependence upon segregated pullout programs for students with diverse learning needs (Adams & Cessna, 1993; Case, 1992).

CONCLUSIONS

Earlier it was noted that no one set of off-the-shelf architectural plans meets the needs of all homeowners who are contemplating home remodeling projects. Similarly, it is not likely that any single approach to collaboration can meet the needs of all schools everywhere.

However, there are architectural plans that have generalized features that meet the needs of most homeowners, especially when fine-tuned to individual needs. Similarly, the cooperative teaching approach to collaboration offers most educators teaching options that help them respond to the problems that are increasingly common to all schools. Cooperative teaching is the only approach to collaboration that

a. simultaneously brings together education professionals in the classroom who possess complementary sets of skills and perspectives, and

b. facilitates those professionals in integrating their varying sets of knowledge and skills into a comprehensive instructional system.

As homeowners seek to remodel their home, an early accomplishment is finding or developing the architectural plans that will meet their needs. Educators are discovering that the set of cooperative teaching blueprints holds great promise for enabling educators to remodel the schoolhouse for the most effective education of all students, including those of varying cultural, ethnic, and linguistic backgrounds, academic abilities, and behavioral characteristics. Chapter 3 describes in detail exactly how the blueprints of cooperative teaching are transformed into the actual brick and mortar of instruction.

CHAPTER 2 ACTIVITY

Self-Examination for Collaboration

This chapter has provided an overview of the features of collaboration and some of the ways in which it can be structured. The following activity will help educators begin a more in-depth, individualized examination of collaboration as it relates to their own school.

As every educator knows, examinations should include material with varying levels of cognitive complexity, from simple recall of basic factual material to using higher level skills as synthesis, analysis, and evaluation. The six levels of Bloom's taxonomy of educational objectives (Bloom, Engelhart, Frost, Hill, & Krathwohl, 1956) often provide educators with a way to structure exam material. These six levels, from the simplest and most concrete level to the most complex and abstract level, are as follows:

Knowledge
Comprehension
Application
Analysis
Synthesis
Evaluation

Unfortunately, many educators find Bloom's taxonomy to be too abstract, requiring too much effort and time to use in their programs. To respond to this complaint, Weiderhold (1991) constructed a question matrix, a user-friendly device based in part on Bloom's taxonomy. Weiderhold's structure moves from simple factual questions in the top left portion of the matrix (e.g., "What is . . . ?") to more complex and demanding questions toward the lower right corner (e.g., "How might . . . ?").

This matrix has been adapted here to help you think about, at a number of levels and in a number of ways, collaboration and its potential to change the way teaching is structured at your school. As you read and consider your response to each question, keep in mind that there are no right answers to these open-ended items. Rather, these 36 questions simply provide an organized structure and framework to help you to more comprehensively analyze yourself and think more deeply about the specifics of your own situation regarding collaboration in your school or district. The matrix is provided in Table 2.1.

TABLE 2.1
Question Matrix

	Event	**Situation**	**Choice**	**Person**	**Reason**	**Means**
Present	What is happening now at your school to cause people to consider beginning collaboration?	When is collaboration scheduled to begin?	Which collaborative structure is best suited for the unique needs of your situation?	Who is most involved in collaboration now at your school?	Why is collaboration being considered now?	How is collaboration going to change the way your school's programs now function?
Past	What did you think when you first learned of collaboration?	Where (in what situation) and when did the idea of collaboration at your school first emerge?	Which alternative educational approaches have been tried in the past to target problems in your school?	Who in the past has proposed collaboration at your school? What happened?	Why did no one propose collaboration in the past?	How did the initial thinking about collaboration at your school begin?
Possibility	What can be done to introduce the idea of collaboration most effectively at your school?	Where and when would it be best to prepare potential collaborators at your school?	Which of the many reasons for collaboration can be most easily "sold" to educators at your school?	Who can most effectively "sell" collaboration at your school?	Why can collaboration be successful in your school?	How can the administration most effectively support collaboration?
Probability	What would happen if collaboration were universally instituted throughout all schools?	When would involved professionals be able to get together to review and discuss collaboration?	Which collaborative structure would be seen as the most dramatic departure from the present system?	Who in your school would be most resistant to participating in collaboration?	Why would professionals at your school resist becoming involved in collaboration?	How would the school be affected if only a few professionals chose to participate in collaboration?
Prediction	What will happen if the administration provides only partial support for collaboration in your school?	Where in your school is collaboration likely to be most easily established?	Which comments from parents will be most frequently heard when collaboration is implemented at your school?	Who at your school will emerge as the leading advocate for collaboration?	Why will students at your school welcome the implementation of collaboration?	How will the professional responsibilities inherent in the present day "one teacher–one classroom" structure change with collaboration?
Imagination	What might collaboration change in you personally?	Where might collaboration be less appropriate and less effective than the present system?	Which student characteristics at your school might collaboration be especially well suited for?	Who will be the most pivotal person at your school to convince of the benefits of collaboration?	Why might some students at your school initially resist collaboration?	How might successful collaborators best develop collaborative networks with other professionals?

Note. Adapted from *Cooperative Learning and Critical Thinking: The Question Matrix*, by C. Weiderhold, 1991, San Juan Capistrano, CA: Resources for Teachers. Copyright 1991 by Resources for Teachers. Adapted with permission.

Developing the Blueprints:
Planning for Cooperative Teaching

If you fail to plan, you plan to fail.
—Unknown

B y this point the homeowners who have decided to remodel their home have spent a significant amount of time reviewing possible architectural plans and discussing which of these plans and options are best suited for their changing needs. They have identified the one set of plans that appears most promising but also have concluded that those plans may require adaptations. They now must carefully review the plans for the remodeling project, examining the various features and options to determine how each can be adapted to best meet their needs.

Chapter 2 presented several potential sets of blueprints for educational collaboration that schools throughout the country are using to rebuild the schoolhouse. Possible approaches for this project include collaborative consultation, peer collaboration, coaching, mentoring, teacher assistance teams, and cooperative teaching. Over time and through experience, many educators are finding that the features of cooperative teaching make it especially attractive for schools in the 21st century. The next step to implement cooperative teaching is to begin planning for instruction.

PROFESSIONAL ROLES IN COOPERATIVE TEACHING

Diversity in professional backgrounds is a cornerstone of cooperative teaching. Cooperative teaching arrangements often include elementary and secondary teachers working with support services providers such as special education teachers, instructional assistants and paraprofessionals, speech and language therapists, Title 1 and remedial reading teachers, facilitators for gifted and talented students, teachers of English as a Second Language (ESL), occupational and physical therapists, school nurses, librarians, and school psychologists and counselors. These individuals work in pairs, or even in trios.

The essential philosophy of cooperative teaching is a simple one: *sharing*, especially of responsibilities and accountability. In short, in cooperative teaching all educators are responsible for all students. In cooperative teaching, assignments are based on the individual educators' unique packages of knowledge and skills. In this way specific and unique educator capabilities are used most effectively for the benefit of all students.

Most general educators are knowledgeable about curriculum and curricular sequencing, especially in the traditional academic areas. These teachers have extensive experience with educational components such as basal series and literature-based texts in reading and spelling, and mathematics scope and sequence matrices. At the secondary level, these educators typically have expertise in content areas (e.g., English literature, chemistry, social studies).

In addition, general educators traditionally have been skilled in large group classroom management procedures. To function effectively, these educators must skillfully manage students in groups of 20 to 40, ensuring that all students in these large groups are effectively engaged in the learning process. Large group management competencies include skills such as effective whole class presentations and assessments, large group discipline, and records management.

Conversely, the work of support services providers such as special educators evolved to emphasize individuals, not large groups. As a result, these professionals have a significantly different set of skills. For example, most special educators have expertise in highly detailed individual student assessment for determining eligibility and developing subsequent curriculum. An increasingly important skill of support services providers is the ability to target areas of difficulty within the general education curriculum, then design and adapt instructional materials and strategies to maximize the success of diverse students.

Contemporary special educators can pinpoint those components of the general education curriculum and instruction that are presenting the greatest challenges to students with learning, language, or behavioral differences, and design adaptations or modifications of those components to make them more accessible for these students. Furthermore, students identified as gifted or talented also may require accommoda-

tions through enrichment of the standard curricula, as well as possible changes in the manner of instruction. Educators skilled in curricular adaptation are in great demand as general education classrooms contain more heterogeneous student populations.

Most support services providers, especially special educators and school psychologists, also have experience developing individualized positive behavior support programs. Whereas general educators' classroom management strategies traditionally (and understandably) emphasize large group management procedures, special educators and other specialized support services providers have expertise in using systematic positive behavioral procedures to enhance the behavioral and social success of individual students.

In addition, most support services providers such as special educators are already familiar and comfortable with the evolving emphasis on school standards and accountability. The move toward greater teacher accountability, with students expected to reach certain prescribed skill levels, shows no sign of abating (e.g., Kohn, 1999). Although this movement has many in general education concerned, experienced special educators long have worked with such expectations. The enactment of the Education for All Handicapped Children Act of 1975 required special educators to identify beforehand the specific skills that would be acquired by their students over the course of the year, and to identify the specific professional(s) who would be responsible for each annual goal. Special educators now have more than 25 years of experience (a) helping students systematically work toward and achieve identified and measurable goals, and (b) being held accountable when these programs are reviewed annually. This background can be invaluable to general educators as they move into similar sets of expectations.

Other specialized services providers also can make unique contributions. Instructional assistants and teacher aides have great experience in direct program implementation, sometimes more than the educators under whom they work. Title 1 and remedial reading teachers bring specific diagnostic and intervention skills for helping students with math and reading difficulties. Other support services providers such as speech and language therapists and physical and occupational therapists possess unique knowledge and competencies not found elsewhere on a school's staff. Psychologists and school counselors may be especially skilled at facilitating social and emotional growth, as well as bringing professional perspectives to areas of concern such as learning strategies and family dynamics.

In addition, many of these professionals are especially experienced with the diversity of student cultural backgrounds found in the schools today. For example, the intensive language background that English as a Second Language (ESL) teachers bring to a classroom is invaluable in the linguistically diverse classroom. ESL teachers also know how to imbed language instruction in typical classroom activities for all students.

As a result, when general educators work together in cooperative teaching with specialized support services providers representing two or more of these backgrounds, the partners can bring an impressive combination of skills to the integrated classroom.

Traditionally, school decisions regarding the assignment of responsibilities and duties to specific educators have been made primarily based on such considerations as educator certifications or endorsements, labels of students, and so on. For example, typically special educators have worked under the assumption that their only educational responsibility was toward those students found legally to be disabled and eligible for special education services. Similarly, general education teachers often have seen themselves as free of further educational responsibility for such students once a diagnosis of a disability has been made.

These perceptions are changing. Certainly the practical realities of educator certification by state boards of education must be acknowledged. For example, some interpretations of federal and state regulations suggest that special educators should provide services only to students legally identified as eligible for these services. If a special educator teaches thinking skills to an entire fifth-grade class, it might be interpreted as a violation of this regulation, because students not eligible for special education services would nevertheless be receiving services from a special educator.

Perhaps the most effective response to this concern is to examine the federal law governing special education. Specifically, the law states that students with disabilities may be removed from the general education environment only when "education in regular classes with the use of supplemental aids and services cannot be achieved satisfactorily" (Federal Register, August, 1977, p. 42497).

In reading this, the primary intention of the law is unmistakable. Students with disabilities should be taught in general education classrooms with the use of supplemental aids and services. Special educators and other support services providers participating in cooperative teaching are providing such a supplemental service in general education classrooms. Because cooperative teaching facilitates the provision of the legally required "satisfactory education" for students with disabilities, such services are appropriate, warranted, and justifiable. Regulations that are interpreted in a manner contrary to this intent conflict with both the letter and the spirit of this federal law.

BENEFITS OF COOPERATIVE TEACHING

Cooperative teaching has significant immediate and long-term benefits for both students and educators. In the short term, it facilitates the transition of students presently receiving educational programming in segregated educational settings (e.g., ESL students, students with disabilities, and students receiving other specialized services) back into inclusive general education classrooms. The research on inclusion consistently indicates that inclusion is most effective when the classroom teachers adapt curriculum and instruction to make it accessible for all students in the class (e.g., Walther-Thomas, Korinek, McLaughlin, & Williams, 2000). With support services providers such as special educators bringing instructional adaptation and individualization skills to the general classroom through cooperative teaching, the full and successful inclusion of students with a variety of diverse educational needs can be achieved.

In the long term, cooperative teaching proactively facilitates inclusion. At present many special educators are unsure whether they can provide services to students not necessarily found eligible for special education services. However, *all* students deserve special services when appropriate and needed. Through cooperative teaching, any student evidencing behavioral, learning, or other problems can receive needed curricular or instructional support immediately and intensively, decreasing the likelihood of the need for traditional special pullout services. As curriculum and instruction in general education classrooms becomes more individualized, fewer students should be identified as requiring intensive intervention services.

The traditional large group general education classroom is characterized by a single educator trying to simultaneously balance instruction and classroom management. This role juggling often results in the presentation of instruction that is easiest from a classroom management perspective (e.g., lecturing to a group of 25 students). Cooperative teaching, with its provision of two educators in the classroom, eases the classroom management burden of the educators, allowing for instruction to be more creative and student involved. One educator may concentrate on instruction of the class while the other maintains primary responsibility for classroom management.

Students are not the only beneficiaries of cooperative teaching. Every teacher knows the frustration of working in isolation, an especially discouraging sensation when some students are not learning. When two educators with distinct sets of professional skills merge, this frustration is tremendously reduced or even eliminated. Over the long term, cooperative teachers acquire both additional valuable professional skills from their partners and personal supportive friendships.

PLANNING FOR COOPERATIVE TEACHING

There are five key elements to proper implementation of cooperative teaching. When each these five elements is appropriately addressed, true cooperative teaching results. These elements, known as the five Ps of cooperative teaching (Hourcade & Bauwens, 1996), are as follows:

1. Cooperative presence
2. Cooperative planning
3. Cooperative presenting
4. Cooperative processing
5. Cooperative problem solving

Cooperative Presence

Some educators begin cooperative teaching by simply being in the same classroom at the same time. Often this occurs in an unplanned fashion, as the result of unexpected free time or a hallway conversation. For example, after a chat in the faculty lounge or by the water cooler, a general educator might invite a special educator into his or her general education classroom to see what he or she is doing. If this cooperative presence is all that develops, few structural changes occur in a classroom. The only difference is that there are now two adults physically present in the room instead of one. In such cases, the special educator or related service provider working with the general educator may feel like an aide rather than a true teaching partner.

In such circumstances the instructional programs in the classroom continue essentially as they always have. The cooperative partner often is left standing to one side of the classroom, perhaps occasionally wandering over to a student who seems to need help. This "drop-in" approach does not represent significant change.

As educators plan to move into cooperative teaching, they must first be aware of the danger of remaining at the cooperative presence level. They must be committed to ongoing collaborative work, not simply working together when it is convenient. If the latter is the case, then their collaboration is vulnerable, because teachers tend to cancel when unexpected demands arise elsewhere. Although their simultaneous presence is the beginning of cooperative teaching, the new relationship must be sustained over time, and must change in nature, for true cooperative teaching to occur.

Cooperative Planning

In cooperative planning, the educators regularly meet to collaboratively design and prepare unit and lesson plans, to identify and differentiate specific individual roles and responsibilities, and to identify needed resources. Many teachers have found it most useful to schedule these meetings every week or two until their new relationship is well established.

These meetings might begin with a series of discussions about the ways in which the educators might best work together. Initially the two teachers might focus on such issues as values and beliefs about teaching and learning, management styles and techniques, personal teaching preferences, and ways in which to best work with parents.

As they continue, the dialogue begins to shape a unified approach to teaching "their" students. This sets the stage for the educators to build a common language, create a cohesive vision, and develop a consistent management plan that represents the voice of all parties involved in this cooperative teaching venture.

The language used by the cooperative teaching partners is a good indicator of the status of the cooperative teaching relationship, and suggests the degree to which the participants have incorporated the critical concept of sharing into their work. Successful cooperative teachers no longer refer to "my classroom" and "your classroom," or "my students" and "your students." Consistent use of such language as "our students," "our curriculum," "our lessons," and "our class," both in conversations with each other and with students (e.g., "Our goal is for you to . . .") helps develop the strong sharing foundation needed for successful cooperative teaching. Such terminology also exposes students to the increasingly collaborative nature of work in contemporary society.

In addition to initial planning conversations, cooperative teachers should visit each other as they teach solo to gain insight into each other's instructional and management style. The visits help identify the ways to best blend their styles as cooperative teaching partners.

Once the teachers have completed this initial stage of planning, they should begin to plan how their instruction might be structured to best meet the needs of all students. The 1997 amendments to the Individuals with Disabilities Education Act (IDEA) clearly require that students with disabilities have access to the general education curriculum. There are several ways in which schools have responded to this mandate.

One way has been to assign students with disabilities to the special education resource room where they are tutored on their assignments from the general education curriculum and given additional help in completing their homework. This approach has been criticized because it may reinforce students' learned helplessness, does not directly teach them strategies for learning how to learn, and does not encourage self-management strategies (e.g., completing homework on their own).

A second and more recent way in which students are being served has been to physically include them in general education classes. In some cases, however, little or no direct support has been given to either the student or the classroom teacher. For example, some students on IEPs may be supplied with a daily or weekly packet of instructional materials (at the students' intellectual or academic skill level) and asked to independently complete them. These materials may not directly correlate with what is being taught in the general education classroom, except that the materials originate in the same curriculum area.

For instance, a student with a disability included in a ninth-grade math class may be given a packet of math worksheets at his or her current skill level. If included in a history class, he or she may be given a packet of materials that include a story about a famous person, a list of preselected vocabulary words, and a word-search puzzle to complete. Some or all of these materials, however, may be related only indirectly to the content covered in that class session.

Another approach has been to assign a paraeducator to track or shadow a particular student with a disability in general education classes, and assist him or her in acquiring the content information. These paraeducators may not have been involved in planning the units or lessons, and thus, they may not have a vivid picture of the entire unit of instruction, information about the day-to-day subject matter, or the sequence of instructional activities. As a result, the paraeducator's initial role is actually that of a learner in this instructional environment.

These isolated instructional approaches do not provide the level of appropriate cognitive access to the general education curriculum for students with disabilities that is mandated by law. In addition, such arrangements may not effectively prepare students to participate in any state-mandated assessments.

Such approaches additionally have negative results for three major stakeholders. First, the special educator or related service provider struggles with fragmented planning efforts. Second, the general educator experiences fragmented instructional efforts for the diverse students in the class. Last, and most important, the student experiences fragmented learning. Thus, those students who are most educationally fragile may be receiving the least powerful instruction.

Clearly, these outcomes were unintended. These interventions were not designed to be noncompliant with the intent of the law. However, educators must identify and implement more effective methods of providing access to the general education curriculum for all students. As long as students are disengaged, either physically or cognitively, from the general education curriculum, they do not have effective access to it. Therefore, in the second P of cooperative teaching, cooperative planning, educators must shift the way in which they think about and plan for all students, especially those with disabilities.

To begin with, any planning must now be collaborative, not individual. Joint planning represents a significant change for many educators. In this planning, it is imperative that all educators who will be cooperatively teaching begin by meeting to develop collaborative answers to two issues. First, they must plan the *mechanics* of their cooperative teaching. Second, they must develop the shared fundamental *conceptualization* concerning how their instruction should be developed and implemented.

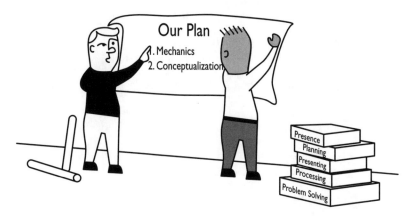

Mechanics

The mechanics of planning refers to the basic nuts and bolts of planning for instruction in cooperative teaching. Specifically, the partners in a new cooperative teaching arrangement should agree on the following six elements.

1. *Who* elements. Sample *who* elements include the following:

   - Who will be ultimately responsible for assigning grades?

   - Who will take the lead in general classroom management?

   - Who will deal with especially challenging behaviors?

   - Who will take the lead role in communicating with parents?

   - Who will take primary responsibility for such tasks as grading papers, taking roll, presenting new information, monitoring activities, and assessing student performance?

2. *What* elements. Sample *what* elements include the following:

   - What are the key components of a shared instructional plan?

   - What will the format for the unit and lesson plans look like?

3. *When* elements. Sample *when* elements include the following:

   - When will planning occur? (Daily? Biweekly? Weekly? Monthly? As needed?)

   - When should the meetings be held? (Before school? After school? During the school day?)

4. *Where* elements. Sample *where* elements include the following:

   - Where will planning occur? (Classroom? Faculty room? Electronically?)

   - If collaboration will take place in cyberspace, how will technology assist? (E-mail? Web site? PowerPoint presentations? Inspiration?)

   - Where can information about the emerging cooperative teaching be disseminated?

5. *Which* elements. Sample *which* elements include the following:

   - Which type of lesson design will be used most frequently? (Direct instruction? Inquiry and discovery? Both equally?)

   - Which materials best support the identified program goals?

6. *How* elements. Sample *how* elements include the following:

   - How much time should be allotted for unit and lesson planning?

   - How might class time be used for planning when students are working collaboratively?

   - How should a planning agenda be structured?

   - How will absences be dealt with?

   - How will planning interruptions be dealt with?

   - How should students be involved in planning?

   - How should information about cooperative teaching be disseminated to parents, students, and colleagues?

Meeting beforehand to decide directions for program planning helps to build a solid framework for working together. In addition, it promotes unity, setting the stage for molding diverse ideas into a unique and extraordinary program that minimizes any "This is how I have always done it" reactions.

Conceptualization

In addition to considering the above mechanics of planning, the second task for new cooperative teaching partners is the development of a shared fundamental conceptualization concerning how instruction should be developed and implemented. In the late 1990s a new perspective on how best to provide access to the general education curriculum emerged, called universal design for learning (UDL; Kame'enui & Simmons, 1999; Meyer & Rose, 1998; Orkwis & McLane, 1998). The following few paragraphs explain the concept of general universal design so that readers can build on these general principles in curriculum planning for diverse classrooms.

The underpinnings of the UDL principles (Kame'enui & Simmons, 1999; Meyer & Rose, 1998; Orkwis & McLane, 1998) originated many years ago in the fields of architecture and product development. The major objective of this work was to design structures and products that were accessible to or usable by the broadest possible range of consumers. For example, drinking fountains that are placed lower and have larger controls for operation are more accessible not only for individuals in wheelchairs but also by short adults and children.

In universal design, the accommodations are built in from the beginning, rather than added on as an afterthought. When accessibility features are planned, adaptations can be more subtle and integrated more smoothly into the overall design (Meyer & Rose, 2000). This is clearly demonstrated in newer buildings where wheelchair access ramps are integral to the design of the building, as opposed to older buildings where a ramp snakes awkwardly around the steps (Orkwis & McLane, 1998).

The incorporation of universal design features typically results in greater access by a variety of users in ways that were not initially anticipated. For example, curb cuts make the sidewalks more accessible not only to individuals using wheelchairs but also to such other sidewalk users as bicyclists, parents with baby carriages, skateboarders, and people using canes (Meyer & Rose, 2000). Buttons that operate external doors make buildings more accessible not only to wheelchair users but also to anyone who is carrying a heavy or awkward load.

UDL has moved from its initial conceptual base in the field of building architecture and product design into a variety of other arenas, including the "architecture" of the ways in which schools organize and deliver curriculum and instruction. Initially UDL targeted physical and sensory access to the curriculum, especially through the use of technology. More recently, the use of UDL principles has been expanded to provide greater cognitive access for students with disabilities, including cognitive impairment and learning disabilities. In education, the fundamental purpose of UDL remains unchanged. It should enhance accessibility to the school's curriculum and instruction for diverse learners, including those with disabilities. This chapter concludes with additional information about implementing UDL principles and tools to plan instruction.

Once cooperative teachers have planned a unit and several lessons, ongoing planning no longer necessarily needs to be face-to-face. For instance, some cooperative teachers select a location in their classroom for a planning board where they publicly develop and display ideas for their units and lessons for the next time they will be teaching together. Each educator writes down ideas on Post-It notes about unit goals, lesson organization, materials, and so forth, then reviews, sequences, and finally secures both sets of notes to a preformatted laminated planning sheet. Once the ideas have been sequenced, the cooperative teachers can identify who will have major responsibility for which specific tasks and topics. This planning approach not only saves time but models to students effective planning strategies.

In addition, many cooperative teachers are beginning to use electronic means of collaboration (e.g., e-mail, fax, file transfer protocol drop box) as an effective alternative to face-to-face planning efforts. Chapter 5 discusses the rapidly emerging potential contributions of electronic approaches to collaboration.

Cooperative Presenting

The third P of cooperative teaching is cooperative presenting. There is little question that having two or more educators simultaneously present and actively involved for a sustained period of time within a general education class offers more powerful instruction. But educators moving into cooperative teaching may be uncertain about how to best take practical advantage of this potential, largely because they have never before experienced such an arrangement. Chapter 4 explores the possibilities for cooperative presenting, and presents a variety of field-tested strategies for effective cooperative presentations.

Cooperative Processing

The fourth P of cooperative teaching, cooperative processing, requires cooperative teachers to determine how they will monitor and evaluate their cooperative teaching and its results. This evaluation requires deep reflection and ongoing mutual debriefings.

The ongoing processing of the cooperative teaching arrangement is composed of two distinct but interrelated dimensions. First, the educators evaluate the overall effectiveness of their cooperative teaching, based in large part on student achievement. The cooperative teachers must give careful consideration to the effectiveness and efficiency of their instruction, as measured by student learning.

Second, and equally important, the cooperative teachers must evaluate the ongoing quality of the cooperative teaching relationship. Although it is easy to overlook or disregard this component, it is critical for building and maintaining a strong interpersonal working bond. Specific issues that should be discussed jointly and evaluated include the following:

- How effectively are we using our individual sets of knowledge and skills?

- What do each of us especially like about our cooperative teaching relationship?

- What (if anything) do each of us dislike about our cooperative teaching relationship?

- What might we do to work more harmoniously?

Cooperative processing requires direct and honest dialogue among the parties involved. It is important that the partners in cooperative teaching talk to one other, not to someone who is outside the cooperative teaching environment (i.e., the building principal). If this processing element is overlooked, then the cooperative teaching relationship is likely to founder.

Cooperative Problem Solving

The fifth and final P of cooperative teaching that requires forethought is cooperative problem solving. The paradigm shift inherent in moving into cooperative teaching inevitably will generate problems. Although the arrival of these problems will seem discouraging, the reality is that any true structural change in a system should result in substantial changes in the attitudes, knowledge, skills, and behaviors of participants involved. The absence of problems would suggest that only superficial and trivial changes have occurred. The partners in cooperative teaching must plan for and develop a proactive, solution-focused approach to dealing with problems.

A particularly useful approach is for the cooperative teachers to concentrate not on the problems but on the solutions. Educators who are solution-focused quickly and optimistically look for creative ways in which to solve the problems that are inevitable when such dramatic changes are underway. Effective problem solvers in education believe that, for any problem, there is at least one solution. Successful problem-solving strategies are presented in Chapters 7 and 8.

As educators move into cooperative teaching, their new relationship can either grow and develop, remain superficial, or actually fail. If cooperative teachers plan for the five Ps of cooperative teaching, they will become more successful professionally, and also will find greater professional and personal satisfaction.

PLANNING AND THE UNIVERSAL DESIGN FOR LEARNING PRINCIPLES

Universal design for learning (UDL) principles hold great promise for helping cooperative teaching partners contribute to the remodeling of the schoolhouse. Its straightforward, proactive approach to educational planning is critical as schools strive to most effectively and efficiently educate all learners. Instead of implementing after-the-fact, costly modifications to the general education curriculum, cooperative teaching partners can design unit and lesson plans and evaluation procedures in such a way that the unique characteristics and needs of *all* learners are taken into account.

The Three Essential Principles of Universal Design for Learning

The first step in planning instruction that effectively addresses the strengths and needs of all learners is to understand and implement the three essential principles of UDL (Orkwis & McLane, 1998). These three elements are applicable when planning for any age group and within any subject area. The three principles are as follows:

- Multiple means of representation
- Multiple means of engagement
- Multiple means of expression

Multiple Means of Representation

Multiple means of representation refers to the format or presentation of the information provided to students during the initial phases of instruction. When cooperative teaching partners plan to introduce a big idea or new concept, they should consider how it might be introduced to students in a variety of distinct yet related ways.

For example, information might be presented to students via a multisensory approach, engaging them visually, auditorally, and kinesthetically. Text presented on a computer (instead of in print) is flexible. It can be changed in size, shape, and color, or even transformed into speech (Orkwis & McLane, 1998). Audio information presented with captions provides greater access for all students than either audio or print alone.

Similarly, educators might invite guest speakers to convey new information in a unique way that is especially likely to capture students' interest. Teachers could use multimedia or familiar objects in novel ways to change drab or abstract instruction to instruction that is more vivid, concrete, and appealing. Multiple means of representation helps ensure that all learning styles are effectively addressed, better meeting the needs of all learners.

Multiple Means of Engagement

Multiple means of engagement refers to how students will interact with and respond to the instruction and lesson. Creative use of technology can help support diverse learner interests by varying content, teaching materials, and response modes. For example, in a computer-based mathematics lesson, within the basic structure of the lesson's objectives, students might select specific content according to their personal interests, and work problems in the context of that choice (Meyer & Rose, 2000).

Another way to approach multiple means of engagement is to vary the social structures for the students as they work. For example, rather than having students always work independently, teachers might provide students opportunities to work in tandem with each other. Students can be assigned to work as partners or in small group configurations.

Another way to provide multiple means of engagement is to give students various ways to get involved in the lesson. For example, after completing a reading assignment, students might deepen their involvement in it by writing a series of questions about the material, completing drawings about it, creating a computer-generated graphic organizer, or paraphrasing their understanding to someone else.

Multiple Means of Expression

Multiple means of expression refers to the outcome and evaluation component of instructional design. Students can document their understanding of newly acquired information and skills in many ways besides traditional paper-and-pencil tests. Providing for multiple means of expression refers to presenting varied options for students to demonstrate mastery of the subject matter.

For example, some learners might create a portfolio of their work in the classroom that documents their learning over time. Others might research and propose a new product as a result of what they learned. Other learners might develop a video, audio, or computer presentation, and share it with another group of students.

Even if all learners are expected to take a paper-and-pencil test, they might be provided with options there as well. Some might write directly on the test itself instead of filling in bubbles on a computer-scored sheet. Others might take the same test on a computer, perhaps by using the touch pad on a computer screen. Still others might dictate their answers into a tape recorder.

Through the creation of multiple means of representation, engagement, and expression, educators can demonstrate serious consideration of each learner's unique characteristics. Cooperative teaching arrangements can help in that each participant can contribute ideas, so that there are more options from which to choose. Through the incorporation of these UDL principles, teachers will provide more successful access to the general education curriculum for all students.

Tools of Effective Curriculum Design

The UDL approach incorporates six basic tools of effective curriculum design (Kame'enui & Simmons, 1999). These are research based and, when thoughtfully implemented, enhance the learning of all students, especially those most likely to experience learning difficulties.

The six basic principles of UDL effective curriculum design are as follows:

1. Big ideas
2. Conspicuous strategies
3. Mediated scaffolding
4. Strategic integration
5. Judicious review
6. Primed background knowledge

Big Ideas

The sheer amount of information in the typical contemporary general education curriculum imposes extraordinary demands on students (Kame'enui & Simmons, 1999). At the beginning of the 21st century it is estimated that the quantity of available factual information about the world is doubling every 24 months. This means that present-day students are exposed to more information in a year than their grandparents were in a lifetime (Longstreet & Shane, 1993). In trying to embrace much more material than in the past, American educators are covering the material at an increasingly shallow level ("International Math and Science Study," 1994, p. 10).

One of the most effective alternative approaches is to concentrate on so-called big ideas (Wiggins & McTigue, 1998). Big ideas are those concepts or principles that facilitate the most efficient and broadest acquisition of knowledge over the course of a particular subject (Carnine, 1994). They are anchoring concepts through which smaller ideas (more detailed information or facts) can be learned and organized more efficiently and effectively. For example, big ideas in history might include topics such as conflict and exploration. Teaching a realistic number of big ideas to a true mastery level helps all students, especially those with difficulties, capture the essence of a subject area, while minimizing the need for teaching relatively isolated facts. Cooperative teaching partners can identify these big ideas by reviewing the curriculum content standards of their respective educational agencies, and by examining research-based areas of curricular convergence (Kame'enui & Simmons, 1999).

Conspicuous Strategies

Most effective teachers reflect constantly on the quality and effectiveness of their instruction. One of the most important considerations in this process is determining to what degree their instruction clearly and explicitly communicates the steps the learner must take to successfully complete the task.

Most students develop their own problem-solving strategies as they go through school. But not all learners are equally efficient at identifying the correct options for all problems. Cooperative teaching partners can help students develop this skill by obvious and direct instruction in the exact and specific steps that the teacher would use to solve that problem. This is teaching using *conspicuous strategies*.

Specifically, teachers explain to students exactly what problem-solving strategy is most appropriate in a situation, and also explain why that strategy is best. Similarly, teachers can overtly model the specific strategy they are employing in a given situation, including "thinking out loud" as they solve a problem. Normally covert mental processes become observable for students.

Some educators are concerned that conspicuous strategies, by being so direct, "dummy down" the curriculum. But this procedure actually makes learners more successful, both at the present task and in future work by enhancing student metacognition, or awareness of themselves as learners.

Mediated Scaffolding

For true access to the general education curriculum, some students will require adaptations in both curriculum and instruction. *Scaffolding* refers to the ways in which teachers provide help to students as they acquire new knowledge. Just as scaffolding supports a building until it can stand upright on its own, educational scaffolding supports students until they can perform independently.

Scaffolding can be provided in a number of ways. For example, when the steps in a task are too complex for a given learner, task scaffolding can be used. In such cases, the task is broken into smaller, more precise segments, similar to the way a complex math problem can be divided into smaller and easier steps. Teachers can carefully select illustrative examples that progressively move from less difficult to more difficult. Instruction can be structured so that early in initial instruction, similar (and thus potentially confusing) facts and concepts are deliberately separated. In addition, the instruction should progress smoothly from teacher-directed activities to student-directed activities, and from easy tasks to more difficult ones.

Human scaffolds include the judicious use of peer tutors. Equipment scaffolds, such devices as calculators and other computer-based assistive technologies, allow students with disabilities to complete tasks that would not be possible otherwise.

Strategic Integration

For the highest levels of mastery and generalization of new knowledge and skills to occur, the new information must be carefully combined and integrated with previously mastered information. *Strategic integration* refers to the carefully controlled combination of what the student already knows with what he or she has to learn so that the relationship between previous knowledge and new knowledge is clear. The result for the student is more complete knowledge (Kame'enui & Simmons, 1999). Strategic integration can be especially useful for combining information across curricular domains (e.g., history and geography, or mathematics and science). For example, a social studies teacher can show how such geographic features as rivers, mountains, and coastlines impact historic events such as exploration and conflict, synthesizing two content areas into a comprehensive whole. Teachers can achieve strategic integration by making explicit connections between past learning and present learning, and between the different components of the new lesson. In addition to generating new learning, strategic information also can help avoid or correct confusing concepts.

Judicious Review

For mastery to occur, newly acquired information must be reviewed to ensure its retention. Effective lesson design includes ongoing practice of newly acquired information in familiar as well as unfamiliar circumstances, as well as periodic revisiting of previously acquired knowledge and skills. *Judicious review* is the creation of opportunities where students do things repeatedly, but not repetitively, and requires thoughtful creativity to ensure academic success for diverse students.

Review is most effective if distributed and carried out over time. Repeated presentations in short increments distributed over time results in higher levels of learning than reviews collapsed into a single long review time period (e.g., Kame'enui & Simmons, 1999). In addition, review is most effective when it is cumulative, varied, and integrated into more complex tasks (Dixon, Carnine, & Kame'enui, 1992).

Primed Background Knowledge

Student acquisition of new knowledge and skills is largely determined by (a) the prior knowledge that the learner brings to the task, (b) the accuracy of that information, and (c) how well the learner accesses that information. *Priming* is a brief reminder or prompt that tells the learner to retrieve needed background information (Kame'enui & Simmons, 1999).

Educators who are effective at teaching diverse learners incorporate appropriate prerequisite background information as a refresher for students in the early stages of the introduction of new material. Students then have access to this newly cued relevant information as they attack the new educational tasks. It is important to remember that students are most successful when they have both the language background skills (vocabulary and concepts) for a new task as well as the component background knowledge, or the prerequisite individual component skills required in the new task (Kame'enui & Simmons, 1999).

CONCLUSIONS

As cooperative teachers begin their new work by developing the blueprints for their new relationship, each must begin by carefully analyzing both himself or herself as well as the partner. In this process each must identify those unique skills and strengths he or she brings to the relationship, and those areas in which help is needed.

Cooperative teaching provides participants with a variety of benefits. Its team approach enables educators to avoid the stress and burnout that often result from working in the unique psychological climate of isolated education settings (Fullan, 1997). By working within an integrated educational setting that contains two (or more) sets of professional education skills and knowledge, educators may enhance their overall job satisfaction and stability. For example, educators who work in collaborative school environments have reported enhanced levels of enjoyment of work and also perceived themselves as more effective in the delivery of instruction (e.g., Gibb et al., 1998; Rainforth & England, 1997).

In a successful construction project, once the blueprints have been developed, the experienced building contractor can review them and get a good sense of how the actual finished project will look. Similarly, this chapter has outlined basic blueprints for developing cooperative teaching arrangements, and suggested what a cooperative teaching relationship might look like and what might be done within it.

New cooperative teaching partners should consider and plan for the five Ps of cooperative teaching. These are (1) cooperative presence, (2) cooperative planning, (3) cooperative presenting, (4) cooperative processing, and (5) cooperative problem solving. As part of their planning, these teachers should consider ways to make the curriculum and instruction accessible to all students, including those with diverse academic and linguistic backgrounds. An especially promising way to structure programs for enhanced accessibility is to incorporate the principles of universal design into their planning.

In any remodeling project, after the blueprints have been developed, the next step is to identify the specific subcontractors who can take on and successfully complete each part of the plan. Chapter 4 provides a variety of field-tested strategies for identifying ways that cooperative teaching partners can work together most effectively.

CHAPTER 3 ACTIVITY

Concerns-Based Adoption Model

Most people react with concern when confronted with the possibility of change in their lives. This apprehension is as true of educators as it is of anyone. Rather than trying to hide them, one should instead seek to learn more about these initial misgivings. This first stage of self-analysis then gives each person an objective point from which to begin adapting to the new idea or procedure.

One approach that has proven to be especially fruitful in this self-analysis is the Concerns-Based Adoption Model (CBAM; Hord, Rutherford, Huling-Austin, & Hall, 1987). The CBAM allows educators to assess their level of concern regarding potential innovations. The results are organized into seven levels, grouped under three major loci of concerns.

Locus of Concern	Levels of Concern
SELF	Awareness
	Informational
	Personal
TASK	Management
IMPACT	Consequences
	Collaboration
	Refocusing

The adaptation of the CBAM in this activity allows educators to assess their concerns about the implementation of cooperative teaching in their schools.

The first of the three loci of concern is Self, which is further broken down into three levels. The first is the Awareness level. At this level respondents either may not know about the innovation or are not interested. Next, at the Informational level, respondents want additional information about the proposed changes. The third level of the Self locus is the Personal level, at which the respondent wants to know what specific impact the proposed changes will have on him or her.

At the second locus of concern, Task, there is one level: Management. Pragmatic concerns such as time, ability, and resources are identified here.

The third locus of concern is Impact. The three Impact levels start with Consequences, in which respondents note the possible effects the change will have on students. In the second level, Collaboration, respondents identify possible concerns about how their working relationships with other professionals will change. Finally, at the highest level, Refocusing, respondents note their interest in adapting and individualizing the proposed changes to their unique needs and characteristics.

Although the three loci of concerns have no specific hierarchical arrangement, the individual levels of concern within each are sequenced deliberately. For example, within the Self locus of concern, respondents at the Awareness level are in an early point of adjustment and thus have different needs than respondents at the Personal level.

The following self-assessment instrument allows school professionals to identify their own levels of concern regarding cooperative teaching. In completing the evaluation, remember that the purpose of this activity is to facilitate your own personal and professional growth. This is best achieved through honest responses.

Some items on the questionnaire may appear to be of little relevance to you at this time. For those items, please circle 0 on the scale. Other items will represent concerns you have in varying degrees of intensity and should be marked according to the following key:

6 = This statement is *absolutely true* to me at this point in time
5 = This statement is *very true* to me at this point in time
4 = This statement is *moderately true* to me at this point in time
3 = This statement is *somewhat true* to me at this point in time
2 = This statement is *slightly true* to me at this point in time
1 = This statement is *not at all true* to me at this point in time
0 = This statement is *irrelevant* to me at this point in time

Please respond to the items below in terms of your present feelings about cooperative teaching.

Rating Scale

1. I am concerned about students' attitudes toward cooperative teaching.   0 1 2 3 4 5 6

2. I now know of some other approaches that might work better.   0 1 2 3 4 5 6

3. I don't even know what cooperative teaching is. 0 1 2 3 4 5 6

4. I am concerned about not having enough time to organize myself each day. 0 1 2 3 4 5 6

5. I would like to help other faculty members use cooperative teaching. 0 1 2 3 4 5 6

6. I have a very limited knowledge of cooperative teaching. 0 1 2 3 4 5 6

7. I would like to know the effect implementing cooperative teaching will have on my professional status. 0 1 2 3 4 5 6

8. I am concerned about conflict between my interests and my responsibilities. 0 1 2 3 4 5 6

9. I am concerned about revising my use of cooperative teaching. 0 1 2 3 4 5 6

10. I would like to develop working relationships with both our faculty and outside faculty using cooperative teaching. 0 1 2 3 4 5 6

11. I am concerned about how cooperative teaching affects students. 0 1 2 3 4 5 6

12. I am not concerned about cooperative teaching. 0 1 2 3 4 5 6

13. I would like to know exactly who will make what decisions in a cooperative teaching partnership. 0 1 2 3 4 5 6

14. I would like to discuss the possibility of using cooperative teaching. 0 1 2 3 4 5 6

15. I would like to know what resources are available if we decide to adopt the cooperative teaching approach. 0 1 2 3 4 5 6

16. I am concerned about my inability to manage all that cooperative teaching requires. 0 1 2 3 4 5 6

17. I would like to know how my teaching or administration is supposed to change. 0 1 2 3 4 5 6

18. I would like to familiarize others with the cooperative teaching approach. 0 1 2 3 4 5 6

19. I am concerned about evaluating the impact of cooperative teaching on students.   0 1 2 3 4 5 6

20. I would like to revise the instructional approach to cooperative teaching.   0 1 2 3 4 5 6

21. I am completely occupied with other things.   0 1 2 3 4 5 6

22. I would like to modify our use of cooperative teaching based on the experiences of our students.   0 1 2 3 4 5 6

23. Although I don't know about cooperative teaching, I am concerned about its use.   0 1 2 3 4 5 6

24. I would like to excite my students about their part in cooperative teaching.   0 1 2 3 4 5 6

25. I am concerned about time spent working out non-academic problems related to cooperative teaching. 0 1 2 3 4 5 6

26. I would like to know what the use of cooperative teaching will require in the immediate future.   0 1 2 3 4 5 6

27. I would like to coordinate my effort with others to maximize the effects of cooperative teaching.   0 1 2 3 4 5 6

28. I would like to have more information on time and energy commitments required by cooperative teaching. 0 1 2 3 4 5 6

29. I would like to know what other educators are doing in the area of cooperative teaching.   0 1 2 3 4 5 6

30. At this time, I am not interested in learning more about cooperative teaching.   0 1 2 3 4 5 6

31. I would like to determine how to supplement, enhance, or replace cooperative teaching.   0 1 2 3 4 5 6

32. I would like to use feedback from students to change my cooperative teaching program.   0 1 2 3 4 5 6

33. I would like to know how my role will change when I am using cooperative teaching.   0 1 2 3 4 5 6

34. Coordination of tasks and people takes too much of my time.   0 1 2 3 4 5 6

35. I would like to know how cooperative teaching is better than what we do now.   0 1 2 3 4 5 6

SCORING

Each of the seven individual levels has five questions related to it on the instrument. After responding to each of the 35 items, transfer the rating for each item to the indicated space on the score sheet, then add the scores for each level as shown. The item number from the instrument appears under the blanks where that item's rating should be recorded.

Self

Awareness ___ + ___ + ___ + ___ + ___ = _____
(test items) 3 12 21 23 30 Awareness total

Informational ___ + ___ + ___ + ___ + ___ = _____
(test items) 6 14 15 26 35 Informational total

Personal ___ + ___ + ___ + ___ + ___ = _____
(test items) 7 13 17 28 33 Personal total

Task

Management ___ + ___ + ___ + ___ + ___ = _____
(test items) 4 8 16 25 34 Management total

Impact

Consequences ___ + ___ + ___ + ___ + ___ = _____
(test items) 1 11 19 24 32 Consequences total

Collaboration ___ + ___ + ___ + ___ + ___ = _____
(test items) 5 10 18 27 29 Collaboration total

Refocusing ___ + ___ + ___ + ___ + ___ = _____
(test items) 2 9 20 22 31 Refocusing total

INTERPRETATION

Although there is no fixed system to translate the results of this instrument into specific prescriptions, the following information can help educators become better prepared to respond to the changes inherent in implementing cooperative teaching. Within the Self locus of concern, respondents whose scores are highest at the first level, Awareness, are indicating that up to this point they have heard little about the proposed changes. Such individuals should seek out colleagues who know about cooperative teaching to find out basic information without being overwhelmed.

Respondents with high scores at the Informational level have heard about the change but do not know a great deal about it and thus are in need of more information. These educators should visit sites where cooperative teaching arrangements have been successfully implemented, in particular looking to see how these practices relate to their current work.

A high score within the Personal area indicates that the respondent is especially concerned with the effect cooperative teaching will have on his or her daily functioning. These educators should understand that such concerns are common and legitimate. It may be helpful for them to meet informally with educators who presently are practicing cooperative teaching. These school personnel likely experienced similar concerns and can explain how their personal issues diminished over time as they gained experience.

Respondents recording high scores in the area of Management within the Task locus of concern are saying that they need practical how-to information. These educators should concentrate on the nuts-and-bolts aspects of cooperative teaching, meeting with other educators to generate specific answers to immediate questions and problems.

The final three sets of data come from the Impact locus of concern. High scores in the first of these, Consequences, indicate the respondent is interested in the direct results of implementing cooperative teaching. These educators should visit programs where cooperative teaching has been established for some period of time, so that the effects can be clearly seen.

Respondents with high scores in the Collaboration level of concern are indicating that they have implemented and been successful with cooperative teaching. As a result, they want to spread the news to other professionals. These educators are the obvious choice for helping to provide inservice training activities to those just beginning these new professional relationships. One especially useful system is to have several of these experienced professionals work together to plan training activities and offer assistance.

Finally, respondents with high scores in the Refocusing level of concern represent the most sophisticated implementers of cooperative teaching. These individuals have experience with successful implementation during which they likely identified procedures to customize and revise for even more effective instruction. School professionals at this level should solicit the resources they need to make the system work even better. They also should continually re-examine what they are doing and why, and consider the present and future impact of this work.

Getting Construction Under Way:

Implementing Cooperative Teaching

A journey of a thousand miles must begin with a single step.
—Lao-Tzu

Ith blueprints finally complete, homeowners move into the hammer-and-nails phase of their remodeling project, actually beginning the physical construction of their new structure. The building materials involved in this phase include lumber, drywall, nails and screws, and paint.

Similarly, educators who are remodeling the schoolhouse through cooperative teaching must identify, obtain, prepare, and assemble the building materials necessary for their remodeling project. In the schoolhouse remodeling project the materials include time, scheduling, and administrative support. These three things are frequently mentioned by educators who are moving into cooperative teaching as the most significant needed resources.

When remodeling, it is sometimes difficult to conceptualize what the final project will look like with the limited information contained in blueprints and descriptions. Pictures or models that show the new arrangements can give the homeowners a much clearer idea of the final result. This chapter concludes with several "pictures" of the remodeled cooperative teaching classroom.

THE NATURE OF TIME

Typically people consider time a resource. However, time has a singularly unique quality. Unlike physical resources that educators can control (e.g., money, paper, materials), time cannot be stockpiled or saved for later use. It is irreversible and irreplaceable, and it passes at a fixed and invariable rate, regardless of whether one wishes to spend it or save it.

Imagine that one had a bank account into which $86,400 was deposited every day. Further imagine that whatever residual amount had not been spent was canceled every evening. In such a situation, the only reasonable thing to do would be to spend every cent every day. In reality, each person has a "time account" into which 86,400 seconds are deposited each morning, all of which are gone by midnight. Whatever has not been invested in productive use is lost forever (Drawbaugh, 1984).

The term *time management* is actually something of a misnomer. The passage of time is beyond the ability of people to control or manage. It passes regardless of the actions or inactions of people. Thus, instead of managing time, it may be more accurate to speak of managing one's own behaviors with respect to time (Mackenzie, 1972).

As educators begin to work collaboratively in the schools, their schedules and use of time will change dramatically. One of the most essential ingredients for successful collaboration is time (e.g., Cramer, 1998; Murphy, 1997; Walther-Thomas, Korinek, McLaughlin, & Williams, 2000). Setting aside the time to plan and implement cooperative teaching is critical, especially in its early stages. One way to more effectively find and use time is to assess present patterns of time usage.

ASSESSING TIME USAGE

Teachers have a near-universal sense that time slips away from them, and they often have little idea of where the time is going. One way school professionals can begin to understand their time use is to keep a daily time log.

In its most basic form, a time log contains two columns: one for recording a specific time, and one for recording the activity that occurred at that time. Starting with awakening, one records time and activity. When an activity is completed and a new one started, the new time and new activity are recorded, and so on. Alternatively, a time log might contain preexisting blocks of time (for example, 15-minute blocks). In each block the educator can record the activity that occurred during that block. (See the appendix for a sample time log.) After completing time logs for several days, teachers typically are surprised to find how much time they spend on activities they seldom think about and how little time is devoted to those functions that they anticipated to make up the largest part of their work and lives.

In self-assessing time usage many educators have discovered the following (Drawbaugh, 1984):

- Much time is spent on routine tasks and activities of low priority.
- Little time is spent planning and working toward established goals.
- Uncommitted time during the typical school day is limited to about 1 hour.
- Time is wasted in roughly the same way each day and each week.

Another way that professionals in the schools can determine if they are using time productively is to complete a time questionnaire. A sample time questionnaire is provided at the end of this chapter.

A final step in analyzing time usage is to identify the most significant wasters of time. There are two types of time robbers: external and internal (Mackenzie, 1972). External types are those largely beyond the educator's control, including meetings, paperwork, unscheduled activities, and so forth. Internal time robbers are those under the direct control of the teacher, and include lack of planning, procrastination, lack of organization, inability to say no, refusal to delegate work to others, and personal and outside activities. Internal time robbers are the biggest wasters of time.

Most school professionals have certain structural limitations on their time. For example, they are expected to be at the school by a certain time before classes start and to remain a certain amount of time after classes end and students leave. However, these limitations may be less restraining than they appear.

Bartholomew and Gardner (1982) calculated that educators spend an average of 45.9 hours per week on all teaching duties. They also noted that educators directly control at least 2 hours of each of their 8-hour workdays and also directly control the 60 nonteaching days per year (weekdays in the summer). These hours yield educators a total of 852 hours per year (more than 100 eight-hour days) over which they have direct control. (The question of whether educators are paid for professional activities during the summer aside, the reality is that this time is indeed available for such use.)

FINDING PLANNING TIME

Beginning cooperative teachers frequently are concerned with finding time to plan. In elementary schools planning can occur during student specialty classes such as art, physical education, or library time (Murphy, 1997). If the activities are blocked back to back, then periods of 60 to 90 minutes become available (Walther-Thomas et al., 2000).

Another possibility is to convert several instructional days per year into staff development days, parts of which might be reserved for planning cooperative teaching (Kochhar, West, & Taymans, 2000). In some states and districts, the school day has been lengthened by 20 to 30 minutes, with equivalent early dismissal of students on Fridays. School professionals then use Friday afternoons for planning, including planning for cooperative teaching (Raywid, 1993).

Many middle school schedules are designed with one or two planning periods, thus facilitating planning by cooperative teaching partners (Walther-Thomas, 1997). Some educators involved in cooperative teaching have found that scheduling a common daily lunch period and a common preparation period immediately thereafter can yield a shared hour and a half every day (Raywid, 1993).

Other schools have instituted regular assemblies conducted by the principal, assistant principal, or community volunteers. In these programs a school's aides and administrators take attendance and monitor the students during the assembly and then escort them back to their classes afterward. During this time the rest of the school's staff arrive early and go directly to planning meetings. Year-round schools with 3-week breaks between quarters allow collaborating educators intensive 2- or 3-day planning meetings (Raywid, 1993).

The occasional combining of classes for activities that apply to a variety of students (e.g., viewing of videotapes or selected cable programming) also can give educators time to plan their cooperative teaching efforts (Watson, Buchanan, Huyman, & Seal, 1992). Some teachers have found it useful to combine classes in a special "quiet time," where students can work on projects independently, but must do so in silence (Young, 1994). Such an atmosphere makes it easier for cooperative teaching partners to plan.

Other individuals such as retired educators, professionals from the business community, state employees, college students, and parents often volunteer in the schools.

An education intern from a college might assume instructional responsibility for monitoring group work while the cooperative teaching partners meet in a quiet area of the classroom for a short period of time (Kochhar et al., 2000).

USING PLANNING MEETINGS EFFICIENTLY

Home remodelers must plan ahead to make best use of their building materials. Similarly, cooperative teaching partners must plan ahead to make best use of the scarce resource of time. By some estimates, half of all time spent in meetings is wasted (Mackenzie, 1972). Efficient meetings do not happen automatically; there are a number of strategies that can make them more productive.

Establish an Agenda for the Planning Meeting

Creating an agenda is perhaps the single most important step for a successful meeting. The agenda should include a point-by-point outline of exactly what is to be accomplished at the meeting. Each point to be covered should be worded as a question, to encourage the educators to think about answers. If one person has special responsibility for any point, that person's name should be listed by that point. A sample agenda for a meeting of cooperative teaching partners is shown in Figure 4.1.

---

1. Reflection: How did we do last week?
   a. What were the best things that happened in our cooperative teaching this past week?
   b. What did either of us make mental notes to talk about improving?

2. Goal-setting: What could we do, and what should we do, this next week?
   a. What are the possible things we might do?
   b. Which of these things will help us effectively teach all students?

3. Resources: Based on the goals we've set for this next week, what are the resources we'll need to achieve these goals?
   a. What are the physical resources (materials, equipment, and so forth) that will be required?
   b. What are the personnel resources that will be required?

4. Responsibilities: Which of us will be responsible for which goals and activities?

Figure 4.1 Agenda for a cooperative teaching meeting.

Ongoing issues should continually be included in meeting agendas to allow the educators to identify and resolve small problems early. Perhaps the single most important agenda item is the regular review of the quality and quantity of the interactions between the cooperative teaching partners.

Follow the Agenda

Imagine professional house remodelers coming to work at a remodeling site, beginning their workday by reviewing the architectural plans, and then ignoring those plans for the rest of the day. Predictably, chaos would result. Yet most educators have participated in meetings where this happens. The discussion drifts off the agenda, meanders, and wanders aimlessly. Participants bring up tangential points that disrupt the continuity of the meeting, cause the entire meeting to drift, and ultimately result in the goals of the meeting not being accomplished. In cooperative teaching planning meetings, educators should be aware of this tendency and stay with the agenda.

After each point is discussed and resolved, it should be checked off the agenda, and the agreed-upon actions to be taken should be noted. Before the meeting ends one person should summarize the decisions made and conclusions reached. This ensures that all meeting attendees leave with a common sense of accomplishment, purpose, and direction. Alternatively, one person can keep a record of decisions and, using carbon paper, a computer, or a copy machine, distribute results to attendees before adjournment.

Establish Priorities

To ensure that the most important items are covered at the meeting, the agenda preparer should use the classic newspaper "reverse pyramid" ordering style. The most important item to be discussed and resolved should be first on the agenda, the second most important item should be discussed second, and so on. This "top loading" of the agenda with the most important items first ensures that the meeting addresses and resolves the most important questions.

Set Time Limits

Different items on the agenda will require differing amounts of time. A common problem is to spend 30 minutes on some unimportant issue or detail, leaving only 15 minutes for more critical items on the agenda. Each item should have time limits for discussion, as well as an overall time limit for the meeting. One person might serve as timekeeper, noting how much time is left for any given item, and how much time remains for the entire meeting.

Control Interruptions

To minimize interruptions, meetings should be held in a relatively out-of-the-way location, a quiet corner that is not highly visible. Cooperative teaching partners should minimize interruptions during their planning times, including shutting the door, turning off or ignoring the phone, and keeping others from distracting the participants.

Be on Time, Start on Time, End on Time

It is unfair to all participants involved for a person to be late for meetings. A school professional who is consistently late for meetings is saying, "My time is more important than your time. I do not consider this meeting, or you, important." Chronic tardiness for meetings inhibits the development of the mutual respect and trust that is fundamental to effective professional partnerships.

One way to resolve tardiness is to target it as an issue to cover at the next meeting. In this discussion, the on-time partner must communicate effectively to the tardy partner the specific sorts of problems (both functional and interpersonal) that the late behavior is causing.

During the informal moments at the beginning of meetings it is important that the teaching partners take a few moments to reestablish social contact, especially if they have not seen each other for a while. However, this should not take more than a few minutes. Although collaborating educators should enjoy each other's company, meetings will not be productive if they become primarily social get-togethers.

Plan the Next Meeting

Planning the next meeting, including time, place, and agenda, should be the final item on each meeting's agenda. This ensures ongoing continuity.

DEVELOPING SCHEDULES

Scheduling difficulties are a frequently reported barrier to collaboration (Kochhar et al., 2000). Cooperative teaching requires major shifts in the way a school's professional personnel work throughout the day. Support services providers, who historically have worked via pullout programs independent from their general education colleagues, now will be spending the majority of their professional workdays working directly with other educators in general education classrooms.

Scheduling Considerations for Support Services Providers

In cooperative teaching, support services providers (e.g., school counselor, special educator, psychologist, speech–language therapist, school social worker, gifted and talented facilitator) typically go into general educators' classes for varying periods of time. In developing schedules for their work with their general education partners, support services providers first should consider the following questions.

1. How much does the support services provider wish to participate in cooperative teaching, especially at first? This is perhaps the single most important question. Some are eager to become heavily involved. Others are more comfortable beginning in small doses.

2. How much time does the support services provider have available for cooperative teaching? Often these professionals have a variety of other duties (e.g., counseling, therapy, testing, meetings). Whereas many of these duties can be restructured or rescheduled, others simply must be worked around.

3. In which classrooms are the students who might benefit most from cooperative teaching? (In other words, how many general educators will be involved initially, and how many might be involved ultimately?) Some schools cluster such students with just a few educators, whereas others subscribe to a "natural proportions" philosophy, in which students with special needs are dispersed throughout all classes. Although the former option may enhance the ease and efficiency of services delivery, many educators have come to see this segregation as another way that access to the general education classroom is prevented.

4. To what degree is the school's general education curriculum and material appropriate for students with special needs? How much adaptation and modification of this curriculum (and accompanying materials) will be required? To a large extent this determines the amount of time the support services provider will be engaged in active preparations for cooperative teaching. That is, some general education curricula may be structured such that they are already relatively accessible to almost all students, with little or no modification required. Other schools with more traditional and less flexible curricula may require greater amounts of work from the support services providers to make the curricula accessible for all students, especially those with linguistic or academic differences.

5. What are the wishes of the students with special needs? Especially in middle school and high school, some students feel singled out and isolated when it is time for them to leave the general classroom and go to the resource room. This problem can be minimized through extensive in-class cooperative teaching where the special services provider works with many or all students, not just those with disabilities.

6. How much support is needed by the students? This is one of the most critical determinations in developing a cooperative teaching schedule. As a general rule, the greater the student needs, the more time the support services provider might spend in that general education classroom. At one extreme, classrooms with one or more students with severe disabilities might have a support services provider in the room for the entire school day. Conversely, classes with students with mild disabilities may have a support services provider working in the room for only a brief period, and not necessarily on a daily basis.

7. What are the general education teacher's wishes and comfort level with cooperative teaching? Some may wish to participate extensively, whereas others may prefer initially lower levels. Needless to say, this topic should be thoughtfully discussed early on, with both partners able to disclose their true feelings about the new approach.

8. What are the wishes of the parents of the students with special needs in terms of the types of educational programs they would like their children to receive? Historically many parents battled to win specialized services for their children (e.g., pullout programs with specialized resource rooms). Understandably, some may be reluctant to give up such programs for the unknown entity of cooperative teaching. Other parents will actively encourage cooperative teaching, which they see as supporting inclusion efforts and programs (Kochhar et al., 2000).

Scheduling Considerations for General Educators

1. Does the general education teacher truly believe that all students can learn? In many ways, traditional pullout and segregated special education developed because of the absence of this belief. Successful cooperative teaching requires that all educators involved agree that all students can learn.

2. How much does the general educator want to participate in cooperative teaching? At least at first, some general educators may feel defensive about other educators entering their rooms. In the past, the infrequent professional visit to the classroom usually was to evaluate the teacher, leaving him or her with mixed feelings about visitors. Others pragmatically welcome any additional educational support in the classroom.

3. How much support does the general education teacher need? Some educators will have the knowledge and skills necessary to teach a wide variety of students, whereas others may lack the preparation, experience, or disposition to teach increasingly diverse groups of students.

4. How flexible is the educator? Working with a second professional requires more flexibility than working alone. After years of having sole responsibility for classroom instruction, some teachers may be uncomfortable with the more flexible arrangements that cooperative teaching requires.

5. How will parents of all students in the classroom feel about the implementation of cooperative teaching in the classroom? The provision of two school professionals in the classroom simultaneously should help assure parents that *every* student who needs help will receive it.

Scheduling Considerations for Both Cooperative Teaching Partners

As general educators and support services providers develop schedules for their new cooperative teaching arrangement, they must jointly consider the following questions. (Adams & Cessna, 1991):

1. What are the needs of all students in the school?

2. What curricula, instruction, and assistive technologies can best ensure access to the general education curriculum for all students in the school?

3. What resources (human and otherwise) are available in the school that can be incorporated into the educational program?

4. What outside resources (e.g., university faculty and students, consultants, parents and other adults, supplementary materials) might be drawn in as needed?

5. What supports do general education teachers require to best meet the needs of all their students in appropriate settings throughout the day?

6. What are the unique strengths of the individual educators involved in cooperative teaching, and how can scheduling best use these?

The eventual schedule that evolves should reflect consideration of these questions. Perhaps needless to say, these schedules will have to be flexible. Although some cooperating educators might be more comfortable (especially initially) with a fixed schedule, they should acknowledge from the beginning that the schedule will be fluid and subject to change.

Types of Schedules

The educators who have been most successful in cooperative teaching have found it easiest to begin simply. In planning for their cooperative teaching, the partners first should determine how much time per day and how many days per week will be spent in cooperative teaching.

Paired Stable Schedules

The least complicated cooperative teaching arrangement is one support services provider working with one general educator. Their schedule for cooperative teaching is fixed; for example, every day for a particular period. Figures 4.2 and 4.3 illustrate paired stable schedules, one for a daily schedule and one for a 3-day-a-week schedule, respectively.

Paired stable schedules offer several advantages. The consistency is easier on students, and facilitates educator planning and the development of solid professional relationships. There is less possibility for confusion because follow-up by the special services provider can be more consistent. Downtime during which the support services provider must catch up on what has been accomplished since the last time she or he was in the room is minimized.

	Monday	Tuesday	Wednesday	Thursday	Friday
8–9:00	X	X	X	X	X
9–10:00	X/I	X/I	X/I	X/I	X/I
10–11:00	X	X	X	X	X

(*X* represents the general educator in the education classroom; *I* represents the support services provider in the general education classroom.)

Figure 4.2 Cooperative teaching schedule: Daily basis.

	Monday	Tuesday	Wednesday	Thursday	Friday
8–9:00	X	X	X	X	X
9–10:00	X	X/I	X/I	X/I	X
10–11:00	X	X	X	X	X

(*X* represents the general educator in the general education classroom; *I* represents the support services provider in the general education classroom. Many cooperative teaching partners have found Mondays and Fridays too unsettled and variable to work consistently.)

Figure 4.3 Cooperative teaching schedule: Clustered basis.

However, there also exists the possibility of burnout or boredom, because the cooperative teaching partners are together day after day. This staleness can be avoided by the participants' switching roles from time to time. This consistent pairing may result in the participants' becoming dependent on each other, rather than learning to carry out certain tasks independently. Under this schedule the support services provider will be able to work only with a small number of students and general educators. Finally, some students may become dependent on these intensive levels of support services instead of acquiring more independent learning skills.

Rollover Schedules

As the support services provider becomes more comfortable with the cooperative teaching arrangement in a general education classroom, she or he likely will wish to expand cooperative teaching to more than one general classroom and more than one general educator. Moving from classroom to classroom during the day is referred to as a rollover schedule. Figure 4.4 illustrates the rollover concept.

Rollover schedules provide one very significant advantage over paired stable schedules. This schedule allows a single support services provider to work with a greater number of general educators and students, sharing his or her specialized skills with a larger group. More general educators can acquire the specialized skills the support services provider brings to the general education classroom. In addition, more students will be able to receive these specialized services.

Having the support services provider come in on certain days introduces variety into general education classrooms. By being exposed to different teaching styles, students can acquire more sophisticated learning strategies that will generalize to future learning environments. In addition, many educators have found that when support services are provided less frequently, students develop informal cooperative learning arrangements, learning to help one another.

	Monday	Tuesday	Wednesday	Thursday	Friday
8–9:00	X/I	X	X	X/I	X
9–10:00	Y/I	Y	Y/I	Y	Y/I
10–11:00	Z	Z/I	Z/I	Z	Z/I

(*X* represents the first general educator in the first general education classroom; *I* represents the support services provider in a general education classroom; *Y* represents a second general educator in a second general education classroom; *Z* represents a third general educator in a third general education classroom.)

Figure 4.4 Cooperative teaching schedule: Rollover basis.

One disadvantage of rollover schedules is the lessened amount of time that the support services provider has for his or her traditional duties (e.g., special educators have less time for pullout activities, speech and language therapists have less time for direct therapy). Planning is also more challenging with this schedule. The more colleagues with which one works, the more individual styles one must learn to accommodate. Help for general educators is available only at certain times and on certain days, making their planning more difficult. Some students, general educators, and support services providers may find switching back and forth disconcerting and even disruptive. Finally, some general education classrooms and some students may want the support services provider on a daily basis, causing him or her to feel stretched too far and spread too thin to be effective.

Most homeowners prefer to work with creative architects and home remodelers who can provide the homeowners with many options for their project. Similarly, in cooperative teaching, scheduling formats are limited only by the creativity of the cooperative teaching partners. Although hour-long blocks are included in the aforementioned examples for simplicity's sake, the amount of time spent in cooperative teaching may be as little as 20 to 30 minutes, or may extend to most or all of the school day.

ADMINISTRATIVE SUPPORT

When school professionals are asked to explain the success or failure of innovative projects, one of the most frequently reported causes is administrative support or lack thereof. Administrative support is critical for the success in innovation (e.g., Kochhar et al., 2000). School principals are especially influential for the change process inherent in collaboration (Walther-Thomas et al., 2000).

Because the concept of cooperative teaching is relatively new, principals may not know at first exactly what resources to provide. Cooperative teachers need to communicate to their principals the specific supports the teachers need to be effective. The support required will vary significantly depending on the unique personnel who are involved.

Administrative support is a two-way street. As cooperative teaching partners receive support from their administrators, the partners must return that support. Administrators should see that their efforts to support educators in implementing cooperative teaching are acknowledged and appreciated.

The School Principal

In most schools the principal is the primary administrator, and, as such, subject to pressures from both inside and outside the school, many of which are not seen by other school professionals. Educators often attribute a great deal of power to principals, not realizing the substantial restrictions on principals' options. Most effective principals quickly learn that simply asking or telling staff to do a certain thing, or to act a certain way, does not ensure that those changes come about.

There are several ways in which principals can foster collaboration, including cooperative teaching, among teachers. Principals who are effective at this do the following to promote cooperative teaching in their schools:

- communicate a vision for cooperative teaching
- demonstrate that they value cooperative teaching
- lead faculty development for planning
- provide and participate in faculty development opportunities
- provide resources, including time
- assist in creating an action plan
- recognize student and teacher accomplishments (Tindall, 1996)

Developing Administrative Support

As Montgomery (1990) noted, the initial hurdle to any change is inertia. The "we've never done it that way before" syndrome is typical, usually appearing early in the process of seeking administrative support. She additionally concluded that administrators are haunted by two great fears: that they will lose control of a program and that money and other resources will be mismanaged.

One problem is that budgets typically are built on existing service models, not on new and innovative approaches. This almost inevitably results in understandable financial concerns when unpredictable creative approaches are proposed. In most districts funding for the support services providers is based on the number of students technically identified as requiring specialized educational programs. Some principals will be reluctant to approve projects that might serve to reduce the amount of this funding.

This may well be the case with cooperative teaching, at least in the short term, until funding models catch up with service delivery systems as they have in the past.

Another obstacle to administrative support is that neither all the problems nor the answers of any innovation are known at first. This is an understandable concern for principals. Educators implementing cooperative teaching must help the school principal to see the inevitability of an initial period of uncertainty. Although principals and other stakeholders should be kept abreast of the status of the program, full-scale evaluation of cooperative teaching should not come until after this initial period.

As educators seek to implement cooperative teaching, there are a number of ways they can elicit the administrative support necessary for the program's success (Montgomery, 1990). First, cooperating educators should discuss plans with the principal well in advance of the proposed changes. Educators can prepare a short, one-page description that provides information to the principal in a "who, what, where, when, why, how" format.

In addition to this planning, the principal should arrange with the teachers to inform all parents of the students affected by the change about the program. Many cooperative teaching partners have found it useful to write letters to all parents of students in the class explaining the arrangement. (A sample letter is included in Figure 4.5.)

After program implementation, the cooperative teaching partners should share frequent brief written update reports with the principal, especially early on. Whereas these progress notes should highlight successes, any problems also should be noted. Effective principals usually have solid problem-solving skills, and the partners should take advantage of this skill to find solutions. By soliciting the principal's skills, the teaching partners increase the principal's personal and professional investment in cooperative teaching.

Cooperative teaching partners might resist telling colleagues too much about the program at first, instead waiting until it is more firmly established. The cooperative teaching partners might place information about their work on a common bulletin board in the faculty lounge or on the school's Web site so colleagues can read the information at their leisure. Also, the school staff will likely be more interested in hearing about a program that is currently functioning than in receiving an advance presentation of a program idea. A person would not hold a housewarming party for a remodeling project while the walls were unpainted and the roof incomplete.

Cooperating teaching partners should maintain a database that supports the effectiveness of the collaborative intervention. This database might include information about standardized test scores, curriculum-based measurement, or social and behavior skills. A brief numerical or statistical summary of the accomplishments of cooperative teaching provides principals with a report that is easily understood by their superiors.

The support services provider should make special effort to become integrated with rest of the school staff. This includes volunteering for committees (especially those not related to special services), correcting papers, helping with the school newspaper, coach-

Dear Parents:

As some of you know, in the past here at Barr School, whenever students received specialized educational services they almost always left their regular classroom to receive their special programs. However, today there is much research that students do not make as much progress this way as they might with other approaches.

This school year we will begin a different, and what we believe be a better, approach to educating all our students, including those who need extra support. In our new cooperative teaching arrangement a variety of staff professionals will be coming into the general classrooms to work with the students' teachers so that they can combine their skills to teach all students. We believe that this approach will help **all** of our students succeed better in the general class and also will help the students with special needs feel less isolated.

If you are the parent of a student presently receiving special services, please contact your child's teacher at 555-5678. He or she will explain the program in more detail and work with you to make the necessary changes in your child's program. We also have a video available for checkout that will show you this exciting program in action at another school. We are excited about this new approach at Barr School and invite you to come and see the program in action.

Sincerely,

Jim Patent
Principal

Lori Carnick
Teacher

Figure 4.5 Sample letter to parents.

ing athletics, and so forth. Such actions demonstrate clearly to the rest of the school staff that all educators are there for all students.

Once cooperative teachers have shown their principal the advantages, he or she is more likely to support the program. Even when the principal supports cooperative teaching in theory, he or she may not know how to demonstrate it.

Expressions of Administrative Support

There are many ways that principals can show support for cooperative teaching. Although the types of support administrators provide are as varied as the administrators themselves, certain categories or types of administrative support have been identified (e.g., Arends, 1982).

Perhaps one of the most important initial types of support a principal can offer cooperating educators is for the principal to collaboratively develop a clear vision of what the school can be, and the role of each school professional in making that vision a reality (Barth, 1990; Fullan, 1993a). An administrator's understanding of the philosophy of cooperative teaching and the foresight to see how this theoretical philosophy can be translated into practical reality make it easier for educators to sense support from administration.

Ideas concerning organizational problems and solutions are received differently and with greater attention when coming from individuals in positions of authority. A principal's frequent demonstration of support through public actions such as verbal comments, short written notes, and literal pats on the back shows that he or she is thinking about and supportive of the changes.

The implementation of an innovation always introduces instability. The school staff will look to the principal to clarify the professional roles, especially those most directly associated with the proposed changes. This role clarification also extends to the principal, who must clarify his or her new role regarding the innovation.

One of the frequent roles an administrator plays in the implementation of a new program is that of defender of the changes. Defending the changes covers tasks such as helping innovators cut through bureaucratic red tape and facing hostility from staff members who are resisting change. In the absence of such administrative efforts, innovators will find themselves beaten down.

Perhaps the strongest administrative expression of support for change is new allocation of resources. These resources may include release time and planning time; space (especially space with symbolic value, such as space that is large or physically close to the administrator); money; status; suggestions for scheduling; staff development opportunities; freedom to experiment; and dedicated time from, and access to, the administrator. Such resources clearly show that the project has administrative support.

Although many of these administrative displays of support are primarily symbolic (e.g., allocation of space, pats on the back, and so forth), it does not diminish the crucial role they play in the acceptance and ultimate success of innovative projects such as cooperative teaching.

PICTURES OF POSSIBILITIES

Although an architect might describe verbally the way a home remodeling project will look upon completion, those descriptions often fail to adequately convey to the homeowners exactly how the results will appear. A set of artist drawings or even three-dimensional models are much more effective ways of getting this information across.

Similarly, educators moving into cooperative teaching often are unsure of exactly what their new arrangement might look like, or what they might do in it. The remainder of this chapter presents 24 text descriptions accompanied by graphics of field-tested cooperative teaching practices to help educators realize the possibilities. Specifically, these examples demonstrate the differentiation of roles and responsibilities for the cooperative teaching partners. They also reveal ways in which students with special needs are provided access to the general education curriculum.

These 24 cooperative teaching practices illustrate a powerful instructional procedure incorporating four stages of teaching and learning. The first stage, *initial instruction*, is teacher directed, and provides the necessary cognitive framework for subsequent student learning to proceed most efficiently. The second stage, *guided practice*, is characterized by active student learning, either in pairs or in small groups, with teacher support provided as appropriate. In the third stage, *independent practice*, students have the opportunity to refine their newly acquired knowledge and skills without teacher support in structured experiences. Finally, students demonstrate their new competencies in the fourth stage, *individual accountability* (Los Angeles County Office of Education, n.d.).

The 24 possibilities for cooperative teaching arrangements that follow incorporate the three essential qualities of Universal Design for Learning that were discussed in Chapter 3. These three qualities are (1) multiple means of representation, (2) multiple means of expression, and (3) multiple means of engagement (Orkwis & McLane, 1998).

The illustrations are additionally grouped into three categories, based on the specific and unique backgrounds of the educators participating in cooperative teaching. The first set of graphics (Figures 4.6–4.13) depicts a general educator and paraeducator working collaboratively, in both elementary and secondary settings. The second set (Figures 4.14–4.21) portrays ways in which a general educator and special educator might cooperate, also in elementary and secondary settings. The final set of pictures (Figures 4.22–4.29) shows ways in which a trio of educators (specifically, a general educator, a special educator, and a paraeducator) might cooperatively teach in elementary and secondary settings.

General Educator and Paraeducator

When paraeducators are assigned to general education classrooms, too often they are limited to one of two roles: either clerical duties, or working one-on-one with the same student for an entire class period or sometimes an entire school day, entire school year, or even an entire school career (Mueller, 1997). Such assignments are unnecessarily restrictive for the general educator, the paraeducator, and their students. The presence of two educators in the classroom should cause a significant restructuring of the classroom instructional environment, not simply more of the same (Garnett, 1996). Figures 4.6 through 4.13 illustrate how a general and paraeducator might cooperatively teach in an elementary or secondary classroom.

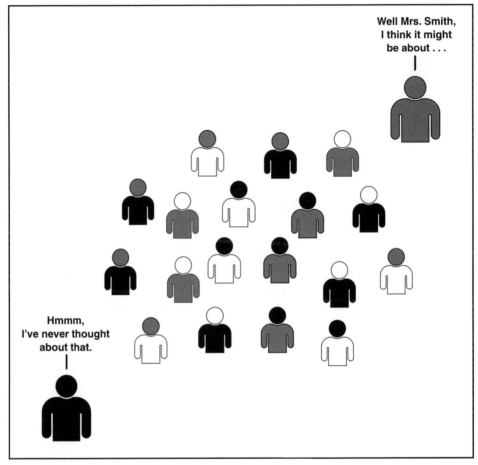

Figure 4.6 Sample 1: General educator and paraeducator, elementary level, initial instruction.

Elementary Level

Sample 1. The general educator introduces a story by showing students the cover of a trade book while the paraeducator models cognitive problem-solving skills overtly by talking out loud about the potential content of the book. Then both educators take turns reading the story to the student. Throughout this activity each educator interjects questions related to the content, again overtly modeling cognitive processes. See Figure 4.6.

Sample 2. During the guided practice stage, students are assigned to work in groups of two or three. Each group is given a bag containing several books with vivid illustrations on the cover. Taking turns, each student selects a book, reads the title and

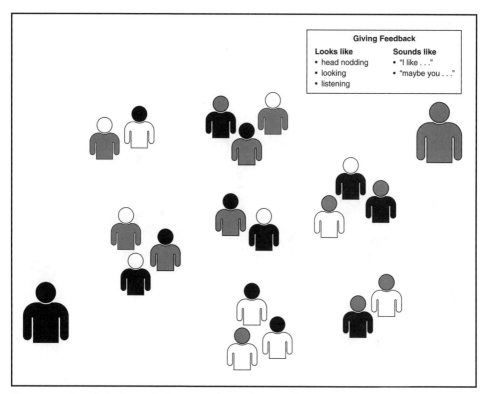

Figure 4.7 Sample 2: General educator and paraeducator, elementary level, guided practice.

reviews the illustration, makes a prediction about the contents of the book, and then receives immediate feedback from his or her group partner(s). The teachers may first model for students how to give feedback. The group then reads the story together, and, finally, compares their predictions with the correct response already written on an index card in the back of the book. The general and paraeducator closely monitor the groups; either teacher spends extra time with any students as needed. See Figure 4.7.

Sample 3. For independent practice, the educators redistribute the books to each student. The students then practice making predictions, while the two educators monitor and coach them as a group by asking questions to individual students. Each student then selects a book, and compares his or her prediction with the actual story line. If a student needs assistance in reading the book, one educator might work one-to-one with him or her while the other educator monitors the entire group. In addition, there may be audiobooks that allow students with emergent literacy skills to participate as well. See Figure 4.8.

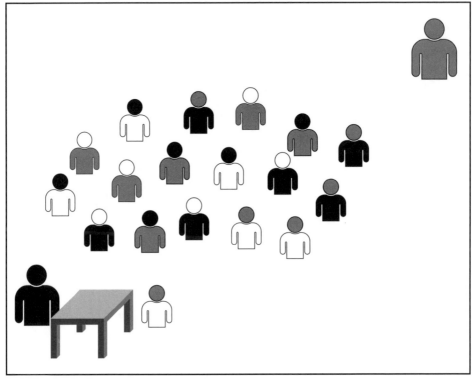

Figure 4.8 Sample 3: General educator and paraeducator, elementary level, independent practice.

Sample 4. For the individual accountability stage, the general and paraeducator have designed a computer-assisted evaluation instrument by scanning in various book covers and multiple-choice questions to measure student skill in making predictions. The general educator calls four students to the back of the room for their individual evaluations, while the paraeducator monitors the remaining students as they read their self-selected trade books. See Figure 4.9.

Secondary Level

Sample 5. In this example, during initial instruction, the general educator introduces the big idea of an instructional unit as the paraeducator orally and visually interjects supplemental information. Then the paraeducator asks students to write down what they want to learn more about on that topic on separate Post-it notes, places the notes on the board at the back of the classroom, and categorizes students' interests while the general educator visually maps out the major topics, tasks, and activities on a planning board for the unit. The general educator then asks students to transfer key tasks and

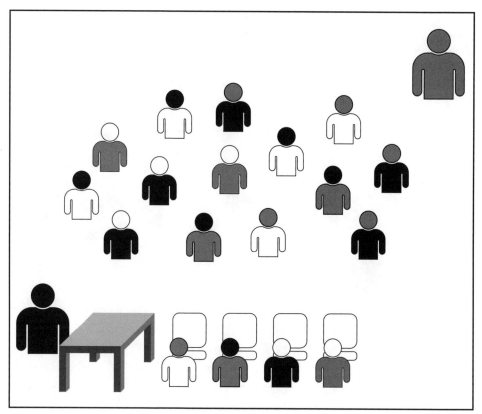

Figure 4.9 Sample 4: General educator and paraeducator, elementary level, individual accountability.

due dates to their personal agendas or calendars. Prior to the end of the day's session, both adults view the planning board to reconfirm future lessons, using the Post-it notes to ensure that student needs are met. See Figure 4.10.

Sample 6. For guided practice, while the general educator takes roll, the paraeducator provides an overview of the day's guided practice activity by describing the jigsaw cooperative learning task and then assigning students to heterogeneous groups. The general educator assigns differentiated reading tasks from a current magazine article to be completed by members of each group. The paraeducator then posts charts in distinct areas of the room and instructs students to move into their focus groups to answer specific questions posted on the charts related to their section of the readings. The general educator then directs students back to their heterogeneous groups to tutor and teach their peers the new information. Students then discuss the information. Throughout these assignments both educators are monitoring activities. See Figure 4.11.

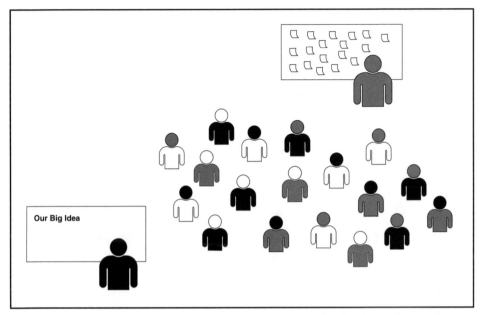

Figure 4.10 Sample 5: General educator and paraeducator, secondary level, initial instruction.

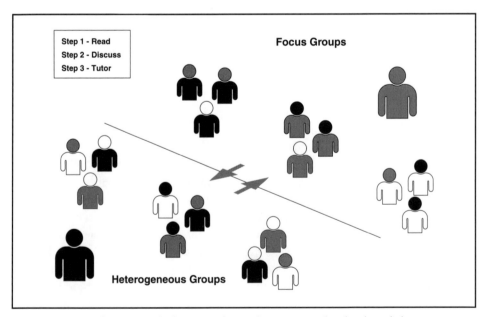

Figure 4.11 Sample 6: General educator and paraeducator, secondary level, guided practice.

Sample 7. For the independent practice stage, the general educator reviews question-writing strategy with the students, and then asks them to independently write several questions about each section of the magazine article discussed during the last class session. While the students are working independently, the paraeducator takes roll and both educators monitor and give students immediate feedback on their questions. After the question-writing task, students pair off to collaboratively answer the questions. Finally the two educators identify students who had difficulty writing questions, and develop a plan for a brief peer tutoring/reteaching opportunity during the next class session. See Figure 4.12.

Sample 8. On the next day, for individual accountability, after a brief reteach/review session, students are given a list of questions at varied levels of difficulty focusing on the article's content, and are asked to respond to one or more questions independently. A four-step writing process (write, check, rewrite, go to checkpoints) is reviewed with the students. Once completed, each student then proceeds to two checkpoints for immediate feedback, one where the paraeducator evaluates the written response for mechanics, and a second where the general educator evaluates the content of their responses. See Figure 4.13.

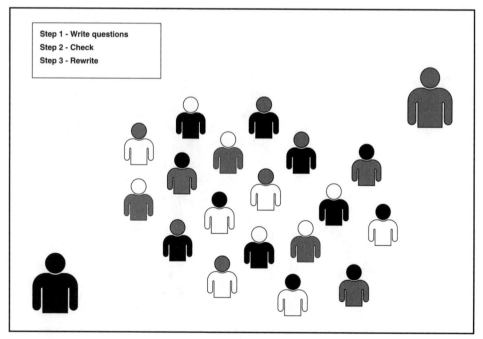

Step 1 - Write questions
Step 2 - Check
Step 3 - Rewrite

Figure 4.12 Sample 7: General educator and paraeducator, secondary level, independent practice.

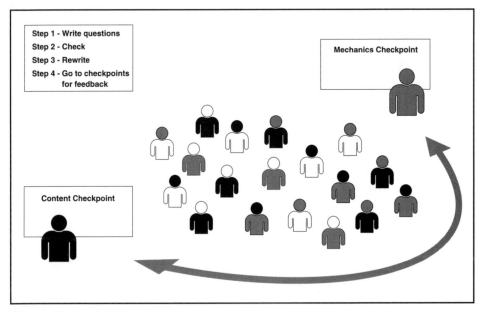

Figure 4.13 Sample 8: General educator and paraeducator, secondary level, individual accountability.

General Educator and Special Educator

Increasingly special educators are joining general educators in regular classrooms (Bauwens & Hourcade, 1995). Unfortunately, too often the special educator waits until the general educator assigns a task, and then relentlessly assists targeted or labeled students in completing that particular task, regardless of the task's suitability, utility, or relevance for the targeted students. Neither the curriculum nor the instruction changes. Instead, the educators simply try harder to fit students into the existing models.

True collaboration should result in a transformation of the curriculum that is consistent with research-based best practices (Zemelman, Daniels, & Hyde, 1998). The following eight examples illustrate how general educators and special educators might implement effective cooperative teaching arrangements in elementary and secondary classrooms.

Elementary Level

Sample 9. In the first example, for initial instruction, the general and special educators begin by introducing a unit on fractions. They break the class into heterogeneous halves and individually continue this initial instruction with the smaller group of students. They debrief at the end of the session while each student meets with a counterpart from the other group to paraphrase what he or she has learned. See Figure 4.14.

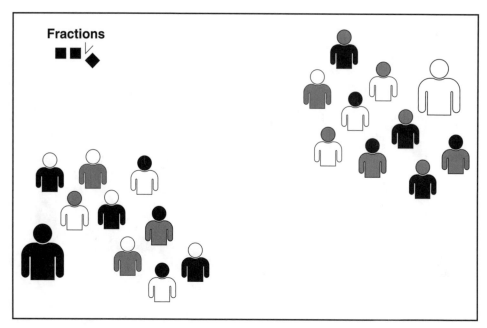

Figure 4.14 Sample 9: General educator and special educator, elementary level, initial instruction.

Sample 10. During the next session, guided practice, the special educator introduces the task and the general educator describes how the students will work together (in pairs, shoulder to shoulder). Using cognitive manipulatives (e.g., kinesthetic hands-on tasks where students think out loud while moving objects), the educators take turns showing and telling about fractional parts and their use in daily situations (e.g., cooking, cleaning, eating). See Figure 4.15.

Sample 11. Figure 4.16 (independent practice) illustrates how cooperative teaching allows for three levels of independent practice of the same task to occur simultaneously. In this example, one group is closely supervised (top right). In another group, students check in with peers if they need one-to-one additional support, while students in the left and bottom portion of the figure work independently. The general educator is working with four students who need the most support (top right), while the special educator is monitoring the other students. Immediate regrouping occurs as the special and general educators notice students who need either more or less support (the arrows in the figure indicate movement between peer work and independent work).

Sample 12. In the final phase of this lesson, students' knowledge of fractions is checked using a simulated pizza picture that contains several tasks for students to show what they know about fractions. Each student meets privately with one of the educators for short evaluation checks. While the students are being evaluated individually, the others complete an art activity applying fractional parts. Upon completion, all students

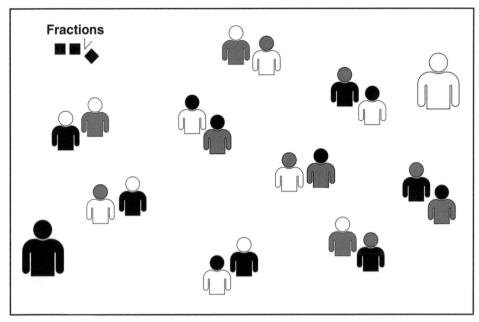

Figure 4.15 Sample 10: General educator and special educator, elementary level, guided practice.

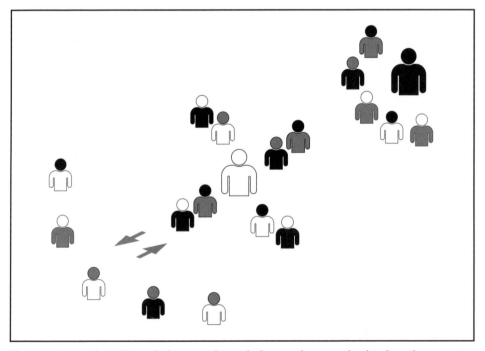

Figure 4.16 Sample 11: General educator and special educator, elementary level, independent practice.

have a pizza party while the educators meet about the results and plan for the reteaching/extension lesson. See Figure 4.17.

Secondary Level

Sample 13. In a high school social studies class, for initial instruction, students are introduced to a new country. Students then count off 1-2, 1-2, and so on. All of the 1s are grouped and asked, "What do you know" about this country, while the 2s group is asked, "What do you want to know" about this country. Students are reminded of the three-step sequence: (1) think about your answer, (2) write your answer, and (3) share your answer with your teachers and classmates. The two groups then exchange tasks so that each student eventually responds to both questions. Then the general educator reviews the written student responses to these questions with students and categorizes them, while the special educator does the same with the other group. Next, the general educator groups students according to interests, and the special educator introduces the students to a group investigation strategy called Co-op/Co-op (Kagan, 1996), wherein students work cooperatively in small groups to complete a project. Then each group shares their unique information with the entire class. See Figure 4.18.

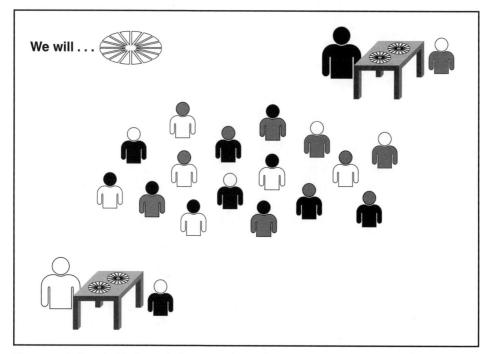

Figure 4.17 Sample 12: General educator and special educator, elementary level, individual accountability.

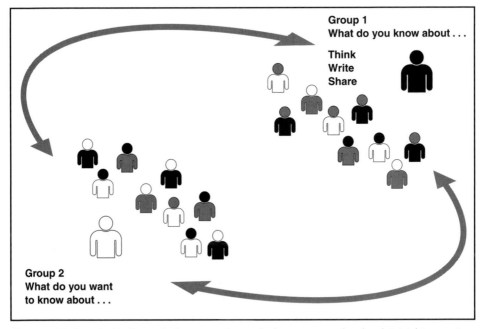

Figure 4.18 Sample 13: General educator and special educator, secondary level, initial instruction.

Sample 14. The next session, guided practice, begins with the students moving into six deep-study groups. The general educator briefly reviews the assignment and test schedule and encourages students to note the critical dates in their agenda books while the special educator monitors. Then the special educator conducts a minilesson about how to retrieve information, while the general educator interjects "what if" thought-provoking statements.

Next, the general educator delineates the specific research tasks for the groups, outlining their goals for their research work, while the special educator distributes written guidelines for this task. Some students go to the library with the special educator to begin their work, while the general educator remains in the classroom to assist groups in differentiating roles or tasks on their contract. See Figure 4.19.

Sample 15. The independent practice session begins with students reviewing their research contracts. Both educators pose questions concerning where students might locate information on their topics. Students then have additional time for research before they return to their group and share their findings. The general and special educators then role-play how to present information collaboratively, rather than in a turn-taking fashion. Next, students brainstorm ways to present their lesson, while the educators debrief and discuss plans for the next lesson. See Figure 4.20.

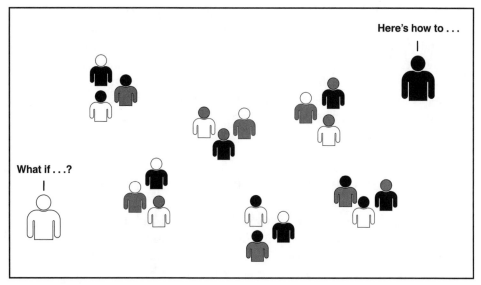

Figure 4.19 Sample 14: General educator and special educator, secondary level, guided practice.

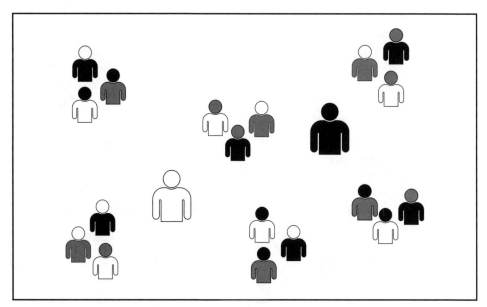

Figure 4.20 Sample 15: General educator and special educator, secondary level, independent practice.

Sample 16. After completing their individual and group research preparation, students are ready to share information with their classmates for the individual accountability stage. The general educator begins by reviewing with the first team of presenters the specified time limits, and ways to monitor their time. Simultaneously, the special educator describes to the audience how to complete the peer evaluation form for each presenter. Once the presentations begin, both educators observe the presentation and complete their evaluations along with the student audience members. See Figure 4.21.

General Educator, Special Educator, and Paraeducator

Cooperative teaching most frequently involves a general and special educator in the classroom simultaneously. Students with disabilities increasingly receive much or all of their educational programs in general education classrooms, with the assistance of those supplemental aids and services he or she requires to be educated alongside peers without disabilities (Turnbull & Turnbull, 2000). One such supplemental aid and service is the provision of a paraeducator in classrooms of students who have disabilities.

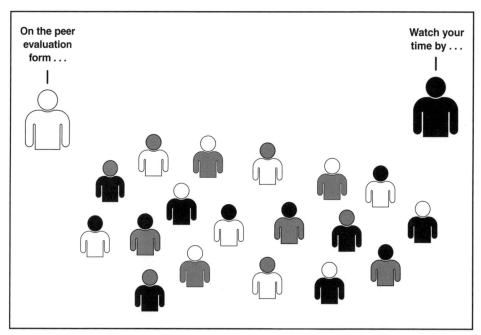

Figure 4.21 Sample 16: General educator and special educator, secondary level, individual accountability.

Although not every classroom will (or even should) have three educators, when the combination does exist it should be used efficiently and effectively.

Too often, when a classroom has several educators present simultaneously, the general educator talks, while the other educators passively listen. It may be analogous to the way many road crews appear to the public: one person doing most of the work while the rest "hang out." The following examples suggest a variety of ways in which three adults can be actively involved in cooperative teaching.

Elementary Level

Sample 17. For initial instruction, a primary classroom can be divided so that three language development skills groups are being conducted simultaneously. Each instructional group uses the same curriculum materials, but each group has specific emphases coordinated by a different educator, depending on the student skill levels and needs. Students who have learning or language difficulties are distributed across all three groups so that all three educators have an opportunity to observe all students. Weekly regroupings are based on regular formative evaluations. The three adults rotate skill group assignments twice a month so they become familiar with all students. That first day's lesson concludes with students participating in various open-ended language interaction activities monitored by students from a nearby university or parent volunteers, while the three educators debrief and plan subsequent instruction. See Figure 4.22.

Sample 18. During the guided practice session, the special educator describes the day's task, while the general educator displays a heterogeneous group assignment sheet and the paraeducator distributes an envelope of pictures. In round-robin fashion, students select a picture, think about what the picture is saying, and then tell a story about it to their peers. Each of the three educators closely monitor targeted students within various groups for application and generalization of language skills previously taught. See Figure 4.23.

Sample 19. For independent practice, student partners sit back-to-back and are given a bag that has a number of miscellaneous objects. One student picks out an object and describes it in five statements to his or her partner. The partner then tries to guess the object. While this activity is occurring, all three educators are conducting informal contextual (i.e., ecological) language evaluations of students. See Figure 4.24.

Sample 20. For individual accountability, the three educators assess specific language skills (e.g., asking questions and initiating conversations). As students participate in a language-oriented application game within triads, the educators conduct a brief language sample to assess present level of language skills for the members of each group. Upon completion, the educators immediately share their data to determine new skill groups. See Figure 4.25.

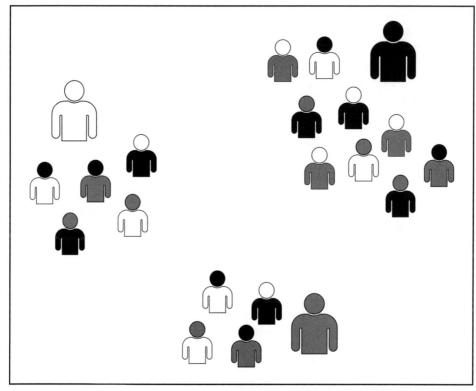

Figure 4.22 Sample 17: General educator, special educator, and paraeducator, elementary level, initial instruction.

Secondary Level

This series of graphics focuses on teaching a miniunit titled "Work Ethics."

Sample 21. In initial instruction, the general educator begins by defining *work ethics*, while the paraeducator and special educator interject ideas. The general educator also asks a series of "what if . . ." questions to which the students respond, while the paraeducator and special educator interject questions that are offshoots of the student responses. See Figure 4.26.

Sample 22. The next session, guided practice, begins with the paraeducator welcoming the students back and setting the stage for the day's session, while the general educator takes roll and distributes 3" × 5" cards coded P (plus), M (minus), or I (interesting) on the floor in strategic locations (de Bono, 1986). Each student also receives a P, M, or I card. The special educator then asks students to identify the letter they have on their 3" × 5" card (P, M, or I), and to move to the area with the placard that matches the letter on their card.

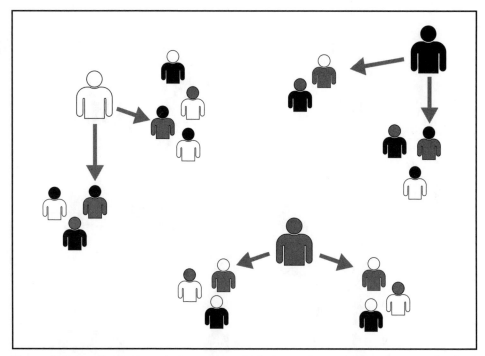

Figure 4.23 Sample 18: General educator, special educator, and paraeducator, elementary level, guided practice.

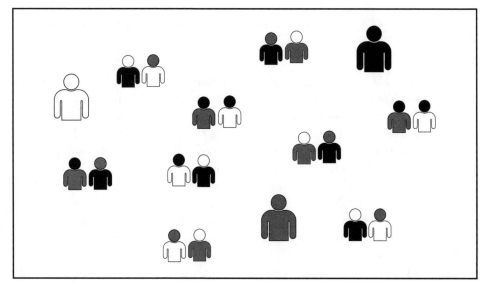

Figure 4.24 Sample 19: General educator, special educator, and paraeducator, elementary level, independent practice.

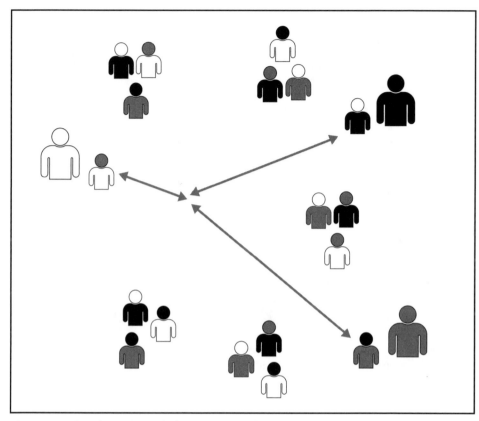

Figure 4.25 Sample 20: General educator, special educator, and paraeducator, elementary level, individual accountability.

Then students brainstorm the pluses (P), minuses (M), and interesting things (I) that they know about work ethics at each of three stations, spending several minutes at each. Then the educators have the students face the center of the room, where the paraeducator has on a suit jacket and tie, and the general and special educator prepare to be interviewees for a job. One educator will depict a well-prepared interviewee, and the other will show a disheveled, unprepared individual. The paraeducator reviews the importance of first impressions with the students, then begins the two interviews. Next, the students form groups of threes and, based on their observation of the good and poor job interviews, take turns role-playing good and poor job interviews, from the initial handshake to the final words. In each group, students rotate between the roles of interviewer, interviewee, and observer. This guided practice session concludes with a minilesson about giving feedback. See Figure 4.27.

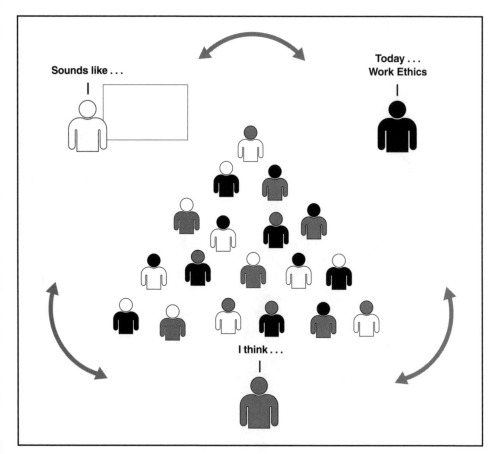

Figure 4.26 Sample 21: General educator, special educator, and paraeducator, secondary level, initial instruction.

Sample 23. The independent practice session begins with the three educators taking turns introducing different parts of the day's lesson on work ethics. The students then are asked to critique three video clips of people applying for a job, using a guided and structured note-taking format specifically created to match the content of the videotape information.

After the video ends, the general educator organizes the students in groups of three for small group discussion, while the special educator rewinds the video and leads the student groups in further analysis of the first video clip. The general educator and paraeducator monitor the students' discussions. The educators rotate between these tasks, taking the lead and monitoring accordingly. The lesson wraps up with a brief overview about the next class featuring business people visiting and discussing with students their impressions of work ethic behaviors. See Figure 4.28.

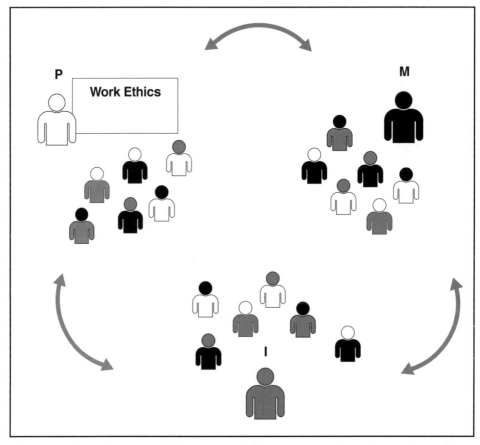

Figure 4.27 Sample 22: General educator, special educator, and paraeducator, secondary level, guided practice.

Sample 24. In preparation for this individual accountability activity of practice conversations with business people, the educators have invited several visitors to class. When students arrive, the stations are set up with the visitors seated. The general educator provides an overview of the day's session. Then the special educator displays and discusses the forms for students to record their observations, while the paraeducator distributes two to each student. As the visitors begin their conversations with individual students, the three educators monitor to make sure the other students serving as observers are watching and writing on the feedback sheets. In closing, each student is given his or her set of completed evaluations, and is assigned to write a self-analysis as an out-of-class activity. See Figure 4.29.

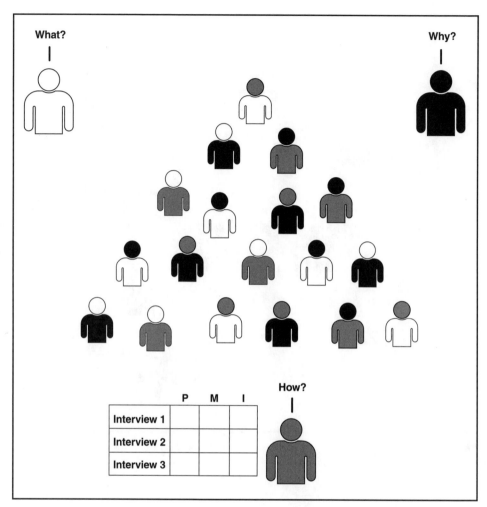

Figure 4.28 Sample 23: General educator, special educator, and paraeducator, secondary level, independent practice.

CONCLUSIONS

Although we may be oversimplifying the process of change, we believe that most educators who have implemented cooperative teaching successfully have done so by deliberately beginning small. Rather than attempting to dramatically reshape their entire school, they initially sought to incorporate occasional periods of cooperative teaching into their work. As they gained familiarity with and experience in cooperative

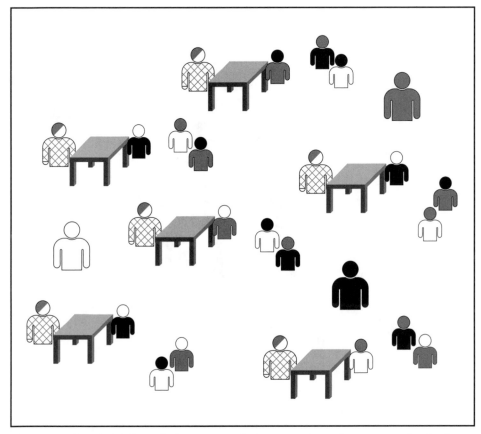

Figure 4.29 Sample 24: General educator, special educator, and paraeducator, secondary level, individual accountability.

teaching, they expanded their efforts, eliciting administrative support as their growing successes were noted.

One way to conceptualize how changes such as cooperative teaching are implemented in the schools is to consider again a home remodeling project. A group of individuals from diverse backgrounds and perspectives jointly develop the architectural plans. The building materials then are brought to the job site and shaped and cut to fit the new plans.

The workers begin their individual jobs simultaneously. Some work on the flooring, others work on the walls, some work on the wiring, and still others work on the ceiling and roof. Thus the remodeling project is carried out from neither a pure top-down nor a pure bottom-up approach. These processes are carried out simultaneously.

Similarly, the development and implementation of cooperative teaching in the schools is most likely to be successful when it is neither solely top down (implemented by direct administrative decree in the absence of educator input) nor bottom up (educators attempting cooperative teaching in the absence of administrative interest, input, or support). When administrators carry out their "ceiling" work as educators construct "walls and flooring," the project is completed quickest and with the greatest sense of unified purpose. Using detailed models and illustrations for aid makes success most likely.

CHAPTER 4 ACTIVITY

Time-Management Survey

The following questions will help you identify your normal time use patterns. Please circle the number that best indicates normal practice. This self-assessment will show those areas where time management is effective, as well as those areas that need attention. If the questions do not apply to your particular situation, circle NA. Mark your response according to the following key:

1 = Always or Yes
2 = Usually
3 = Sometimes
4 = Rarely
5 = Never or No
NA = Not Applicable

1. Do you have a clearly defined list of objectives in writing?　　　　　　1　2　3　4　5　NA

2. Have you recorded your actual time use during the past year?　　　　　　1　2　3　4　5　NA

3. Do you write out your objectives and priorities each day?　　　　　　1　2　3　4　5　NA

4. Do you spend time each day reviewing your daily objectives and priorities with any colleagues who will be affected by them?　　1　2　3　4　5　NA

5. Can you find large blocks of uninterrupted time when you need it?　　　　　1　2　3　4　5　NA

6. Have you eliminated frequently recurring crises from your job?　　　　　　1　2　3　4　5　NA

7. Do you refuse to answer the telephone when engaged in important conversations?　　1　2　3　4　5　NA

8. Do you plan and schedule your time on a weekly and daily basis?　　　　　1　2　3　4　5　NA

9. Do you use travel and waiting time productively?　　　　　　　　　1　2　3　4　5　NA

10. Do you delegate as much as you can
    to others?   1 2 3 4 5 NA

11. Do you prevent your aide from delegating his
    or her tasks and decisions upward to you?   1 2 3 4 5 NA

12. Do you use your aide as well as you can?   1 2 3 4 5 NA

13. Do you take time each day to sit back and
    think about what you're doing and what
    you're trying to accomplish?   1 2 3 4 5 NA

14. Have you eliminated one time waster within
    the past week?   1 2 3 4 5 NA

15. Do you feel really in control of your time
    and on top of your job?   1 2 3 4 5 NA

16. Is your desk and office well organized and
    free of clutter?   1 2 3 4 5 NA

17. Can you successfully cope with stress, tension,
    and anxiety?   1 2 3 4 5 NA

18. Have you successfully eliminated time waste
    in meetings?   1 2 3 4 5 NA

19. Have you learned to conquer
    procrastination?   1 2 3 4 5 NA

20. Do you tackle tasks based on their importance
    and priority?   1 2 3 4 5 NA

21. Have you discussed time-management
    problems with your aide within the past
    month?   1 2 3 4 5 NA

22. Do you resist the temptation to get overly
    involved in your aide's activities?   1 2 3 4 5 NA

23. Do you control your schedule so that other
    people do not waste their time waiting for you? 1 2 3 4 5 NA

24. Do you resist doing things for others that they
    could and should be doing for themselves?   1 2 3 4 5 NA

25. Are you reluctant to interrupt your aide or
    colleagues unless it is really important and
    cannot wait?   1 2 3 4 5 NA

26. Do you meet deadlines and finish all your
    tasks on time?   1   2   3   4   5   NA

27. Can you identify the few critical activities
    that account for the majority of your results
    in your job?   1   2   3   4   5   NA

28. Have you been able to reduce the amount
    of paperwork or the amount of time it
    consumes?   1   2   3   4   5   NA

29. Do you effectively control interruptions and
    drop-in visitors rather than allowing them to
    control you and your time?   1   2   3   4   5   NA

30. Are you better organized and accomplishing
    more than 6 months ago?   1   2   3   4   5   NA

31. Are you able to stay current with all
    your reading?   1   2   3   4   5   NA

32. Have you stopped taking work home in the
    evenings and on weekends?   1   2   3   4   5   NA

33. Have you mastered the ability to say no
    whenever you should?   1   2   3   4   5   NA

34. Are you spending enough time training and
    developing your aide?   1   2   3   4   5   NA

35. Do you feel that you have enough time for
    yourself for recreation, study, community,
    or family activities?   1   2   3   4   5   NA

Total Score _____

SCORING

Add all circled numbers to find a total score. The lower the score, the better one's use of time is. The higher the score, the more indication there is that there are improvements one could and should be making to improve management of time.

Installing the Wiring:
Electronic Collaboration

The Internet is at once a world-wide broadcasting capability, a mechanism for information dissemination, and a medium for collaboration and interaction between individuals and their computers without regard for geographic location.
—Leiner et al. (2000)

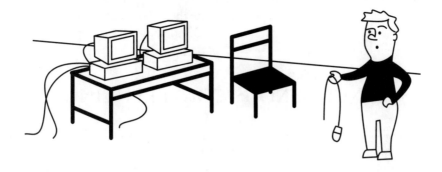

One of the goals of many home remodeling projects is enhanced capability for technology access. The explosion in use of such devices as home personal computers with DSL or cable Internet connections, fax machines, and television cable and satellite services shows few signs of abating in the foreseeable future. As a result, many home remodeling projects involving extensive rewiring for technology, with cable and telephone lines being added throughout the home.

What most of the above technologies have in common is that they facilitate communication between the homeowners and others, especially in the exchange of information. In the cooperative teaching schoolhouse, technology is playing a significant role in how teaching partners exchange information. It is unlikely that the use of present and foreseeable communication technologies will ever completely replace face-to-face meetings. However, skills in technology and in electronic communication are becoming ever more important for teachers. If school professionals choose not to establish electronic links with each other, they run the risk of facing the equivalent of professional extinction, of being unable to do the educational work of the future (Geisert & Futrell, 1995). The thoughtful use of technology can make it easier for cooperative teaching partners to collaborate.

USING TECHNOLOGY FOR COLLABORATION

In terms of technology usage, many teachers today find themselves feeling like recent immigrants to a new land. The customs and language are at best unfamiliar, if not actually disturbing and threatening. However, to be as successful as possible, the individuals must master these new and strange ways (Geisert & Futrell, 1995, p. xv).

In using any new technology, a person faces the first obstacle of learning the initially intimidating new language and terminology. In considering the technology used to facilitate collaboration, one may conceptualize the different approaches as being either *synchronous* or *asynchronous* (Jonassen, 2000). Each of these approaches can be accurately defined very simply.

SYNCHRONOUS CONFERENCING

Sometimes referred to as real-time conferencing, *synchronous conferencing* refers to any form of communication using technology in which individuals interact with each other at the same time (Jonassen, 2000). The exchanges of thoughts, ideas, and emotions are synchronous, or occurring in real time. This is the way that communication occurs in typical face-to-face conversations. Perhaps the most common form of synchronous conferencing (even though it often is not thought of as such) is a telephone conversation.

More often, synchronous conferencing refers to exchanges of information that take place via a computer. There are three ways that cooperative teaching partners can communicate synchronously through computer-based technologies. These include the following:

- chat
- audioconferencing
- videoconferencing

Chat

The chat option is in many ways the most basic, reliable, and widespread form of synchronous collaboration. In its most basic form, individuals "chat" by entering text via a computer keyboard in so-called chat rooms. A chat room is a Web site with an ongoing text-based dialogue where each "speaker" is identified by a name that he or she has chosen to use in that forum. Individuals enter at any time and communicate with whomever else is logged in there at that particular moment. The chat or talk occurs in real time.

As a chat-room participant types text on his or her computer, the text shows up automatically on the screens of all other individuals logged onto that site at the time. Anyone logged on to the chat room at that time can then respond by typing in text on his or her own computer. The flow of information between individuals in a chat room is similar to that of a conversation.

The chat format of exchanging information has a number of advantages. Its text format does not require a fast Internet connection or a powerful computer, making it desirable for many computer users. Some chat software includes a virtual whiteboard on which all participants can draw and make notes, thus enhancing their communication. In addition, chat software sometimes allows for the sharing of applications, so that, in addition to text, the information exchanges also could include a database or spreadsheet on which the chat-room participants might work simultaneously (Thorsen, 2003). Sharing complex applications, however, can significantly slow the speed with which the computers process the exchanges.

More sophisticated versions of chat rooms are emerging, including those with a more graphic environment (Jonassen, 2000). Rather than being text based, these advanced chat rooms allow participants to be identified as visual characters who can dress differently and move around a virtual room or environment. They communicate through pop-up text bubbles, or even actual audio.

Although chat rooms have emerged as a primarily social forum, they do hold potential for helping teachers collaborate electronically. For example, chat rooms might be established for cooperative teachers to share and learn about such issues as the following:

- grading students who require differentiated assignments and tests

- aligning general education curricula with standards while ensuring access for all

- developing IEPs that incorporate both individualization as well as the general education curriculum

- developing creative ways in which roles and responsibilities might be shared in cooperative teaching

Audioconferencing

Every school professional has talked with a colleague over the phone, which in a sense is audioconferencing. Similarly, several teachers around a speakerphone also might be considered to be audioconferencing.

However, computers linked via a small network or the Internet also can be an effective way for teachers to interact and exchange information with each other in synchronous conferencing. Unlike telephone usage, school professionals who are separated by some distance can establish audioconferencing through their computers via the Internet and avoid long distance charges. Audioconferencing requires minimal bandwidth, making it useful in many situations (Thorsen, 2003). (Bandwidth refers to the amount of data that can be transferred in a given amount of time through an Internet connection.)

Audioconferencing requires participants to use microphones hooked into their computers to get their voices out over the network, and speakers hooked into their computers for hearing the voices of other participants. Headphones can be used instead of computer speakers to minimize feedback (a high-pitched squeal) that can occur when microphones are close to speakers (Thorsen, 2003).

Possible uses of audioconferencing for educators participating in cooperative teaching include the following:

- access to national or regional presentations in real time
- access to archived presentations from conferences
- links to educators participating in cooperative teaching at other schools

Videoconferencing

A final type of synchronous conferencing is that of videoconferencing (or video/audioconferencing). The possibility of the video equivalent of a telephone conversation has been around for almost 40 years, but only now, as computers are linked via the Internet, is videoconferencing approaching practical reality.

Desktop videoconferencing allows the transmission of live data between computers over a network, including audio, video, text, files, screens, pictures, and shared applications (Jonassen, 2000). The same software that is often used to enable chat and audioconferencing supports videoconferencing. Two especially common programs are NetMeeting and CuSeeMe.

NetMeeting (http://www.microsoft.com/windows/netmeeting) is free software for video- and audioconferencing that is designed for Windows computers. It is available and downloadable from Microsoft. CuSeeMe (http://www.cuseeme.com) is also free and downloadable from its developer. Unlike NetMeeting, CuSeeMe is available in both Windows and Macintosh versions, though it is considered less powerful than NetMeeting (Jonassen, 2000).

Regardless of the specific software program used, videoconferencing requires microphones and speakers (or headphones) for the audio components of the conferencing, and video cameras for the visual components. These cameras range in price from $100 to $1,000, with the more expensive cameras generating higher quality images. The most common physical placement for the camera is on top of the computer monitor, so that each user can see the other nearly face to face. That is, each user is looking at the monitor, so if the camera is placed there it can capture a full-face image.

Each participant's camera and microphones are plugged into his or her computer. The information that each camera captures is digitized (converted to the digital signals that computers use), and then transmitted over the network to the connected computer(s).

Most software for asynchronous conferencing includes the virtual whiteboard function. Participants can use this helpful feature to draw and make notes for each other. In addition, some conferencing software allows more than two people to participate in the conferencing (Morrison, Lowther, & DeMeulle, 1999).

Possible uses for videoconferencing in cooperative teaching include the following:

- connecting with nonschool agencies as a student's needs warrant

- allowing faculty members in teacher preparation programs to observe students in field-based programs

- giving teacher education students in such programs the opportunity to immediately debrief with faculty members afterward

- conferencing with faculty members at a student's previous school

- viewing real-time examples of cooperative teaching at other schools

When working perfectly, videoconferencing offers exciting possibilities for synchronous conferencing. However, it is rare that all works perfectly. The bandwidth required for the digital transmission of video information, especially moving images in color, is substantial. As a result of bandwidth limitations, the displays of the transmitted pictures are usually small or grainy. In addition, as most experienced Internet users will attest, computer network connections remain to varying degrees unreliable and susceptible to inexplicable crashes. Also, especially when Internet traffic is heavy, both the video and audio portions of the signal may become broken up and characterized by breaks and gaps.

In terms of the technology, the most reliable form of synchronous conferencing is the oldest form, chat. Audioconferencing is relatively reliable, and its speech-based structure (as opposed to the text-based structure of chat) may be more comfortable and easier for many users. In the opinion of many professionals (e.g., Thorsen, 2003), videoconferencing presently offers more promise than usable function. As computer hardware and software continue to advance, videoconferencing will likely improve significantly in the near future.

For the best and most efficient use of synchronous conferencing, collaborative teaching participants should do the following (Gay & Lentini, 1994):

1. Orient themselves by becoming familiar with the communication technology and the task at hand

2. Define the problem

3. Subdivide the problem by defining the task(s), and setting goals, boundaries, and responsibilities

4. Establish roles

5. Seek information by asking questions and finding answers

6. Share information

7. Monitor the responses of the participants

8. Negotiate understandings by ensuring that all involved understand conclusions and agreements

Any evaluation of the quality of synchronous conferencing ultimately must be based on its outcomes. Jonassen (2000) suggested the following three considerations:

1. Is the work on task and relevant?
2. Are the ideas original?
3. Does the conversation stay organized?

Synchronous conferencing is particularly susceptible to one problem: It can be difficult to initially get down to work, or to subsequently stay on task, because conferencing is social in nature. Although it is appropriate and desirable for the partners to enjoy their interactions with each other, too much socializing can inhibit professional productivity. This problem can be minimized by the participants being aware of it and agreeing to monitor themselves and their partner(s). It may be most useful to agree to begin these exchanges with several minutes of purely social time, and then move into professional work.

ASYNCHRONOUS CONFERENCING

In synchronous conferencing, the communication exchanges occur in real time. In *asynchronous conferencing*, only one individual communicates at a time, with pauses of hours, days, or even more between communications. Telephone answering machines and fax machines are examples of asynchronous conferencing technologies. As is the case in synchronous conferencing, in asynchronous conferencing some unit of information (e.g., text, pictures) is entered into one computer where it is encoded digitally, transmitted electronically over a network, then received by another computer or computers where the message is decoded and displayed (Jonassen, 2000). Most forms of computer-mediated communications are asynchronous. The most common forms of computer-mediated communications include the following:

- e-mail
- electronic bulletin boards
- electronic mailing lists

E-mail

E-mail (for electronic mail) is the most common form of computer-based communication, and is a good example of one-to-one communication, where one individual communicates with one another. In its most common form, one person composes text-based communication on the computer using e-mail software, and addresses the e-mail to the recipient. Two effective free and downloadable e-mail programs are Eudora (http://www.eudora.com) and Pegasus (http://www.pmail.com).

When ready, the user sends the e-mail electronically through a network to another computer equipped with an e-mail program, which displays the communication as text. E-mail was one of the first widespread uses of the Internet. Because text can be converted to digital data so easily and compactly, it moves over the Internet quickly and efficiently, and does not require much storage space. Nearly every computer manufactured since 1991 can access e-mail (Thorsen, 2003).

E-mail addresses are structured in a systematic way, as follows: user@host_computer.network. The recipient's user name precedes the @ sign. The name following the @ sign is the host computer to which the e-mail will be sent. This might be a commercial service (e.g., America Online) or a school host computer. The name following the period (the "dot") refers to the particular network carrying the message.

For example, the e-mail address for the first author of this book is: jhourca@ boisestate.edu. In this address, the author's name (Jack Hourcade) is shortened to jhourca (seven letters is the maximum allowed in the particular program that is being used). The host computer is that of Boise State University. Finally, the network is the *edu* (education) network.

Most school-based addresses are in the *edu* network. Other networks include *org* (for organizations), *gov* (for government agencies), *com* (for commercial enterprises), and *net* (for general communications). Sometimes the network will indicate a country other than the United States. For example, e-mail from Britain will typically use the *uk* network designation.

Most e-mail clients have address books built into them, a feature that remembers and makes it easy to retrieve electronic addresses. Also, selected addresses may be gathered together in a group so that one can send a single e-mail message to multiple recipients simultaneously (Thorsen, 2003).

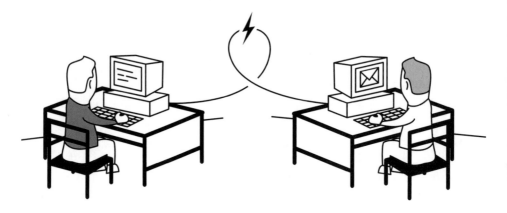

E-mail supports all text characters. In addition, e-mail can include formatted documents, files, and even programs as attachments. This can be especially useful as educators participating in cooperative teaching share their work, such as lesson plans or schedules. Most often, the documents that an educator attaches to an e-mail have been generated on a computer, using a program such as Microsoft Word or PowerPoint. Alternatively, even handwritten plans, figures, and flow charts can be converted into electronic form via a scanner, saved as an electronic file, and then attached to an e-mail. Given its many possibilities, e-mail has been specifically identified as being especially useful in supporting educational collaboration (Paulsen, 1995).

Some of the ways that e-mail can be used between cooperative teaching partners include the following:

- sharing ideas for the next instructional unit to be taught cooperatively

- sharing information gained from professional articles

- inviting student teachers to suggest programs for students they have observed or with whom they have worked

- proposing agendas for upcoming meetings

- arranging meeting times for synchronous conferencing

- reporting the status of students to the other educator when he or she is not present

- sending (as attachments) Internet-based resources or addresses that will be particularly helpful to the other educator

- sending draft versions of IEPs or Section 504 accommodation plans

- communicating with parents of students in a cooperative teaching program

- linking with new teachers to serve as mentors

- sending progress reports to administrators to help them support cooperative teaching

E-mail, however, is not without obstacles. Computer crashes at the sender's personal computer, one of the host computers, or the receiver's computer can result in the loss of the e-mail. Sometimes e-mail messages inexplicably never arrive. Incorrect e-mail addresses caused by typos or address changes cause some e-mail messages to fail to reach their intended recipients (Thorsen, 2003).

Bulletin Boards

Electronic bulletin boards or BBSs (bulletin board services) are special purpose computer programs that enable users to post messages to a metaphorical bulletin board in cyberspace. They serve the same function as a physical bulletin board one might find at the supermarket or on a university campus. On a BBS, any message posted can be accessed by others to read and download. A BBS is housed on a host computer, which can range from a high-speed server computer at a large organization to a personal computer that has been dedicated to this function by an individual (Jonassen, 2000).

A bulletin board (or Web board) is a good example of a one-to-many asynchronous conferencing structure, where one individual can communicate with many others. These boards, sometimes referred to as *newsgroups*, usually revolve around a commonly shared interest. Bulletin boards exist for nearly every imaginable professional and personal interest topic.

A BBS usually has a table of contents, which allows users to access previous messages by titles. These messages are often organized into *strands* or *threads*, which are a series of messages and responses on a particular topic. Electronic bulletin boards can replace traditional print publications as a vehicle for getting information to a targeted group of individuals. Its advantage is the immediacy with which the information can be disseminated.

Possible uses for a bulletin or Web board in a cooperative teaching program include the following:

- Educators can create a site that targets a particular challenge in cooperative teaching that has emerged at a school. Colleagues can review the data, and send in ideas and suggestions.

- Experienced cooperative teachers can develop a mentor site that targets educators just beginning to move into cooperative teaching. The site might include model lesson plans, effective behavior management strategies, and other examples of contemporary best practices.

One emerging use of the BBS is computer conferencing, an alternative to traditional physical conferences in which participants travel long distances and pay the high costs of travel, meals, and lodging to attend. Computer conferences are asynchronous discussions, debates, and collaborative efforts among people who share an interest in some topic. In some ways a BBS offers significant advantages over face-to-face meetings, in that the asynchronous format may provide increased potential for more thoughtful responses because individuals have the opportunity to reflect on ideas or look up information before responding (Jonassen, 2000). In addition, a complete record of any discussion is available immediately.

Electronic Mailing List

Electronic mailing lists (one particular program is called LISTSERV) are essentially a specialized form of e-mail. Like electronic bulletin boards, usually electronic mailing lists target one particular topic of interest to its participants. One subscribes electronically to an electronic mailing list as one would to a physical newspaper or magazine. At that point the user begins regularly receiving e-mail from other subscribers. Each e-mail sent in by a subscriber on the electronic mailing list is automatically forwarded to every other subscriber.

These messages may be sent individually to subscribers, as soon as the writer has submitted it, or the messages may be compiled into a digest that is sent out to all subscribers regularly, typically once a day. In the dissemination of this information, threads typically develop. A thread is a topic that provokes significant interest and a number of responses, and may be kept alive for several days or even weeks.

Possible uses of a school-based electronic mailing list for school professionals participating in cooperative teaching include the following:

- maintaining communication between all teachers who have a particular student with significant needs in their programs

- keeping all members of an inclusion team updated on a student's progress

- providing follow-up information to all teachers who attended particular staff development program

- providing an ongoing professional dialogue and resource for any teachers who encounter a common or shared problem

- informing parents about cooperative teaching and upcoming instructional units

- communicating with interested colleagues about the developing status of a cooperative teaching venture

In some ways electronic bulletin boards are more practical than electronic mailing lists. Web boards categorize submissions so that readers can simply go to the particular thread or strand of interest, rather than wading through every submission from every participant. Subscribers to an electronic mailing list receive everything, regardless of interest or usefulness.

In general, asynchronous conferencing offers a number of significant advantages for partners in cooperative teaching over both synchronous conferencing and even face-to-face meetings. The asynchronous format encourages more reflective levels of thought, rather than spur-of-the-moment responses. Participants tend to stay more task focused (Jonassen, 2000). One may interact when it is convenient and best fits into one's schedule. One of the socially revolutionary developments in this sort of communication structure is that participants are more likely to be judged by the quality of their exchanges and contributions, rather than by such irrelevant factors as appearance, ethnicity, or gender.

There also are disadvantages of asynchronous conferencing. Participants may respond to one idea and let other ideas that are less interesting slide by. In addition, because participants can change topics at will, continuity, decision making, and task completion may suffer. Also, without the social cues that are available in face-to-face meetings, misunderstandings can develop. Text is simply unable to communicate certain subtleties as effectively as people do when communicating face to face. Finally, the present level of technological reliability continues to leave much to be desired (Jonassen, 2000).

ELECTRONIC COLLABORATION INFORMATION ON THE WORLD WIDE WEB

In addition to facilitating communication between teachers, technology is providing greatly expanded possibilities for acquiring professional information. In recent years a variety of Web sites have emerged that target the development of enhanced electronic collaboration between school professionals. Although Web sites are often transitory, in the year 2001 several especially useful sites included the following:

- http://www.lab.brown.edu/public/ocsc/collaboration.guide/. This user-friendly handbook provides a wealth of information about electronic collaboration, including such information as designing a collaborative environment and choosing appropriate technologies. It also includes a list of additional resources.

- http://onlineacademy.org. This site provides online courses, including a comprehensive course on collaboration and cooperative teaching.

- http://education.boisestate.edu/keyiscollaboration. This site provides a PowerPoint-based overview of collaboration.

- http://www.powerof2.org/. This site provides staff development programs about collaboration and cooperative teaching.

- http://www.learningspace.org. This site provides educators with opportunities and tools to develop, implement, and share effective uses of technology to improve student learning.

CONCLUSIONS

Skills in electronic collaboration are likely to become required of professionals in the schools. As Bill Gates (1999) noted, "Electronic collaboration redefines the roles of all, and streamlines the process for everyone involved" (p. 86). Just as professional collaboration is changing the ways teachers work, technology is changing the way they will collaborate. With the remodeled schoolhouse now wired for technology, it is now time to begin the work of cooperative teaching.

CHAPTER 5 ACTIVITY

The Electronic Collaboration Readiness Scale

In Chapter 1 we presented a self-quiz designed to help the reader determine his or her readiness for collaboration. That activity was important because many educators have not yet developed extensive experience in professional collaboration.

Similarly, the idea of using technology, especially for collaboration, is new to some school professionals. Complete this self-examination quiz to determine your readiness for using technology for professional collaboration. This quiz is adapted from a similar one in the area of readiness to use technology in the field of human resources from the Web site of William M. Mercer (http://www.mercerweb.com/readiness_quiz/readiness_quiz.htm).*

For each of the statements below, rate the extent to which the statement is true in your school on a 0 (Not True) to 5 (True) scale. Then total the points for each response.

	Not True					True
1. The administration at my school has demonstrated strong support for electronic communication and collaboration.	0	1	2	3	4	5
2. A significant percentage of professionals at my school (60% or more) has or will soon have access to electronic communication at work.	0	1	2	3	4	5
3. The administration and staff at my school have a solid understanding of the school activities and functions that could be achieved through electronic communication and collaboration.	0	1	2	3	4	5
4. At my school we have intregrated electronic communication into our overall communication and administration strategy.	0	1	2	3	4	5
5. The staff at my school is Web literate (i.e., comfortable using a Web browser and search features).	0	1	2	3	4	5

*Note. Adapted with permission from William Mercer Resources Consulting.

6. The technology infrastructure and systems
resources at my school can support electronic
communication and collaboration.   0   1   2   3   4   5

Your total score: _____

SCORING AND INTERPRETATION

The results from this self-examination are designed only to offer general guidelines. Each school and its needs are quite different, as are the possibilities of electronic collaboration.

Total score of 0–10.
Scores in this range suggest that the possibilities for electronic collaboration in your situation are just beginning. The possibilities for the sucess of future electronic collaboration will depend in large part on your next steps. Concentrate on reviewing your objectives for electronic collaboration, and aligning your plans with those objectives. There are essentially two questions that should be answered: What are you ready to do now and what might you want to add in the future?

Total score of 11–20.
Scores in this range indicate that either you have a picture of what your electronic collaboration might look like, or you have begun some electronic collaboration. Now is the time to establish or review your objectives for electronic collaboration. Take advantage of the technological resources your school offers now, and consider how you might be able to build in the future as the resources grow and new technologies emerge. It is important to keep in mind that not all potential collaborators have access to (or are comfortable with) electronic communication and collaboration. You may wish to integrate your online communication with other media, such as print.

Total score of 21–30.
Scores in this range suggest great success for electronic collaboration. It appears that your school has embraced the strengths and potential of electronic collaboration.

ITEM COMMENTS

The following comments are offered to gain additional insights into each of the statements in the quiz.

1. *The administration at my school has demonstrated strong support for electronic communication and collaboration.*

   As with most initiatives, electronic collaboration will either become stagnate or fail unless the school administration lends its ongoing support. For electronic communication and collaboration to remain effective, school administrators must stand behind the effort, providing the necessary financial, technical, human, and other resources.

2. *A significant percentage of professionals at my school (60% or more) has or will soon have access to electronic communication at work.*

   To reap the benefits of electronic communication, school professionals need access to the Web. Educators who do not routinely use computers in their classrooms (yes, there are some!) can still take advantage of electronic communication through kiosks and loaned computers. Many teachers have computers at home that can be used for electronic collaboration.

3. *The administration and staff at my school have a solid understanding of the school activities and functions that could be achieved through electronic communication and collaboration.*

   Many schools use their intranets to provide basic information. Although this information dissemination is an important function, you may be able to take better advantage of features of intranets and the Internet. For example, often scheduling can be done online more efficiently than through phone messages.

4. *At my school we have integrated electronic communication into our overall communication strategy.*

   Unless the goals for the electronic communication and collaboration are clearly defined and aligned with the school's overall communication strategy, you may have groups of people working cross-purposes, delivering different messages through different communication channels targeting different groups of people. Schools need to determine what messages they wish to convey online, and then build an integrated technology solution that takes full advantage of a variety of media to deliver a consistent message.

5. *The staff at my school is Web literate (i.e., comfortable using a Web browser and search features).*

   You cannot assume that all colleagues will be as comfortable with using technology for collaboration as you are. You may need to nudge some colleagues into this new arena by going slowly and offering support as they begin to learn. For ongoing communication and collaboration, the technology must be reliable and easy to use.

6. *The technology infrastructure and systems resources at my school can support electronic communication and collaboration.*

An electronic communication system that has unbearable download times or awkward navigation, or is unreliable, is destined for failure. Be sure to draw on the best minds from your school for the technological know-how to avoid these problems.

Inspecting the Job:
Evaluating Cooperative Teaching

*The facts will eventually test out all theories, and they form,
after all, the only impartial jury to which we can appeal.*
—Jean Louis Rodolphe Agassiz

After deciding to remodel their house, homeowners usually spend hours reviewing potential plans and blueprints, ultimately selecting those that appear best suited for their purposes. When construction starts, some walls come out while others are built, new framing and flooring is added, and so on. During this process the homeowners frequently pause to evaluate the work accomplished to that point, as they envision how each step contributes to the overall project. After project completion, the homeowners and remodelers usually take great pride in stepping back to admire their work, imagining how the new structures will improve the homeowners' quality of life.

Sometimes, however, after moving back into the newly remodeled house, the occupants find the results unsatisfactory. Traffic patterns may be awkward, the newly renovated rooms may feel more crowded than anticipated, there may be too much or too little light, and so forth. These unexpected results can lead to dissatisfaction with the project's outcome.

One way to minimize unexpected and unpleasant developments in the rebuilding process is to decide beforehand exactly what outcomes are desired, and what jobs, features, and specifications are necessary to yield those outcomes. This information then serves as a point of comparison for the ongoing construction, with regularly scheduled checks continuing along the way to make sure that all is progressing as planned. As educators remodel the schoolhouse through the implementation of cooperative teaching, they must begin with a clear sense of what it is they hope to accomplish. The potential outcomes might include benefits for all students, for the overall educational system, for educators in the school, and for parents and the general public. Each of these critical dimensions is discussed in this chapter, with suggestions offered for the evaluation of each.

EVALUATING VERSUS COACHING

It is intimidating for many educators to have another educational professional visit their classroom to observe his or her teaching and offer feedback. The intimidation can be attributed to the fact that such visits typically are infrequent and involuntary, conducted by a superior or an administrator using a predetermined set of official criteria. The results of a classroom visit often carry significant career implications, such as job retention or dismissal. This approach to professional development is *evaluation.*

There is little question that the evaluation of teachers will continue for the foreseeable future. An emerging supplementary practice, however, that holds great promise for substantial professional development is *coaching.* In coaching, classroom visits are ongoing, and the observed teacher volunteers to be coached. The coach, who is usually not an administrator but a skilled knowledgeable educator, prepares feedback based on criteria and outcomes that the observed teacher has identified beforehand, not some arbitrary set of standards. Prior to the visit, the coach asks questions of the teacher to ascertain what it is that the teacher hopes to gain from the visit.

Before beginning any evaluation of cooperative teaching, it might be useful for the cooperative teaching partners to first solicit coaching from experienced cooperative teachers. The suggestions gathered from this coaching will be invaluable to the new cooperative teachers in (a) improving their ability to work more cooperatively and effectively, and (b) helping them to identify and solve problems prior to more formal evaluation.

UNDERSTANDING PROGRAM EVALUATION

McLaughlin and McLaughlin (1993) outlined a strong conceptual framework for thinking about evaluation. As they noted, evaluation is a process through which information is collected that allows people to make comparisons with predetermined standards. This evaluation process is most useful if several points are considered during the development of an evaluation program.

First, evaluation must be designed with a specific purpose (or purposes). The essential purpose(s) of any evaluation can be identified by answering two questions:

1. Who are the potential consumers of the information to be generated by the evaluation?

2. What is it they should know?

In schools where personnel are preparing to implement or expand cooperative teaching, there are a number of potential consumers of evaluative data. Some possible users of this information include the following:

- parents

- educators at the school involved in cooperative teaching

- educators at the school not involved in cooperative teaching

- educators at other schools involved in cooperative teaching

- educators at other schools not presently involved in cooperative teaching but considering whether to become involved

- professors in teacher preparation programs at universities

- staff development professionals and educational consultants in school districts or educational support centers

- school building administrators

- state department of education staff and administrators

- school district administrators

- state legislators

- educational researchers

These potential users have different questions they would like answered through evaluations of cooperative teaching. Without first identifying who should receive evaluative data, it is impossible to design a useful evaluation system.

Second, the evaluation design should address the essential underlying theory of the approach being evaluated. Many professionals involved in program evaluation report that they are not sure how best to apply the results of their evaluation to subsequent decisions about their programs. This uncertainty can be minimized if the evaluation procedures are consistent with the basic purposes of the program to be evaluated. For example, one might anticipate that an evaluation of cooperative teaching will include the collection of data on (a) the relationship between the cooperative teaching partners, and (b) the overall educational effectiveness of the arrangement.

A third point is that a person designing an evaluation program should recognize that changes in evaluation procedures likely will become necessary once the evaluation has begun. As data are collected, new questions often emerge, and unanticipated problems with the evaluation procedures become apparent. If the involved parties realize that the evaluation procedures are likely to change over time, the changes will be less stressful.

EVALUATING COOPERATIVE TEACHING

Evaluation procedures for cooperative teaching must focus on the specific issues that led to its implementation. These issues will be as varied and individualized as the schools or educators themselves.

One way to think about an evaluation of cooperative teaching is to remember how homeowners might evaluate their home remodeling project. For example, during the construction phase of the project, the homeowner might determine whether each of the different subcontracted jobs (e.g., electrical, flooring, painting) is being done as per the agreed-upon specifications. In addition, after the work has been completed, the homeowner will likely check to see that the plans (e.g., dimensions, specifications) that were chosen beforehand actually were achieved. Thus, a homeowner is undertaking two evaluations: the specific work going on throughout the project, followed by the results. These two evaluations are *processes* evaluation and *outcomes* evaluation.

In addition to evaluating both processes and outcomes, the homeowner may conduct an *objective* evaluation, measuring such things as the number of paint coats applied, the size of the windows, and so on. In addition to collecting objective data, however, the homeowner usually measures *subjective* factors, such as whether the selected colors actually feel as pleasant as was expected, whether the window size is providing the sense of airiness that was hoped for, and so on.

One way to think about the evaluation of cooperative teaching is to conceptualize a two-cell by two-cell matrix containing possible types of information. One half of the matrix includes two specific aspects: (1) the processes that are being used in the program and (2) the outcomes of those processes. The other half includes the two forms of the information that might be collected: (1) objective information (conclusions based on impersonal data) or (2) subjective information (conclusions based on personal perceptions). As illustrated in Figure 6.1, this matrix yields four possible types of data about cooperative teaching:

1. objective analyses of the processes involved
2. objective analyses of the outcomes
3. subjective analyses of the processes involved
4. subjective analyses of the outcomes

		Types of Data	
		Objective	Subjective
Dimension Evaluated	Processes	objective processes	subjective processes
	Outcomes	objective outcomes	subjective outcomes

Figure 6.1 Types of information that might be gathered to evaluate the effects of cooperative teaching.

Objective Versus Subjective Information

Any evaluator of cooperative teaching will face a significant decision. Should the evaluation be based on objective (impersonal, data-based) information, subjective (personal perception and opinion) information, or some combination of both? Because each has potential advantages, a comprehensive evaluation procedure might incorporate both types of information.

Objective information consists of observable data that is not influenced by personal opinion. Teachers everywhere are encountering increased calls for professional accountability. At the core of accountability is *count*, or numerical data.

For example, to evaluate the planning component of a cooperative teaching arrangement, evaluators could review written records to learn that cooperative teaching partners had met every week for the previous 3 months. These data would be identical for any observer, and are only minimally subject to personal interpretation (i.e., "Are you counting that as a meeting? I thought we were just chatting!"). Other possible types of objective data might include the following:

- the number of hours the two educators actually spent cooperatively teaching in the same classroom

- standardized test scores of students in classrooms where cooperative teaching was implemented compared with those not so taught

- time spent in training for cooperative teaching

- amount of money spent to support cooperative teaching

Subjective information provides less clear-cut data than objective information, but it can provide valuable insight. Subjective evaluation often includes asking significant individuals to record their personal impressions of various aspects of a program, typically using a Likert-type scale. These scales provide a number of items to which respondents give their reaction by indicating a degree of agreement or disagreement. To construct a Likert-type scale, evaluation designers follow a series of relatively straightforward steps (Adams & Schvaneveldt, 1985):

1. Develop a pool of items or questions relevant to the program being investigated. This pool of items should contain approximately equal numbers of favorable and unfavorable items in a random mix.

2. Provide a response category for each item. The typical 5-point response categories for each item include 1 = *strongly agree*, 2 = *agree*, 3 = *undecided*, 4 = *disagree*, 5 = *strongly disagree*.

3. Phrase some items positively and others negatively. This minimizes the tendency of respondents to simply mark one column down the page without fully reading the items.

4. Choose approximately 20 to 30 items to use in the evaluation. This number provides a good sample without being too cumbersome for the respondant.

5. Administer the instrument and analyze the data. Usually this analysis is based on numerical values (1 to 5) being assigned to each of the five responses, typically with a score of 5 representing a most favorable response. These individual item scores then can be analyzed.

Subjective data might be gathered on both educator and student perceptions of a variety of aspects of cooperative teaching, including the following:

- the quality and effectiveness of help that students who are struggling receive

- the perceived clarity of lessons that are presented

- the overall level of personal and professional satisfaction of the educators engaged in cooperative teaching

- the overall level of personal and professional satisfaction of the students

For example, if the cooperative teaching partners respond to an item that says, "I learned new instructional strategies from my partner," and the average score for this item among the respondents is 1.9 (with a 1 indicating strong disagreement), then one might conclude that the potential for cooperative teaching to allow participants to learn from one another is not being fully achieved. In addition, an evaluator could sum all scores from each respondent to obtain an overall subjective interpretation of how effective cooperative teaching processes have been, and to gain a sense of how favorably any particular respondent feels overall about cooperative teaching processes.

Neither purely objective nor purely subjective evaluative information can provide a comprehensive and accurate picture of the effectiveness of the various processes involved in cooperative teaching. The combination of both kinds of information yields the most complete picture.

To effectively interpret data there must be a point of comparison. Evaluators collect information on the issues or concerns that school personnel had identified as significant prior to implementation of cooperative teaching. (A number of possible factors to evaluate are provided later in this chapter.) This initial set of data serves as a baseline, or beginning point of reference. A second set of data is collected after the program has been in operation for a while. A comparison of these two sets of data allows evaluators to determine where the program is having greatest effect. Additional ongoing evaluations provide an even better picture of how the impact of the program is evolving over time.

Process Evaluation Versus Outcomes Evaluation

Most educators have had the experience of implementing some program that was described as "can't miss," going through the prescribed training and subsequent instructions and procedures exactly as specified, only to find the results disappointing, discouraging, or unsuccessful. Given the inexact nature of education, it simply is not possible to develop school programs that possess the degree of specificity and predictability of results that one finds in sciences such as physics and chemistry.

Given this reality, it may be useful for evaluative purposes to distinguish between two distinct and different aspects of cooperative teaching—processes and outcomes. Evaluation of both these dimensions may be necessary to gain the most knowledge.

Process Evaluation

To be useful, a successful program should be replicable by others. This requires program implementers to clearly identify for others the critical steps, procedures, and processes that they followed. For example, effective implementation of cooperative teaching requires (among many other things) that the cooperative teaching partners meet regularly to discuss, plan, and analyze their work. In the absence of planning, cooperative teaching is unlikely to succeed.

Thus one approach toward evaluating cooperative teaching is to identify and evaluate the various component processes involved. For example, the evaluators might base their analysis in part on such processes as the frequency of planning for cooperative teaching, the productivity of those sessions in generating practical plans, and so forth.

At its simplest level, process evaluation involves two steps. First, the evaluators (along with the cooperative teaching partners if these are not the same individuals) must identify and agree upon the component processes that the program requires. (Chapter 3 provides a starting point for identifying the essential components or processes required in cooperative teaching.)

Second, those identified processes are then evaluated. This stage of the evaluation may involve the use of objective information, subjective information, or both.

Outcomes Evaluation

School professionals design and implement new programs to respond to perceived needs that presently are unmet, and to achieve a desired result. Evaluation of any program should determine how well these needs were met, and to what extent the desired outcome was achieved.

As is the case in process evaluation, the evaluation of outcomes can be based on objective information, subjective information, or both. Typically the implementation of cooperative teaching is designed to achieve both objective and subjective outcomes.

For example, a cooperative teaching effort may be implemented to provide students with more effective instruction in basic academic skills. Measures of the effectiveness with which that outcome is achieved might include such objective data as schoolwide scores on standardized achievement tests, informal reading inventories, curriculum-based assessment measures, and so forth.

However, another desired outcome of the implementation of cooperative teaching might be to foster a sense of camaraderie among educators, a feeling that they all share the same goal (that is, the effective education of all students in that school). Evaluating this personally subjective outcome might require the construction of a Likert-type scale that includes items such as, "After having participated in cooperative teaching, I now believe that I have greater professional responsibility for all students at this school." Individual participants' responses to this item can yield a database from which to judge whether the desired outcome of shared responsibility among all educators is being achieved.

Like process evaluation, outcomes evaluation requires two steps. First, the desired outcomes that were anticipated from cooperative teaching must be identified. Second, those identified outcomes must be systematically evaluated to determine if they were achieved.

DETERMINING SOURCES OF INFORMATION

As previously noted, the evaluation of cooperative teaching should be guided largely by a review of those factors that led the educators to adopt cooperative teaching in the first place. One way to begin is to group all the possible sources of information into four general categories. These sources of information include data gathered from and about the following groups:

1. students
2. the educational system
3. professional educators
4. parents and other outside parties

It is typical for a program to show greater success from some of these types of data than from others. The relative importance of these four types of data should be decided before the evaluation based on each individual school's desired outcomes of cooperative teaching.

Student Information

A near-universal theme in the professional literature is that the purpose of school restructuring must be the enhancement of student learning (e.g., Barr & Parrett, 2001; Elmore, Peterson, & McCarthey, 1996; Newmann & Wehlage, 1995), an idea with which it is difficult to argue. Student outcomes might include both subjective and objective sources of information.

Subjective Student Information

One subjective source of information might be a Likert-type scale to be given to students. Such an instrument could include such items as the following:

- "Cooperative teaching is helping me learn how to study better."

- "When both teachers are in the room our class has to slow down more for kids who are having trouble learning."

- "I think other teachers should come into our class to help kids who need help, instead of the kids leaving our class for help."

This instrument could be administered to all students involved in cooperative teaching.

Objective Student Information

Policymakers throughout the country increasingly are asking that schools be held accountable for their work. School accountability often is defined as objective data from state-mandated student achievement assessment scores (e.g., Barr & Parrett, 2001).

Objective quantitative data is often easier for evaluators to collect than subjective data. Objective data may also carry greater weight with initially skeptical audiences, especially those who are not directly involved in education.

Objective sources of information can be obtained from students in cooperatively taught programs, then compared with that obtained from similar students not participating in these programs. Possible sources of objective student information include the following:

- standardized test scores

- passing rates on tests required for moving from grade to grade

- curriculum-based measurement results

- grades on homework, tests, and other educator-based evaluations of student performance

- proportions of assignments completed

- observations of rates of students' social interactions with each other, both inside and outside of class

- observations of rates of on-task and other academic behaviors

- mastery of IEP goals and objectives for students receiving special education services

System Information

In addition to better meeting student needs, many schools implement cooperative teaching to respond to perceived problems in the way contemporary schools are structured. For example, many educators express concern about the level of physical, social, and professional isolation from their colleagues that they experience. Thus, a second source of information about the impact of cooperative teaching is its effect on the overall school system. Again, like student data, evaluators may want to collect both subjective and objective information.

Subjective System Information

Personal opinions about the effects of cooperative teaching on the educational system can be solicited from a variety of professionals, including general education teachers, support services providers, and administrators. A Likert-type scale developed to gather this information might include items such as the following:

- "Fewer students 'fall through the cracks' in classes where cooperative teaching is implemented."

- "Cooperative teaching is less effective than the present arrangements in preventing small problems from becoming large ones."

- "Cooperative teaching is a less efficient use of teachers' time than is the present system."

- "Cooperative teaching makes it more difficult to maintain consistent communications with parents."

Objective System Information

There are a variety of objective data sources that can be reviewed to evaluate the impact of cooperative teaching on the overall educational system. These include the following:

- frequency of suspensions, expulsions, and similar behavior-management interventions

- absenteeism and drop-out rates

- retention rates

- numbers of students on IEPs

- numbers of students removed from the general classroom for segregated support services (e.g., Title 1, special education, speech and language, gifted and talented)

Educator Information

A third source of information about cooperative teaching is the professionals providing educational services in the schools. Some of these individuals include the following:

- general education teachers
- special education teachers
- school administrators
- Title 1 teachers
- gifted and talented teachers
- speech and language therapists
- occupational therapists
- physical therapists

- school psychologists
- school counselors
- paraprofessionals, teacher aides, and instructional assistants
- specialized area teachers (e.g., art, music, physical education)

Subjective Educator Information

Subjective data gathered from educators can provide valuable information about the effects of cooperative teaching on the participants. The specific questions to include in a Likert-type scale might be based on those factors that led to the decision to implement cooperative teaching in the first place. Possible items on the scale include the following:

- "I enjoy cooperative teaching more than I enjoyed working by myself."

- "I believe I have lost some degree of professional independence since beginning cooperative teaching."

- "I now am spending more time in planning than I was before I began cooperative teaching."

- "Cooperative teaching allows me to make better use of my unique teaching and professional skills."

- "After working in cooperative teaching, I now believe students with disabilities can succeed in general classrooms."

- "I feel more stress working under cooperative teaching than I did under the previous system."

Objective Educator Information

Objective data on the impact of cooperative teaching on the professionals in the schools that may be gathered include the following:

- educator burnout and retention rates

- rate of transfer requests

- number of educators interested in cooperative teaching (e.g., how many sign up and attend training sessions or volunteer to participate)

- number of workshops, staff development seminars, and graduate courses educators pursue and complete

- number of referrals for special education made by educators

Each school will have specific educator-based data that can indicate the effects of cooperative teaching on its professional staff.

Parent and General Public Information

One of the hallmarks of the 2000 presidential campaign was the extraordinarily high profile of public education. Seldom has education been such a large issue in national elections. For better or worse, the public schools are under great scrutiny by politicians as well as society at large.

From the perspective of many in society, the educational system should be held more accountable to the public. The recent growing emphasis on high-stakes testing is perhaps the most dramatic evidence of this development. Many would argue that the primary emphasis of the schools should be to graduate an educated and literate citizenry.

It is understandable that educators are being asked to be accountable to the major stakeholders in the schools. The significance of evaluating the impact of cooperative teaching on these individuals should not be overlooked. Major stakeholders can include the following:

- parents of students without special needs
- parents of students with special needs
- members of parent–teacher organizations
- school board members
- politicians

- employers
- other citizens in the community

As is the case with other sources of information on the impact of cooperative teaching, both subjective and objective parent and general public information can be useful.

Subjective Parent and General Public Information

Subjective data on perceptions of cooperative teaching can be gathered through Likert-type scales completed by parents and others. For example, after having had some experience with cooperative teaching in their children's school, parents could be surveyed about such items as the following:

- "Students with special needs are not likely to have their needs best met in the general classroom, even when a support services provider is there."

- "My child is best educated in a classroom characterized by diversity."

- "Cooperative teaching may be effective for less able students but is not as good for the more able students."

- "I believe that cooperative teaching allows all children to receive a better education."

Objective Parent and General Public Information

Parents can be very responsive, positively or negatively, to changes in the schools. Objective data about the effects of cooperative teaching on parents and others might include information such as the following:

- attendance at parent–teacher meetings
- rates of responsiveness to school messages sent home
- attendance rates at IEP meetings
- voting patterns of school board members and politicians

Perhaps the single most important aspect of evaluation data is its use on an ongoing and proactive basis to shape and determine the future of cooperative teaching. In the absence of this function, evaluation has questionable utility.

The data collection process is incomplete until the data have been synthesized, analyzed, interpreted, and disseminated to appropriate audiences. Chapter 10 identifies forums and audiences appropriate for this dissemination.

A RUBRIC FOR EVALUATING
THE EFFECTIVENESS OF
COOPERATIVE TEACHING

Chapter 3 introduced the five Ps of cooperative teaching. These were the five key elements necessary for the effective implementation of cooperative teaching and included the following:

- Cooperative presence
- Cooperative planning
- Cooperative presenting
- Cooperative processing
- Cooperative problem solving

One way to approach the evaluation of cooperative teaching is to review each of these five elements, determining for each whether the teacher is at a beginning level, an intermediate level, or an advanced level. A rubric for such an evaluative process is outlined in Figure 6.2. This rubric is useful for administrators as they evaluate the work of staff members involved in cooperative teaching, and also is effective in helping educators participating in cooperative teaching conduct self-evaluations, either individually or (preferably) jointly.

Cooperative Presence

Cooperative presence refers to two educators simply physically being in the same classroom at the same time. At the beginning level, the cooperative educators are together only sporadically. At the intermediate level, they work together consistently over a longer period of time, perhaps for several days or weeks as an instructional unit is presented. Finally, at the advanced level, the educators work together regularly long term, either the entire semester or the entire academic year.

Cooperative Planning

In cooperative planning, the two educators meet to collaboratively design and prepare unit and lesson plans, to identify and differentiate specific individual roles and responsibilities, and to identify needed resources to make their instruction most effective for all students. At the beginning level, the educators individually plan for their work together, or one educator plans for both. At the intermediate level, the educators meet on a regular basis to plan their work. However, those plans target a traditional instructional model of making adaptations and modifications of the instruction the educators would typically present. At the advanced level, the cooperative educators base all planning

Cooperative Teaching Skill Evaluation

Place a check in the column that best describes your skill level for each element.

	Beginning	Intermediate	Advanced
1. COOPERATIVE PRESENCE			
2. COOPERATIVE PLANNING			
3. COOPERATIVE PRESENTING			
4. COOPERATIVE PROCESSING			
5. COOPERATIVE PROBLEM SOLVING			

Figure 6.2 A rubric for determining skill level in cooperative teaching.

around universal design for learning features (see Chapter 3), a dramatic departure from traditional instructional planning.

Cooperative Presenting

Cooperative presenting involves two or more educators simultaneously present and actively involved for a sustained period of time within a general education class, with shared responsibilities for delivering instruction. At the beginning level, the educators only occasionally take advantage of the unique instructional opportunities that are available when two or more skilled educators are present simultaneously. They do not vary curriculum and instruction effectively to best meet the needs of all students. Though they may know about emerging best practices in making the general education curriculum more accessible to all, they are not yet implementing these practices. At the intermediate level, the educators sometimes take advantage of their dual presence in the room, and occasionally implement emerging best practices to help students access curricula. At the advanced level, the educators nearly always effectively capitalize on their joint presence, and routinely incorporate best practices to make their instruction accessible to all. At this level they typically employ several universal design tools simultaneously, including such approaches as conspicuous strategies, mediated scaffolding, judicious review, and priming background knowledge (see Chapter 3; Kame'enui & Simmons, 1999).

Cooperative Processing

In cooperative processing, the educators assess their new relationship, considering both its professional and personal effectiveness. This requires deep reflection and ongoing mutual debriefings. At the beginning level, the new partners in cooperative teaching do not regularly discuss their new relationship, trying to anticipate and head off problems. When the inevitable interpersonal problems surface, their first response is to immediately go to an administrator for a solution. At the intermediate level, they are able to resolve many of their relationship problems without going to an administrator, and from time to time meet to review their work together. At the advanced level, the cooperative teachers rarely find it necessary to go to an administrator for help in resolving interpersonal issues, finding instead that they have acquired the skills and experience necessary to solve most of their problems themselves. They meet regularly and often to review their work and their relationship.

Cooperative Problem Solving

Like anyone trying anything new, educators in cooperative teaching will encounter unexpected obstacles and problems. These educators must plan for and develop a proactive, solution-focused approach to dealing with problems. At the beginning level, the educators seldom use data in their decisions, nor are they effective at finding win–win solutions. Rather than identifying each educator's desired outcomes, then identifying ways to merge those desired outcomes, they instead fixate on their personal desired means toward those outcomes, means that frequently are incompatible between the two educators. At the intermediate level, the educators incorporate more data into their problem solving, and have grown more successful at identifying areas of commonality in their desired outcomes. At the advanced level, the cooperative partners consistently use data as they engage in problem solving, and are usually able to identify win–win situations.

CONCLUSIONS

In any remodeling job, the process goes more smoothly when the homeowners first identify the desired outcomes, and then decide how those might be evaluated. In evaluating cooperative teaching, educators must decide (a) who will use the information, and (b) what those individuals need to know. Two dimensions that might be evaluated are (a) the *processes* of cooperative teaching (i.e., what the participants do), and (b) the *outcomes* (i.e., the effects of their work). In addition, these data can be either objective (based on numbers and data), or subjective (based on personal perception and emotional response). Objective data are usually the most effective answer to calls for educational accountability, whereas subjective data are especially useful when dealing with sensitive issues such as personal and professional relationships in the schools.

There are a variety of sources of information that can be used in evaluating cooperative teaching, including students, the school, educators, and parents and the general public. In addition, educators developing cooperative teaching relationships can evaluate themselves as beginning, intermediate, or advanced on each of the five Ps of cooperative teaching.

At this point the schoolhouse remodelers have evaluated the schoolhouse remodeled with the cooperative teaching blueprints, and determined that it is now ready to occupy. However, when homeowners move into their remodeled homes, often a certain period of adjustment is necessary before the new surroundings truly feel like home. Similarly, educators moving into classrooms with cooperative teaching often experience an initial period of uneasiness. The next chapter examines this phenomenon in greater depth, and suggests ways in which the moving-in process can be accomplished most smoothly and successfully.

CHAPTER 6 ACTIVITY

Cooperative Teaching Outcomes Evaluation Guide

One of the more difficult aspects of evaluating a cooperative teaching program is determining exactly what should be evaluated. Again, the two dimensions of cooperative teaching that should be evaluated are its various individual processes and subsequent outcomes.

The following evaluation guide is presented in an *if . . . then* format, and will assist in the evaluation of cooperative teaching.

I. If You Are Interested in Student Changes in . . .

a. **grades,** then review grades of students in cooperatively taught classrooms with those of similar students in traditionally taught classrooms.

b. **social interactions,** then compare levels of social interactions of students in cooperatively taught classrooms with those of students in traditionally taught classrooms.

c. **behaviors,** then compare levels of those behaviors of students in cooperatively taught classrooms with those of similar students in traditionally taught classrooms.

d. **self-concepts,** then administer tests of self-concept to students before they join cooperatively taught classrooms and again after learning in cooperatively taught classrooms for a period of time.

e. **attendance,** then compare attendance records of students in cooperatively taught classrooms with those of similar students in traditionally taught classrooms.

f. **attitudes,** then construct and administer to all students a school attitudes instrument, comparing the results from students in cooperatively taught classrooms with those from similar students in traditionally taught classrooms.

g. **skills acquisition and academic achievement,** then administer either a curriculum-based or a commercially available academic skills test or academic achievement test to all students, comparing the skills of students in cooperatively taught classrooms with those of similar students in traditionally taught classrooms.

h. **attitudes toward diversity,** then construct and administer to all students a survey measuring attitudes toward diversity, comparing the results from students in cooperatively taught classrooms with those of similar students in traditionally taught classrooms.

II. If You Are Interested in System Changes in . . .

a. **referral rates for special education and other support services programs,** then compare the numbers of referrals generated by educators who are participating in cooperative teaching with the number of referrals generated by educators who are not participating.

b. **placement rates in pullout programs,** then compare the number of placements of students from classrooms participating in cooperative teaching with the number of placements of similar students from traditionally taught classrooms.

c. **amount of time students with disabilities are integrated with students without disabilities,** then review Individualized Education Plans and other data to determine the amount of time students with disabilities who are in cooperatively taught classrooms are participating in general education versus similar data from similar students who are in traditionally taught classrooms.

d. **suspension and expulsion rates,** then compare data from students in cooperatively taught classrooms with data from similar students in traditionally taught classrooms.

III. If You Are Interested in Educator Changes in . . .

a. **attitudes toward student diversity,** then construct and administer to all school professionals an informal survey measuring attitudes toward student diversity, comparing results from educators participating in cooperative teaching with results from educators not participating.

b. **teaching behaviors,** then identify a list of specific characteristics sought (e.g., time spent in direct teaching, time spent in individualized instruction, number of explanations given), measure those behaviors in educators participating and educators not participating in cooperative teaching, and compare.

    c. **collegiality,** then identify behaviors associated with collegiality (e.g., time spent in professional discussions, materials loaned and shared), measure those behaviors in educators participating and educators not participating in cooperative teaching, and compare.

    d. **job satisfaction,** then construct and administer to all school professionals an informal survey measuring overall job satisfaction, comparing results from educators participating in cooperative teaching with those from educators not participating. Alternatively, compare resignation and transfer rates of educators participating in cooperative teaching with those of educators not participating.

    e. **stress,** then administer to all school professionals a stress survey, comparing results from educators participating in cooperative teaching with those from educators not participating.

IV. If You Are Interested in Parent Changes in . . .

    a. **attitudes toward the school,** then construct and administer to a sample of parents an attitudes-toward-our-school survey, comparing results from parents of children in cooperatively taught classrooms with those from parents of children in traditionally taught classrooms.

    b. **responsiveness,** then compare the ratio of parent responses to educator communication in classrooms that are cooperatively taught with the ratio in traditionally taught classrooms.

    c. **overall parental involvement,** then compare the frequency of behaviors such as attendance at parent–teacher meetings, participation in parent–teacher organizations, and classroom volunteering of parents of students in cooperatively taught classrooms with parents of students in traditionally taught classrooms.

Using the above format as a model, you should develop a similar *if–then* guide to use in evaluating the specific processes you employ in your cooperative teaching and the desired outcomes of those processes. To do this, you should first determine the following:

    a. exactly what specific outcomes of cooperative teaching are most significant, important, or desirable in your program

    b. exactly what processes make up your individual cooperative teaching effort (e.g., identify cooperative teaching partner, develop schedules, decide on the frequency and duration of meetings, describe the nature of interactions over time, and determine the specific nature of cooperative teaching arrangement)

c. the most desirable or useful nature of the evaluation of each of these individual processes and outcomes (i.e., objective data, subjective data, or both).

Moving In:
Resolving Issues in Cooperative Teaching

Trust is the result of risk successfully survived.
—Jack Gibb

When a home remodeling project is completed, homeowners eagerly move back into their remodeled residence, anticipating the great advantages the renovated structure will now provide. It usually takes some time, however, before the homeowners are completely comfortable in their new surroundings. The revised physical arrangements of the home are likely to disrupt their previous routines, and may lead to unanticipated problems. In most cases, a period of adjustment is necessary before the new structure feels like home again.

Similarly, educators have lived in a schoolhouse that has remained fundamentally unchanged for the last 100 years. The basic structure of the schoolhouse has been one general educator in one classroom with near-total responsibility for one group of students, either for the entire day (at the elementary level) or for one class period (at the secondary level). Various groups of special-needs students were removed from the classroom from time to time, with educational responsibility for these students parceled out to various specialists (e.g., ESL educators, special educators, remedial reading teachers). These specialized professionals worked in isolation from their general education counterparts.

Remodeling the schoolhouse using the blueprints of cooperative teaching results in a substantially changed teaching environment. In implementing cooperative teaching, school personnel dramatically redefine themselves and their professional roles, especially in the area of interpersonal relationships.

Historically, teaching has been a profession characterized by great isolation from colleagues (and in fact from all other adults). Many educators see colleagues only briefly before the start of school, again momentarily during a short lunch break, and perhaps again for a short time after school. This is in stark contrast to almost all other professions, which require coworkers to cooperate with colleagues actively and intensively as integrated teams to complete work projects.

As educators move into cooperative teaching, they construct a new work environment that is radically different from the one to which they have become accustomed. The most significant difference in this remodeled schoolhouse is that educators are faced with new interpersonal issues. Perhaps the best way to understand these changes is to see them in terms of a paradigm shift.

PARADIGMS AND PARADIGM SHIFTS

Futurist and educator Joel Barker began talking about paradigms and paradigm shifts almost 20 years ago as a way to understand the behavior of people as they encounter inevitable changes in their worlds (Barker, 1992). A paradigm is the way in which an individual perceives and understands his or her surroundings. It is the set of written and unwritten rules that establish the boundaries and behavioral expectations of one's world. The paradigm that is dominant to a person at any certain time is so fundamental, so established, so taken for granted, that it is unquestioned.

From time to time powerful changes develop in the perceptions held by a society, the ways a society thinks and acts. Barker referred to these changes as paradigm shifts. Paradigm shifts represent changes in the rules and ways in which a society operates.

Any given paradigm is maintained by an individual because it has been useful for solving problems. In the initial stages of a new and emerging paradigm, its usefulness is limited because many individuals continue to cling to comfortable (though increasingly inappropriate) old ways of thinking and responding. As the new paradigm becomes more established and more clearly understood, its problem-solving potential increases rapidly. Although it does not resolve all problems, the new paradigm does so often enough, and with enough success, that the few problems it does not seem to effectively address can be put off.

At this point the new paradigm becomes widely accepted. Even though still newer alternative paradigms may begin to emerge during this period, the ongoing success of the present paradigm keeps new ones from becoming accepted. As time goes on, however, seemingly intractable problems remain or emerge, and the existing paradigm cannot resolve these problems effectively. It is at this point that the next paradigm begins to emerge, becomes accepted, and ultimately evolves into the widely accepted paradigm for its time.

A major paradigm shift in the mid-20th century in American society was that from racial segregation to integration, a shift that is still evolving. A similar shift toward inclusion of increasingly diverse groups of students in the educational mainstream is presently occurring in the nation's schools.

A paradigm of public education that existed at least since the establishment of compulsory education in the early 1900s through most of the 20th century included the following established rules and boundaries:

- One educator works with, and has responsibility for, only one specified group of students.

- Educators work alone, not together, as they teach.

- As educators work in isolation, they are responsible for (especially at the secondary level) and teach in primarily one discipline.

- An educator works with any group of students for only 1 year.

- There are at least two clearly discernible and distinct groups of students: typical students and students with special needs.

- The two distinct groups of typical students and students with special needs have entirely different requirements in terms of curriculum and instructional techniques.

- Only educational specialists have the skills that students with special needs require; thus, general educators are not appropriate educators for these students.

- Educational specialists have little to offer typical students.

When most countries instituted compulsory education in the early part of the 20th century, usually only average to above-average students were admitted to or stayed in school. At that time the schools' organizational structures were based largely on the assembly-line paradigm of factory production. Thus, students with significant differences were excluded routinely from participation in public school programs.

In most places, exclusion of these students was the paradigm that dominated educational thought and practice through the 1980s. Since then, however, a switch to a paradigm of education that emphasizes inclusion has rapidly emerged.

For example, through the 1940s and 1950s there was great debate about whether students with disabilities should even be in the public schools. Similar debate occurred in the early 1970s concerning students with severe disabilities. When both groups of students initially were admitted into the public schools, often it was only to separate segregated schools for students with special needs. With the advent of legislation in the mid-1970s mandating that students with disabilities be educated in the least restrictive environment, many public schools instituted separate classes in the schools for these students, maintaining functional segregation and exclusion.

Through the 1980s, students with diverse learning needs began to be placed into general education classes for much (though rarely all) of the school day. As this occurred, it became more and more obvious to many school professionals that the existing general education paradigm (which included such rules as "educators work by themselves" and "educators lecture to large groups of passive students") was not the most effective for the increasingly diverse student needs found in contemporary schools. School professionals began to see that education of all students must be a shared responsibility (e.g., Dettmer, Thurston, & Dyck, 2002; Pugach & Johnson, 2002).

Students in general education classrooms were no longer all of average and above-average ability, as they had been for much of the past century. Instead, student populations contained much greater linguistic, ethnic, cultural, learning, and behavioral diversity. Schools were becoming significantly more heterogeneous, as was the greater society. Faced with these diverse student needs, educators increasingly encountered problems that could not be solved using the existing educational paradigm. A new paradigm that could respond to these new problems was required. The emergence and widespread acceptance of cooperative teaching is perhaps the most significant indicator of this new emerging paradigm (Pugach & Johnson, 2002, p. 6).

ROLE CHANGES

As Sarason and his colleagues noted in 1966, teaching is a lonely profession. Rarely do educators have the opportunity to discuss problems or successes with colleagues (Sarason, Levine, Goldenberg, Cherlin, & Bennet, 1966). Similarly, Rudduck (1991) noted that education is among the last vocations where it is still acceptable to work alone. Based in the old educational paradigm, professional and social isolation has characterized the professional experience of most educators.

The old educational paradigm of professional isolation led to a number of consequences, including the following:

- made it difficult for educators to share new ideas and better solutions

- inhibited the recognition of success

- permitted incompetence to exist and persist to the detriment of students and educators (Fullan & Hargreaves, 1991)

- allowed (if not produced) conservatism and resistance to innovation in teaching (Lortie, 1975)

An especially significant consequence of this isolation is the absence of feedback concerning one's performance. Although most school personnel receive pro forma evaluations, they occur infrequently and typically contain little of substance that can actually be used to improve skills.

Rosenholtz (1989) concluded that the typical pattern of educator isolation results in educational settings where learning potential is diminished. The combination of isolation and individualism contributes to and sustains educational conservatism, because educators have little access to new ideas and the opportunities associated with them. School personnel feel comfortable in their familiar, safe practices, which do little to respond to rapidly changing student needs (Fullan & Hargreaves, 1991).

Professional isolation is so inherent in the old educational paradigm that many educators are unable to imagine, and have never actually considered, any working arrangement other than teaching alone. The physical architecture of many schools contributes to the traditional paradigm, as one educator is assigned to one physical classroom and space.

The emerging new educational paradigm, one in which educators work cooperatively, has significant and fundamental implications for redefining the very nature of their work. As Barker (1992) noted, when a paradigm shifts, all concerned go "back to zero." In other words, no matter how skilled an educator was at doing his or her job under the old paradigm, under the new paradigm all participants essentially learn their work all over again.

To understand this more clearly, one need only imagine manufacturers of horse-drawn wagons at the turn of the century, as the transportation paradigm was just beginning to shift. Two possible options for carriage manufacturers at that time were to (1) concentrate on making bigger, stronger, and more deluxe horse-drawn carriages;

or (2) acquire the skills and machinery necessary to survive in the emerging horseless carriage paradigm. The futures inherent in each of these options are clear in hindsight. Regardless of their skill in producing the very finest horse-drawn carriages, those companies that failed to understand and adapt to the new paradigm failed.

Similarly, school personnel cannot ignore the reality that the old educational paradigm of educator isolation is increasingly ineffective at meeting the increasingly diverse needs of present and future student populations. As the old educational paradigm falls, educators will be asked to work in the way almost all workers do throughout society, that is, as part of a cooperative team.

Under a new paradigm, one's past record of achievements becomes less important, much as one's skills in manufacturing horse-drawn carriages became essentially irrelevant in the 20th century. What is more important is how well one can adapt to, and professionally thrive under, the new paradigm. This has great implications for school personnel.

Under the new educational paradigm as exemplified by cooperative teaching, the daily professional interactions of school personnel will be expanded from one-way interactions with students to include more symmetrical and balanced ongoing two-way interactions with peers. In this new paradigm, educators will be help receivers as well as help givers. In addition to the traditional role of giving help to others, educators now will be actively receiving substantial amounts of assistance from their partners in cooperative teaching.

INTERPERSONAL SKILLS

For most educators, the single most significant change involved in remodeling the schoolhouse using cooperative teaching blueprints is the new professional relationships they must develop with their teaching partners. This may well represent the single greatest challenge in implementing cooperative teaching and pose the greatest difficulty for educators accustomed to working in isolation. It takes work and skill to develop and maintain a harmonious and productive working relationship with another professional.

One way to think about the growth of the relationship is to see it as an ongoing process, characterized by several steps. In step 1, *warming,* two people begin to learn about each other, their styles, preferences, quirks, and so on. In step 2, *storming,* the relationship has moved past the initial superficial politeness, with significant issues emerging. The two are comfortable enough with each other and with the relationship that they are able to express disagreements, an inevitable step in successful relationship building. Last, in step 3, *norming,* the degree to which they share a common worldview continues to grow.

Effective interpersonal skills allow people to initiate, develop, and maintain productive relationships. Johnson (1990) identified the following four basic interconnected and overlapping components of interpersonal skills:

1. knowing and trusting each other
2. communicating with each other accurately and unambiguously
3. accepting and supporting each other
4. resolving conflicts and relationship problems constructively

Coming to know and trust another person requires that each discloses how he or she feels and thinks. This in turn requires that each knows himself or herself well. This process of self-awareness followed by self-disclosure is fundamental for the development of trust over time.

There are a number of ways to develop self-awareness. Much as educators learn to watch students to determine who they are, they also can learn to watch themselves objectively, taking note of their own behaviors to learn more about themselves. Using other school professionals as benchmarks or comparison points in these observations, especially those who are similar in key ways, also helps to enhance self-awareness.

Any social relationship requires at least two individuals. For a balanced relationship, each must be open with, and be open to, the other. An individual who is open with another shares personal ideas and feelings, letting the other know who he or she is. One who is open to another must learn who that person is and accept him or her. These processes require self-disclosure.

Self-disclosure is the deliberate revealing of information about oneself that is significant and that normally would not be known by others (Adler & Towne, 1996). It does not necessarily mean revealing intimate details of one's past or present life. What it does mean is sharing one's honest reactions to events both are experiencing in their cooperative teaching relationship. Only through mutual self-disclosure can individuals truly get to know one another, a mandatory requirement for effective cooperative teaching. In doing this the two people build a similar and consistent view of their shared world.

Although there is potential risk in self-disclosure, as one repeats the process and begins to trust the other, the risk diminishes. In addition, the act of self-disclosure makes it easier for the other also to self-disclose, again enhancing and building the level of mutual trust.

Information that is shared through self-disclosure has two dimensions: *breadth* and *depth* (Altman & Taylor, 1973). Breadth refers to the variety of subjects that are discussed. For example, two educators beginning in cooperative teaching are likely to start their relationship by sharing information on such topics as where each went to school, previous jobs, and so forth. As their relationship grows these topics are likely to growth in breadth, expanding into their lives away from work, into their hobbies, families, and so forth.

Depth of self-disclosure refers to the degree to which the information that is shared is personal and revealing. As trust develops in a cooperative teaching relationship, each member becomes more secure and thus more comfortable sharing information that is potentially sensitive. One way to consider depth of self-disclosure is in four levels: social clichés, factual self-disclosures, opinion-based self-disclosures, and personal feelings (Adler & Towne, 1996).

The first of these levels, social clichés, are those verbal exchanges people use routinely with each other, such as, "How are you?" "I'm fine; how are you?" and "Oh, I can't complain." Nothing personal is revealed, and nothing is risked.

Somewhat deeper are self-disclosures based on facts. A statement such as, "Math has always been difficult for me. My grades in my college math courses were my lowest," are factually based and convey a deeper level of self-disclosure than social clichés.

The sharing of opinions is a still deeper and more intimate level of self-disclosure than fact-based self-disclosures. In sharing opinions one more clearly reveals exactly who one is, while simultaneously exposing oneself to greater risk of a critical or hurtful response from the other. A statement such as, "I've never participated in cooperative teaching before" is factual. However, saying, "I'm not sure that cooperative teaching can work in our school" is a much more revealing.

The deepest self-disclosures are those describing one's personal feelings. One partner in a cooperative teaching relationship might say to another, "When you say you'll finish a task and you don't, I feel angry and taken advantage of." This level of self-disclosure is intimate, and opens one up to criticism at a very vulnerable level. However, when accomplished in a mutual atmosphere of trust, it also provides each participant with an additional sense of togetherness.

Qualitative values should not be assigned arbitrarily to these four levels. Each is appropriate in certain circumstances and inappropriate in others. What is important in a relationship such as cooperative teaching is that all participants are able to self-disclose and communicate at all four levels.

The process of self-disclosure is most effective when deliberately and moderately paced. Too rapid self-disclosure early in a relationship can scare another away. Strong relationships usually are built gradually.

Self-disclosure that occurs too slowly, however, hinders the development of mutual trust. Essentially the pace of advancement along the continuum of depth of self-disclosure depends on the level of mutual comfort with each other that is being established.

In self-disclosure a person describes his or her feelings and reactions. In doing so the person typically finds that these thoughts and feelings become clearer and easier to understand. In addition, as the person self-discloses, the reactions of others to those disclosures help the person become more aware of the nature of his or her beliefs and actions. This effect can be enhanced by soliciting feedback concerning self-disclosures, simply following a self-disclosure from time to time with the question, "What do you think?"

TRUST

In a 1989 study of team effectiveness, Larson and LaFasto found that teams are most productive when the teams' surrounding atmosphere is one of trust. They identified several reasons that explain why trust is necessary for teams to function well together.

First, when team members trust each other, they can stay problem focused and goal oriented, rather than concentrating on guarding and protecting themselves. In the absence of trust, team members' personal agendas may surface, and considerable energy may be expended in developing and protecting against personal attacks.

Second, an atmosphere of trust yields a more efficient use of time. Individuals can speak frankly and directly, without others trying to decipher hidden meanings.

Finally, when team members trust each other, each person feels comfortable proposing answers or solutions that may be risky, or proposing possibilities that may fail.

Participants will contribute ideas and suggestions freely, without worrying about potentially hurtful personal criticism. In social interactions characterized by mistrust, people tend to propose only those ideas that are conservative and safe, if they propose any ideas at all. This self-censoring results in the suppression of potentially valuable contributions.

Self-disclosure in the absence of trust is risky. If one does not trust the person to whom self-disclosure is being made, one anticipates rejection and ridicule. Self-disclosure can result in either harmful or beneficial consequences. Trust exists when one person expects that another person will respond in a way that produces beneficial consequences.

Mutual trust builds as two individuals increasingly self-disclose to each other, receiving acceptance and support in return. Trust grows as each participant learns that (a) no self-disclosure will be criticized, and (b) all concerned will guard the self-disclosures made in that context, and will not share those self-disclosures with others. Expressions of warmth, accurate understanding, and cooperative intentions all serve to increase trust in a relationship, even when the involved parties have unresolved conflicts.

Trust can be lost or destroyed in several ways. If one's self-disclosures are met with rejection, ridicule, criticism, or nonacceptance, any trust that has been built up will be damaged. In addition, to develop mutual trust, both participants must self-disclose. If the degree to which the two are willing to self-disclose is significantly unbalanced, the person who is more often self-disclosing may begin to feel overexposed and vulnerable.

To a large extent trust functions as a self-fulfilling prophecy. If one enters into a relationship expecting rejection, one's behaviors are likely to be suspicious and guarded, interfering with the development of mutual trust. If one enters into a relationship, however, anticipating that the other person will be warm and worthy of trust, and if one expresses support and acceptance of the other person, it is likely that one will receive such support in return.

THE EMOTIONAL BANK ACCOUNT

In his 1989 book *The 7 Habits of Highly Effective People*, Stephen Covey introduced a concept called the Emotional Bank Account. This metaphor describes the amount of trust that has been built up in a relationship. One can build up a balance in this relationship account through kindness and trustworthiness, and can deplete or even overdraw the account through discourtesy or betrayal. If the account balance is low, then the relationship is threatened.

To build and maintain positive balances in their Emotional Bank Accounts, cooperative teaching partners must make frequent and major deposits. Covey outlines six ways that this can be done.

Understand the partner. Cooperative teaching partners should understand that their values may differ greatly. Behavior that is seen as inconsequential for one might actually be seen as substantial for the other. For example, one teacher might find being a few minutes late for a meeting to be no big deal. However, his cooperative teaching partner finds such behavior a powerful symbol of disrespect, and each time it happens she grows a bit angrier at him, depleting the account. What must happen is for him to value her wish for promptness as importantly as he does their overall relationship. He must see that although promptness is not valuable to him, it is extremely valuable to her, and so he must respect the values that she holds. In so doing, he demonstrates understanding of her, and makes an important deposit in the account.

Attend to the little things. In relationships, little things mean a lot. One cooperative teaching relationship observed by the authors blossomed after one partner began bringing donuts to the other on Monday mornings. The emotional message behind that small gesture facilitated the development of trust that carried the partners quickly to an effective rapport.

Keep commitments. Keeping a promise is a major deposit in the account, whereas breaking one is a major withdrawal. Covey (1989) asserted that the most massive withdrawal is failing to follow through on a commitment. People make plans and build on the promises of others. When those promises are not kept, subsequent promises will be discounted. In cooperative teaching, each partner must trust that the other will honor his or her commitments. Each time a promise is broken, the relationship suffers. Failure to keep commitments is perhaps the most frequent cause of cooperative teaching "divorces."

Clarify expectations. Many relationship difficulties result from conflicting or ambiguous expectations of roles and goals. Often expectations are implicit and unspoken in relationships, based on the past experiences of the individuals. In such a new social relationship as cooperative teaching, however, the expectations may not be clearly understood by all because of the absence of experience. Cooperative teachers can make substantial contributions in the Emotional Bank Account by making their expectations clear and explicit in the beginning. Although it may be easy for partners to ignore differences in expectations, the relationship ultimately will be undermined by such an approach.

Show personal integrity. Integrity includes honesty, but goes further. Covey (1989) suggested that the best way to manifest integrity is to be loyal to those who are not present. When one defends those who are absent, he or she gains the trust of those who are present. For example, if a cooperative teaching partner criticizes another colleague to her partner, then the partner must wonder if he is similarly criticized at other times when he is not around.

Apologize when making a withdrawal. People make large withdrawals from the account when they are discourteous or break a trust. When this happens, the only way repairs can be made is to sincerely apologize. The simplest words ("I was wrong," "I was disrespectful to you, and I'm deeply sorry") are best. It takes strength and inner security for a cooperative teaching partner to apologize to the other partner. An insincere apology only further depletes the account.

As teachers move into cooperative teaching, perhaps their most challenging issue is the maintenance of their interpersonal relationship with their teaching partner. The Emotional Bank Account concept can help the partners see the subtleties of their relationship in a more direct and practical way.

TURF

In many places, ongoing violence associated with youth gangs revolves around the issue of turf. Often a gang will identify a section of the city as its own, mark that section with identifying symbols, and defend that turf from other gangs. When the turf is violated, the gang uses aggressive retaliation against intruders. Although this is an extreme example, many people similarly come to identify physical or social space as their own, and feel uncomfortable when others invade it.

This is no less true for school personnel than for anyone else. One of the more difficult adjustments educators must make in implementing cooperative teaching is shifting from professional autonomy to professional sharing. After having had sole responsibility for, control over, and personal and professional privacy within one classroom, educators must adjust to a psychologically different climate, one in which another adult is present. Having a colleague move onto one's turf is often unsettling, even for the best-intentioned educators.

There are a number of turfs that cooperative teaching partners must learn to cohabit. The first of these is the actual physical environment that the two will now share. Most educators view a particular classroom as their own, and have decorated and personalized it. Many will actually confess to a bit of discomfort when another school professional is in that space for any length of time.

In addition to the physical space, a second type of turf that must be shared is that of educational materials. Over the years the typical educator assembles a set of customized curricular materials, often purchased with the educator's personal monies.

Yielding sole control and ownership of a set of materials laboriously compiled and assembled over the years is difficult.

An interesting indicator of the success (or failure) of cooperative teaching partners in overcoming these issues of turf is their use of language over time. Shared language as, "we" and "our," instead of autonomous language such as, "I" and "mine," suggests that the cooperative teaching partners have internalized the shared ownership and responsibilities inherent in cooperative teaching.

One of the authors conducted a follow-up training workshop for educators who had been involved in cooperative teaching for a complete academic year. The participants were enthusiastic about the results of their work and were eagerly awaiting the next year. One of the cooperative teaching partners had been a general education teacher, while the other previously had been a special educator working with students who had mild disabilities. The two educators spoke wonderfully of "our" classroom, "our" curriculum, "our" materials, and "our" program. But the former special educator went on to say, "But on the statewide academic competency testing, her kids did better than mine." Although this educator had adopted almost all aspects of the philosophy of shared ownership and responsibility, it was obvious that, when it came to students with disabilities, she still clearly saw those students as hers, with educational responsibility for those students falling primarily on her and not jointly with her cooperative teaching partner.

Given individuals' natural tendency to look for the easiest solutions, when two educators move into cooperative teaching they frequently decide to work in the previous classroom of one or the other. Although such a decision initially appears to be reasonable and logical, what follows naturally evolves from the fact that one educator is at home while the other is a visitor. Though this idea is covert and often not even recognized (much less stated), it nonetheless can have a significant and detrimental impact on the desired goal of shared educational ownership and responsibility.

Many couples marrying later in life experience similar problems when one moves into the home of the other. To avoid this, it is often best for the two to purchase a new home together, one that will be "theirs" from the start. Similarly, if possible it is advisable for the two new cooperative teaching partners to move into a new room, one in which neither previously has worked. The new physical environment provides an atmosphere more suitable for the fresh beginning the educators seek in their professional work, and neither educator can be considered a visitor.

If a new classroom is not possible, the next best solution is for the new teaching partners to dramatically rearrange the physical environment of the existing room. Both educators should substantially rearrange (or even exchange) furniture, work together on room decorations, and so forth. The room becomes less clearly identified as belonging to the previous tenant and instead comes to be seen as shared space. What is sought is a sense of shared ownership, of the room being not "yours" or "mine" but "ours."

FLEXIBILITY

As educators begin cooperative teaching, a consistent theme that emerges as their relationship develops is the need for mutual flexibility. Professional and personal flexibility is essential as school personnel adopt the new educational paradigm of shared responsibilities. No matter how extensively one plans ahead, it is simply not possible to anticipate and plan for the nearly infinite variety of problems that are encountered in a new paradigm.

Any home remodeler can tell stories of plans going astray when pipes or wires were not where they were expected to be, when walls could not be moved, when required materials became unavailable or prohibitively expensive, and so forth. Acknowledging beforehand that such unexpected developments are virtual certainties in any remodeling project makes their inevitable appearance less stressful and disturbing.

Many problems encountered by educators implementing cooperative teaching cannot be solved in familiar ways. Without flexibility, cooperative teaching partners may find these problems to be insurmountable obstacles.

Flexibility includes substantial tolerance for ambiguity. Flexible school professionals can receive conflicting information without forcing premature closure on a situation. Educators who are flexible can look at problems from many perspectives and adopt new ways of thinking easily.

School professionals who are flexible and can adapt to changing situations experience less stress in their professional lives than others. The ability to respond easily and smoothly to changing situations without worrying endlessly helps any educator handle the day-to-day surprises that emerge in school programs.

 ## CASE STUDY: HOLLY H. AND LAURI B.

The following case study is based on a situation encountered by one of the authors during a consulting visit to a school. It illustrates several issues related to the establishment of a new and different sort of professional relationship with a colleague.

Background

Holly H. was the new young special educator hired at Starr Middle School, a school serving a middle-class neighborhood. Holly had 2 years of experience at another middle school where she had had a great experience working in extensive cooperative teaching arrangements with several teachers. She brought the same expectations to her new position at Starr. Prior to Holly's hiring, the special educator at Starr Middle School had provided most special education services primarily through a pullout approach, though some cooperative teaching had taken place. The school principal, Michael H., expressed support for Holly's proposal for more extensive cooperative teaching.

At the first faculty meeting of the school year prior to the students' arrival, Holly talked about her wish to implement cooperative teaching at Starr Middle School, and asked if any of her general education colleagues would like to work with her on this. Lauri B., a male eighth-grade teacher with 15 years of experience, expressed interest, so the two decided to develop a cooperative teaching approach.

Lauri's eighth-grade class had 31 students, 4 of whom were on IEPs, 5 on Section 504 Accommodation Plans, and 3 who were English Language Learner students. Each of the 4 students on IEPs had a diagnosis of learning disability and was reading and writing at a second-grade level or below. Lauri and Holly anticipated that her daily time in the eighth-grade classroom would especially target these 4 students, but that all students would benefit from the presence of both teachers in the room simultaneously.

Initially things went well. The two met every Wednesday after school for 30 to 60 minutes to plan for the next week's work. In these planning meetings they outlined the curriculum to be covered in the next week, as well as who would do what in the presentation of the instruction.

However, as the weeks went on Lauri began coming later and later to their scheduled planning meetings and began leaving earlier and earlier. He even failed to show up twice for scheduled meetings. Less and less time was being spent planning for their work.

In addition, Lauri began to suggest that maybe so much planning was not necessary, because as experienced educators, he said, they could wing it. Holly became increasingly concerned that the students with special needs were not receiving the systematic instruction she believed they needed, due to the lack of planning. Holly became so frustrated that she began regularly pulling these students into the resource room and providing specialized instruction there.

Holly was feeling frustrated, but so was Lauri. He did not realize beforehand that he was committing to regular planning meetings, especially after school on his own time. His experience with cooperative teaching in the past was that the special educator came in as support for what he had planned to do that day. He did not see the need for or the value of extensive planning, and he was beginning to resent it. Indirectly, he was beginning to resent Holly and cooperative teaching.

Given this background, stop for a moment to consider the following:

- What deposits and what withdrawals have been made in Holly's Emotional Bank Account?

- What deposits and what withdrawals have been made in Lauri's Emotional Bank Account?

- What issues might Lauri and Holly ask a colleague or coach to help them with?

- What questions might the coach ask Lauri and Holly?

Analysis

In this case each teacher came to the cooperative teaching experience with unspoken but significantly different expectations. For Holly, cooperative teaching represented a substantial paradigm shift from traditional educational structures. For her, cooperative teaching was an entirely different way to go about education. Lauri, on the other hand, did not perceive such a change. As he saw and understood cooperative teaching, his role in "his" classroom remained essentially unchanged.

The failure of these two individuals to self-disclose their beliefs early on about such important issues as their relative roles in the classroom, and the importance (or lack thereof) of planning, presented a major barrier to their ongoing work. Had Holly known that planning was unimportant to Lauri, she might well have chosen to work with someone else. Similarly, had Lauri known how important planning was to Holly, he might have been less eager to participate. More optimistically, if each had known the other's beliefs beforehand, each might have been more flexible, jointly looking for win–win solutions.

Lauri's tardiness and generally lax attitude toward meetings caused Holly to abandon her cooperative teaching efforts to some degree. She could not see how she and Lauri might work together effectively without regular and detailed planning meetings. As noted, she began pulling the students on IEPs into the resource room for regular work. More important, she began to lose trust in Lauri.

Turf also played an unspoken role here. Planning helped Holly feel more comfortable in Lauri's classroom. Without the planning sessions, increasingly she felt like a visitor to "his" classroom, not a peer.

Resolution

The particular paradigm or worldview that each person holds is so inherent, so deeply ingrained, that it usually goes unnoticed and unquestioned. In this case the two teachers had not adequately discussed the basic issue of what each believed cooperative teaching to be. This discussion should have included such related questions as the role of planning, how instructional roles and responsibilities in the classroom might look, and so on.

To make the cooperative teaching situation work, Holly and Lauri engaged in significant self-reflection, and came to some conclusions. Holly concluded that Lauri was a successful teacher, doing many appropriate things and helping all students in his classroom learn. She came to see that his many years of experience provided him with enough background that planning was less necessary for him than it was for her, a relative newcomer. She acknowledged that, whatever Lauri was doing, it was effective. She began to explore possibilities within cooperative teaching that might require less systematic and extensive planning.

Through ongoing chats with Holly, Lauri began to see how his actions might have unintentionally communicated an "I don't care" attitude to Holly. He also came to see how important planning is in special education, where systematic instruction is inherent in the entire IEP process. Given Holly's deep background in special education, then,

Lauri began to see how important planning was to her, and how it might be especially useful for students with learning differences.

Both Lauri and Holly realized and agreed that their cooperative teaching relationship was important enough that it deserved significant attention. Michael H., the principal, concurred, so much so that he dedicated resources to Lauri's classroom in the form of a teacher's aide to free the two teachers for 1 hour a week to meet. Because this time was not coming out of his personal time, Lauri felt much more comfortable with the planning process.

Holly realized that, professionally speaking, she was powerfully driven. However, also realizing that cooperative teaching relationships are as personal as they are professional, Holly concluded that she should not cram too much work into her planning meetings with Lauri, and was careful to establish a pleasant tone from the beginning of each meeting. The two began their meetings with social exchanges about what each had done the past weekend, and they offered praise to each other on especially noteworthy work that they had seen in each other over the past week. They made efforts to keep things light, and tried to maintain a humorous perspective on their work together. As they did this, their trust began to be reestablished. Their professional relationship is stronger today than ever.

CONCLUSIONS

Moving back into the schoolhouse that has been newly remodeled based on cooperative teaching blueprints presents educators with a novel set of challenges. Specifically, they will now be working with colleagues in very different ways. This requires new skills in interpersonal relationships that the previous educational arrangements did not require, including the building of trust through self-disclosure. The metaphor of the Emotional Bank Account allows partners in cooperative teaching to better understand how to build and sustain their professional and personal relationships, and offers a number of practical suggestions to help educators do this. Related new interpersonal issues include turf, or ownership of physical environment, materials, and programs; and flexibility, the need to adapt when faced with the inevitable ambiguities and unexpected developments associated with a paradigm shift.

After homeowners move into their remodeled house, they gradually become comfortable with the changes resulting from the remodeling. They may find, however, that the previous arrangements of their furniture and other furnishings no longer work as well in the newly remodeled structure as they did in the old. Either the old furniture and furnishings must be rearranged in a new way to better fit the newly remodeled area, or new furnishings must be obtained. The next chapter explores how educators moving into cooperative teaching must similarly examine their social arrangements, shifting and rearranging them as necessary to maximize their professional effectiveness in the remodeled schoolhouse.

CHAPTER 7 ACTIVITY

Assessing Flexibility

As noted in this chapter, flexibility is key to successful implementation of co-operative teaching. It is helpful to know one's own flexibility before trying to blend with a partner in cooperative teaching.

Raudsepp (1990) developed a self-survey of overall flexibility that has been adapted here to allow an educator to determine his or her own level of educational flexibility.* Although the adapted survey has not been empirically validated, many educators nonetheless have found it a useful and enjoyable exercise in personal analysis.

First, estimate your own perceived level of flexibility, from very flexible to very rigid, and mark it on the continuum below.

very flexible   very rigid

Now complete the exercise below.

For each item:

    A = Almost Always
    B = Sometimes
    C = Rarely
    D = Never

These responses should reflect your own personal reality, not the way you wish you were. The accuracy of your self-awareness is an important first step in developing a productive and fulfilling relationship in cooperative teaching.

_____ 1. It is important for me to have a specific place for everything.

_____ 2. I make strong demands on myself.

_____ 3. I feel very uncomfortable when I have to break an appointment.

_____ 4. When leaving home or work I find I have to check and recheck doors, lights, windows, the desk, and so on.

_____ 5. It bothers me when people do not put things back exactly as I left them.

---

*Note. Adaptsed from "Are You Flexible Enough to Succeed?" by E. Raudsepp, 1990, *Working Woman*, 15, pp. 106–107. Copyright 1990 by *Working Woman*. Adapted with permission.

_____ 6. I do not like to stray very much from my planned and scheduled activities.

_____ 7. I get upset if things do not go as planned.

_____ 8. After completing a task, I have doubts about whether I did it right.

_____ 9. I do certain things over and over again even though I know it is pointless to do them.

_____10. I don't dwell on my problems too long.

_____11. I worry about a lot of things.

_____12. I react quickly to unexpected situations.

_____13. I am meticulous with most of my possessions.

_____14. I strive for perfection in what I do.

_____15. I don't care if people laugh at my ideas.

_____16. I feel I miss out on a lot of opportunities because I don't act quickly enough.

_____17. I find time to relax and simply do nothing.

_____18. I move, walk, and eat rapidly because I don't like wasting time.

_____19. I go back and forth searching for the right decision.

_____20. I'm very punctual.

_____21. Stress makes me disorganized.

_____22. I like to make detailed lists of my daily tasks and activities.

For the remaining questions simply score A for Agree and B for Disagree.

_____23. I often feel anxious or apprehensive even though I don't know what has caused the worry.

_____24. I frequently get rattled or annoyed at others for not keeping on schedule with plans we've made.

_____25. I seldom act without critically thinking.

_____26. I sometimes get a kick out of breaking the rules and doing things I'm not supposed to do.

_____27. I tend to dwell on things I did but shouldn't have done.

_____28. I'm frequently tense or nervous.

_____29. There is frequently a discrepancy between the way I want to behave and the way I actually behave.

_____30. My work tends to pile up so much that I have difficulty completing it.

SCORING

After all answers are recorded, they should be scored according to the following key:

1. A=5	B=3	C=2	D=1
2. A=6	B=4	C=2	D=1
3. A=4	B=3	C=2	D=1
4. A=6	B=4	C=2	D=1
5. A=6	B=4	C=2	D=1
6. A=7	B=4	C=2	D=1
7. A=7	B=4	C=2	D=1
8. A=5	B=3	C=2	D=1
9. A=5	B=3	C=2	D=1
10. A=1	B=2	C=4	D=6
11. A=7	B=5	C=2	D=1
12. A=1	B=2	C=4	D=6
13. A=6	B=3	C=2	D=1
14. A=7	B=4	C=2	D=1
15. A=1	B=2	C=4	D=7
16. A=6	B=3	C=2	D=1
17. A=1	B=2	C=4	D=7
18. A=7	B=4	C=2	D=1
19. A=7	B=4	C=2	D=1
20. A=6	B=3	C=2	D=1
21. A=7	B=4	C=2	D=1
22. A=5	B=3	C=2	D=1
23. A=6	B=1		
24. A=5	B=1		
25. A=6	B=1		
26. A=1	B=6		
27. A=7	B=1		
28. A=6	B=1		

29. A=6   B=1
30. A=6   B=1

Total score_____

The total score should be recorded on the following continuum.

Actual score

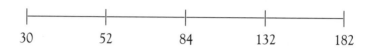

30	52	84	132	182

Now compare your pretest estimate of flexibility to your actual score obtained after completing the self-survey.

INTERPRETATION

Individuals who score from 30 to 52 have very high levels of flexibility, and can make adaptions to new situations relatively easily. People who score from 53 to 84 have some inflexibility. People who score from 85 to 132 have a significant degree of inflexibility, which is likely to cause problems from time to time in new situations. These individuals may pay too much attention to insignificant details, which may hamper success. People who score from 133 to 182 have very high degrees of inflexibility, often accompanied by feelings of nervousness that "things aren't right" because not every *i* is dotted and *t* crossed. Unless they take steps to become more flexible, school personnel with scores at this level are unlikely to be able to deal effectively with rapid and substantial change, such as cooperative teaching.

IMPLICATIONS

Many educators are surprised to find that their scores suggest that they are less flexible than they anticipated. Such findings can serve to guide further thinking, planning, and mutual growth as partners in cooperative teaching begin working together.

Educators whose scores suggest a high degree of inflexibility can take deliberate steps to become less rigid, primarily by taking more risks. Such activities as speaking out early on a controversial school issue, changing one's routines, and going out of one's way to interact with people normally not encountered all serve to "shake things up" and allow one to achieve a fresh perspective. By changing daily routines and moving into unfamiliar territory one can become more comfortable with change in general. In doing so, educators will become better prepared to benefit and grow from the inevitable innovation and change in the schools.

In addition, many cooperative teaching partners have found it useful to share their flexibility ratings with each other, specifically noting and commenting on areas of special flexibility as well as on areas of rigidity each may have identified in this exercise.

Rearranging the Furniture:
Adjusting to Cooperative Teaching

Change is inevitable; pain is optional.
—Anonymous

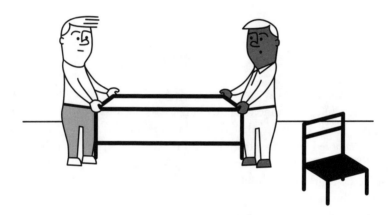

omeowners who have completed an extensive home remodeling project experience an inevitable and often uncomfortable period of change and adaptation to the new surroundings. Various placements and combinations of the furniture, paintings, wall hangings, and plants must be tried out before the right fit is achieved. In addition, the homeowners may notice that there are gaps at the base of a wall that the molding does not completely hide, that one corner of a room has an unpainted spot, or that a door does not swing freely.

The appearance of these problems can cause great distress in the homeowners. Given the magnitude and complexity of any substantial remodeling or rebuilding project, however, such developments must be expected. Indeed it would be rare not to find any problems after a large remodeling job is completed.

When educators move into a schoolhouse that has been remodeled following a set of blueprints for cooperative teaching, they encounter inevitable discrepancies between the ideal situations they had hoped for when they planned the project and reality, which contains the educational equivalents of unpainted walls and gaps that molding fails to cover.

After living in the newly remodeled collaborative schoolhouse for a while, school professionals must spend some time doing the educational equivalent of moving furniture around, patching holes, and painting. The significance of the changes that will be necessary following a rebuilding project of this magnitude should not be underestimated. Educators must realize beforehand that they will probably have to make changes before the new arrangements in the schoolhouse feel natural. One way educators can better prepare for adaptions is to understand the nature of change.

CHANGE

For many educators a paradox emerges between the obvious need for change in the schools and the reality that fundamental changes in education are slow and difficult to achieve. Some have concluded that the problem is that Western culture historically has been preoccupied with *how* things work, not *why* (e.g., Knoster, Villa, & Thousand, 2000). Such a mechanical orientation to change causes people to think more about what to do than why it should be done. For successful change to occur, both the why as well as the how must be understood.

Another way of understanding how this paradox has emerged is to look at how educators view the status of the overall education system versus how they view their specific schools. In general, many educators agree that there are significant problems in general with the schools at present. However, when asked in the same survey about their own schools, these same respondents conclude that their schools are fine, and doing good work in difficult circumstances (Elam, Rose, & Gallup, 1996). It is in this way that one can see how educators both believe that change is imperative and are reluctant to change themselves.

This paradox becomes especially critical as the nature of knowledge, and even society, continues its rapid evolution. In the 21st century the world of information, and especially the sources of that information, will become increasingly complex and interdependent. Individuals whose work involves information (as is the case with teachers) will find that new skills, and new ways of approaching information, are critical to survival and success. The ability to change has perhaps never been so critical to professionals in the schools as it is today.

THE NATURE OF CHANGE

Professionals studying change in general, and school change specifically, have identified three underlying principles that are critical for understanding how change works (Hord, Rutherford, Huling-Austin, & Hall, 1987; Walther-Thomas, Korinek, McLaughlin, & Williams, 2000). These three basic principles are as follows.

1. *Change is a process, not an event.* People often see change as something to get done, at which point the change is over. The reality is that change is ongoing. Significant changes in the schools that will withstand the test of time require that time be measured not in weeks or months, but in years (Walther-Thomas et al., 2000).

2. *Responses to change are highly individualized and personal.* It is individual people who must change, and their responses to change will be as different as they are. Although some educators find change exciting and invigorating, others find it unsettling and disturbing. Both reactions should be considered normal.

3. *The process of change is most successful when those involved understand its practical implications.* It is easier for individuals to accept change when they understand exactly how it will affect their day-to-day lives. When school professionals understand how a proposed change will affect them and when they can grasp the concrete details of how their lives will be altered, they are more likely to support the change.

MANAGING CHANGE

Given the intricacies of the education system, any change process involving it will be complex. Ambrose (1987) proposed a model to understand the factors that are necessary for effective change, and the probable outcomes when one of those factors is absent. Ambrose's model was further refined by Knoster (1993) and by Knoster et al. (2000), and is represented by Figure 8.1. The following paragraphs describe the factors necessary for effective change as presented in Figure 8.1.

Vision. What is the goal that the change is designed to achieve? What will the school look like and how will it function after the change has been implemented? For cooperative teaching to be successful, the vision must be shared by those involved, include the belief in comprehensive inclusion of diverse students, and accept shared responsibility for all students. In the absence of shared and accepted vision, the likely result is confusion.

Knowledge and skills. Do the participants most involved in the change have the basic competence to carry through with the difficult tasks that lie ahead? Cooperative teaching requires new knowledge and skills in planning and problem solving. Without these skills, the probable result will be anxiety; the involved parties will find themselves apprehensive about every bump along the road of change.

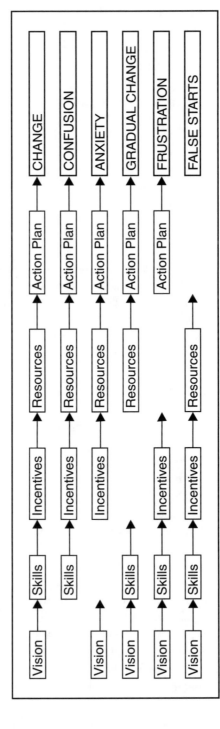

Figure 8.1 Managing complex change. *Note.* From "A Framework for Thinking About Systems Change," by T. P. Knoster, R. A. Villa, and J. S. Thousand, 2000, in *Restructuring for Caring and Effective Education* (p. 97), by R. A. Villa and J. S. Thousand (Eds.), Baltimore: Brookes. Copyright 2000 by Brookes. Reprinted with permission.

Incentives. A truism is that people do not resist change; they resist *being* changed. That is, change is most likely to be successful if the involved individuals are committed to the process, with internal motivation as their driving force. If the participants have a compelling reason for undergoing change, the result is likely to be successful. Absent such incentives, the probable outcome is change that is gradual at best, and at worst nonexistent.

Resources. Over time people fall into habitual behavioral patterns that evolve largely due to efficiency. Change disrupts these efficient patterns. Maintaining the same level of productivity under conditions of change requires more resources, such as, in the case of cooperative teaching, time, training, and administrative support. Without additional resources, the probable outcome is frustration because the participants will be physically unable to move from planning to action.

Action Plan. A difficult journey requires a map. Educators beginning cooperative teaching must be able to analyze both themselves and their work environments, and use that information to map a route to their destination. Without a well-conceived and flexible action plan, the likely result is a series of false starts. As the old saying holds, "If you don't know where you're going, any route will get you there." However, if a map has not been developed in advance and followed, it is doubtful that the destinations will be acceptable.

When all five elements (vision, skills, incentives, resources, and action plan) are present, the likely result will be the desired change. Key to success is the realization that change is about *individuals* and their beliefs and actions, not about programs or equipment. Change is highly personalized and subjective (Knoster et al., 2000).

LESSONS OF CHANGE

In a substantial analysis of change in the public schools, Fullan (1993c) identified a number of lessons that have been learned as school systems have implemented change over the last 50 years. Several of these, along with other findings from studies of change, have direct implications for school professionals as they move into cooperative teaching.

Problems Are Friends

Life is change. Change usually brings unexpected new developments, sometimes in the form of problems. Thus, problems are nearly inevitable in life. These problems emerge and persist, regardless of whether people acknowledge them. When ignored, problems stay and even grow until a solution is found. Unfortunately, when many individuals face problems resulting from change, they retreat to the security of their old ways.

In a massive study of almost 300 schools that were attempting major reform programs based on the effective schools literature, Louis and Miles (1990) found that in general, the schools had greater successes in some indicators of improvement (e.g., student behavior, image of the school in the community) than in others (e.g., drop-out rates, subsequent employment). In any case, the least successful schools were those that simply continued on in the usual ways, ignoring the growing problems. The most successful schools were those that actively sought solutions to the problems.

So how are problems friends? It is that problems hold the key to their own solutions. They contain within themselves the answers. To identify effective solutions, one must first become absolutely familiar with a problem, including all its components. It is only by becoming intimate with the problem that educators can find solutions.

As educators work together in cooperative teaching, problems are inevitable. In fact, an absence of problems would suggest that change was superficial and trivial. When problems emerge, solutions can be developed only by discussing the problem thoroughly and coming to know it as well as one knows a friend.

Connection with the Wider Environment

When homeowners are dissatisfied with the results of a remodeling project, they commonly seek outside help. They may get ideas for fine-tuning their new arrangements by talking with friends, architects, or interior decorators. They may also read home design books or pick up the latest copies of *Architectural Digest* or *Better Homes and Gardens*.

When moving into cooperative teaching, educators will be examining themselves, their students, their classrooms, and their schools, seeking to develop the best implementation strategies for their unique situations. Nias, Southworth, and Campbell (1992) reported that schools effectively implementing collaboration also were responsive to innovations in curriculum and instruction. These effective schools incorporated those developments so that they became a part of their program. In this way the schools came to develop ownership of the entire package as an integrated whole.

As educators implement cooperative teaching at their own schools, they should remember that ideas gleaned from other schools, consultants, books, professional workshops, the Internet, and other sources can only enrich the good ideas they develop in-house. Effective and successful programs stay connected with outside sources of information.

COLLEGIALITY

Perhaps the single most significant change educators experience when moving from traditional service delivery systems into cooperative teaching is the switch from being an isolated individual to a team member. This means that many school professionals will need to develop new interpersonal skills for working with colleagues. Although the ability to work with students has always been an obvious necessity for educators, the equivalent ability to work with other adults in the school, or collegiality, has not been a significant part of their work.

Collegiality refers to productive work completed through interpersonal interactions in which all participants contribute. When effectively developed and implemented, it possesses great power. Unfortunately, some analysts (e.g., Barth, 1990) have suggested that collegiality may be the least common type of relationship among educators. Collegiality is not the same as congeniality, which simply refers to friendly and cordial relationships; collegiality has greater substance, depth, and complexity.

In 1981, Little identified the following characteristics of collegiality that are particularly applicable to partners in cooperative teaching.

First, collegial educators talk about their practice. They discuss what they are doing, analyzing both their teaching and their students' learning. These conversations are concrete, direct, and ongoing.

Second, collegial educators observe each other as they work. These observations provide the material for their ongoing discussions about their work. To facilitate the development of collegiality, these observations must be supportive while being accurate. To be observed while teaching is one of the most threatening experiences in an educator's professional life because such observations typically are followed by evaluation, if not criticism, from a superior. In a collegial relationship, the educator must see that the other educator's observations are being conducted in an atmosphere of mutual trust, and that the information that emerges will be used constructively.

Third, collegial educators work together on curriculum and instruction issues; they design and evaluate *what* they present to their students and *how* they present it. The work is the product of a team, not of separate individuals.

Finally, collegial educators teach each other what they know. Almost every professional who works in the schools has some unique expertise, talent, or skill that other educators would profit from learning. Collegial educators share their unique skills with others, and likewise learn from their colleagues to improve their own professional competence.

When collegiality exists in a school, better decisions are made and more effectively implemented. In addition, educator morale is higher, with educator learning more likely to be sustained. Some evidence even suggests that student motivation and achievement rise in collegial schools (Barth, 1990).

CONFLICT

Any change combines new advantages with new drawbacks, new possibilities with new pitfalls. When educators remodel their schoolhouse with a set of cooperative teaching blueprints, they discover the many advantages of working with another professional in the classroom. But the simultaneous presence of two school professionals with different values, beliefs, perceptions, and ideas in the same classroom can cause conflict that did not occur previously.

For example, if an educator's primary criterion for implementing cooperative teaching was initial ease, then he or she could easily find a colleague who has similar beliefs and professional practices. Though easy to implement, this arrangement would be professionally sterile. It would not offer the potential for professional growth that comes through developing working relationships with collaborators with differing practices and perceptions.

Most educators know how to work effectively with administrators or superiors, following their suggestions, directions, and guidelines. Similarly, most educators also have learned how to work with aides, volunteers, and other educational assistants, outlining work responsibilities and directions for these individuals. In both cases, however, the relationships are hierarchically structured. In each, one person is clearly the superior and the other a subordinate.

Learning to work intensively and extensively with a peer, one who is neither a subordinate nor a superior, requires a new set of professional skills for most educators. Chief among these is the ability to resolve differences by developing win–win solutions. The ability to understand and resolve conflict among peers is new to many school professionals.

Conflict occurs when one person (or group) perceives that another person (or group) is interfering with his or her goal attainment, when there is disagreement resulting from incompatible demands between or among two or more parties (Friend & Cook, 1992; Maurer, 1991). Although conflict is usually perceived negatively, it may be constructive for an organization (Walther-Thomas et al., 2000).

Some degree of conflict is inevitable whenever two or more human beings interact. In the rush to minimize conflict, the potential growth that can result from conflict should not be overlooked. Conflict forces people to become active, to think. Many significant social developments, including labor unions, civil rights legislation, and even the United States of America, emerged from conflict. Thus the task is not necessarily to eliminate conflict, but instead to understand it, minimize its risks, and maximize its benefits (Bolton, 1979).

Possible benefits of successful conflict resolution include stronger working relationships and higher levels of caring or trust. Conflict can result in growth, opportunity, and success. In fact, a moderate level of conflict is considered constructive, whereas a complete absence of conflict may reflect stagnation or lack of energy (Walther-Thomas et al., 2000).

There are three basic types of conflict (Coombs, 1987). The first of these is conflict between individuals with different goals. For example, in an elementary classroom, one cooperative teaching partner might want students to work in small groups, while the other believes fervently that students must learn to work alone. At the secondary level, one educator may feel the need to cover all content in the textbook, while his or her partner in cooperative teaching believes that it would be more useful and practical to focus on a few select concepts. In either of these cases, if one participant entirely wins, the other loses.

A second type of conflict is between individuals who have the same goal that cannot be achieved by both partners. Scheduling problems often fall into this category. For example, two cooperative teaching partners at a high school both may want to take a professional day to attend the same districtwide workshop. However, the school principal has decided that only one can go. Similarly, an elementary teacher may want to reserve the time immediately before morning recess for content instruction, while the cooperative teaching partner may want to use that same period for learning strategies instruction.

A third type of conflict, and one that is a bit beyond the scope of this discussion, is internal conflict. For example, a cooperative teaching partner has spent years pulling together a rich source of materials to use in teaching science. Although in cooperative teaching it might be expected that those materials would be shared with one's partner, he or she may be reluctant to simply give away the materials she had worked so long to put together. This internal conflict can result in external conflicts.

Because conflicts naturally arise from all interpersonal relationships, conflict-resolution strategies are required competencies for partners in cooperative teaching.

CONFLICT-RESOLUTION STRATEGIES

After remodeling, homeowners might be happy with nearly everything, except the unexpected question of where their oversized sofa should now be placed. There are a number of diverse strategies that can help resolve this and other conflicts. Unfortunately, not all of these strategies are equally effective (Bolton, 1979).

Less Effective Approaches to Conflict Resolution

Denial. ("There's no problem with the sofa location.") Every individual who has ever been in conflict has at some point sought to resolve the problem by telling himself or herself that there really is no problem. One pretends that everything is all right and deliberately ignores the reality of the situation. On rare occasions this strategy may actually work. Sometimes conflicts really do not exist, or they exist for only a very short time and then disappear on their own. However, more often the denial strategy simply causes conflicts to grow larger, more complex, and ultimately more difficult to resolve. When this occurs in cooperative teaching, educators retreat to their previous roles of educational isolation, concluding that cooperative teaching does not work.

Avoidance. ("I'll just watch TV in the other room.") In employing avoidance, people acknowledge that a problem exists, but they simply avoid the situations where the conflict is likely to emerge, withdrawing either physically or emotionally. If two cooperative educators have very different beliefs about appropriate behavior-management strategies for their students during school assemblies, one way to resolve this is for only one of the educators to be at an assembly at any time. This way the conflict can be avoided.

In some cases avoidance may be temporarily appropriate. When conflicts are extremely serious and emotionally laden, avoidance can buy time to allow things to cool down a bit (Friend & Cook, 1992). It also may be a useful strategy when more time is necessary to think through complex issues, when the issue is trivial, or when the difficulties of confrontation outweigh the benefits of any potential resolution (Walther-Thomas et al., 2000).

In general, though, avoidance is ultimately unproductive. Avoidance appears to allow people to go on with their lives despite conflicts. What is actually happening, however, is that the involved individuals also are withdrawing from each other, so that all that is left of their relationship is a hollow shell. The involved parties have both re-treated from further interactions. Avoidance also facilitates the development of denial.

Capitulation. ("Okay, put the darn sofa wherever you want it.") Because conflict is unpleasant for most people, some will simply give in. Regardless of how unreasonable or illogical the other's position is, some people will almost automatically go along with whatever the other person wants. Although capitulation may be appropriate when the issues are of minimal consequence, its consistent long-term use is unproductive.

In practice, individuals who routinely use capitulation as a conflict-resolution strat-egy typically allow themselves to be interrupted frequently in interactions with others. They withhold information or opinions they may have, and make many apologies. Their indecisiveness and lack of contributions make them unproductive team members.

Capitulation may appear to minimize conflict, but this result is achieved at the expense of the integrity of the capitulator, who ultimately will conclude that he or she is being devalued in the process. Results consistently achieved through capitulation fail to take advantage of the potential of all involved parties.

Domination. ("I said, 'The sofa goes against the back wall!'") Domination involves one person imposing his or her will on another. The domineering individual generates a solution designed to meet his or her needs and then pushes and pushes the other per-son, ignoring all protests, until the person submits. People who use this approach seek to achieve their goals at all costs. The victory is more important to the dominator than the relationship. Although domination may allow one to gain a particular result, overall it destroys the relationship between the individuals.

In practice, people who often use domination as a means to settle disputes tend to interrupt their colleagues. They often have intense, if not glaring, eye contact, and their physical posture and demeanor is invasive and arrogant. They tend to be poor listeners and frequently resort to sarcasm and accusation to achieve their ends.

There are times when this domineering approach could be defensible. In situations where significant ethical issues are at stake, the ultimate acceptance of one's position might justify such an approach. When an individual is absolutely, beyond the shadow of a doubt, positively convinced that he or she is right, domination may be the only means to the correct end. Finally, when a decision must be made for which one person will have ultimate responsibility, then that individual may be justified in using this approach.

However, these would be rare circumstances. A more likely outcome of domina-tion is the development of two-directional resentment. The person who is being dom-inated comes to dislike and distrust the dominating partner and usually will withdraw from further interactions. Conversely, the dominator comes to see the other person as weak, not to be respected, and ultimately not a true peer. Thus, a relationship in which one party dominates the other sacrifices all advantages that can be gained through cooperative teaching.

Individuals who are being dominated may strike back through sabotage, passive resistance, and emotional distancing. In addition, any agreements reached through domination are unlikely to be actively implemented by the individual who was not allowed to participate fully in the decision-making process.

Both capitulation and domination are win–lose propositions, in that for one person's needs to be met, another person must sacrifice his or her own needs. Given actual outcomes, in practical terms both capitulation and domination ultimately end up as lose–lose approaches.

Deference to expertise. ("We agreed that we'd do what the decorator said.") In cooperative teaching the two educators bring different sets of skills and areas of expertise to their work. For example, often special educators have expertise in differentiation of curriculum, and individual behavior-management and learning strategies. General educators often have skills in large group instruction and management techniques, and curricular sequencing.

Thus one approach to resolving conflicts is for the partners to defer to the more knowledgeable of the two, depending on the situation. For example, if the conflict is one of maintaining discipline of the entire class, then the special educator might defer to the general educator's suggestions, because he or she likely has had more experience in such matters. Conversely, if the management conflict centers around the behavior of one or two students, the general educator might defer to the special educator, whose training and professional experience likely has emphasized procedures useful in the management of individual behaviors.

However, this deference model of conflict resolution has some problems. Its basic premise distorts to some degree the essential philosophy of cooperative teaching: that the two individuals involved are peers. In addition, as the partners learn from each other and gain knowledge from the expanded range of educational experiences in which both are now involved, the question of who is the expert and most knowledgeable about any given situation may not be so easy to answer.

Compromise and negotiation. ("Okay, you can put the sofa there, but your guitars and amplifier have to go in the garage.") In negotiating and compromising, people reach agreements by each yielding to some degree on their initial wishes. It is a frequent solution to conflict; in fact, most of the world's democratic societies depend heavily on compromises for their governments to function. A compromise, however, means that neither party actually obtains what it wants. Each party usually ends up only partially satisfied.

Compromise is usually a better strategy than avoidance, capitulation, or domination. It may be appropriate for two individuals who both tend to be competitive or dominating. Often the solution generated through compromise is at least workable, if not the best or first choice of anyone concerned. It can be successful if each person believes that the sacrifices and gains of each person are equal.

Although compromise can work, it is not terribly powerful, nor does it often result in the best solution. Each party essentially ends up in a partial win–partial win arrangement. Because neither is completely satisfied, conflicts may emerge from the same issues later. What is needed is a truly win–win resolution strategy. One such strategy is collaborative problem solving (Bolton, 1979).

A More Effective Conflict-Resolution Strategy: Collaborative Problem Solving

All of the previously noted approaches to conflict resolution share a common characteristic: they are me-versus-you, one-winner-and-one-loser scenarios. Because the two individuals involved see themselves in competition with each other, only one person can be completely satisfied.

Many people believe that in conflict situations not all involved can have their needs met simultaneously. That is, for someone to win, someone else must lose. However, this need not be the case. There truly are conflict-resolution strategies that can consistently generate win–win outcomes. When people are able to move away from viewing conflicts as win–lose scenarios, and instead accept that all parties can have their needs met effectively and completely at the same time, great progress in conflict resolution has been made.

Conflicts present another way of sharing. By working together and pooling their talents and skills, cooperative teaching partners can generate effective solutions.

Collaborative problem solving is philosophically consistent with cooperative teaching. In cooperative teaching the partners commit to professional sharing: sharing responsibilities, students, and instruction. As part of this professional sharing, when the inevitable conflicts emerge, they too can be shared through a collaborative problem-solving process.

For many people facing conflicts, their first reaction is to immediately try the first possible solution that comes to mind. The tendency to try almost anything in order to be doing at least something is natural and understandable, but it does not result in the most effective resolutions. This is especially true for collaborative ventures.

Bolton (1979) offered an especially effective collaborative problem-solving process, a system based on Dewey's (1916) rules of logic in problem solving. The six steps of this simple yet effective process are as follows.

▶ **Step 1: Define the problem in terms of needs, not solutions.**

Much of the tension in conflicts comes about when two individuals propose different solutions to a problem. When these two solutions are incompatible, arguments and animosity develop. Instead, each person should describe the problem in terms of the person's primary needs, or the desired outcomes, not in terms of the solutions each person developed to meet that need. In collaborative conflict resolution, participants must be careful to keep the distinction between (a) the ultimate desired result, and (b) the means that one has identified to reach that goal. Confusing these elements can cause much tension.

For example, assume that a general education teacher has several students in need of speech and language therapy. The support services provider (the school's speech therapist) has proposed that she work with each of these students individually on a pullout basis in the therapy room. However, the teacher is opposed to this proposal, arguing instead that the students should stay in the classroom.

At this point each educator is arguing from a solutions perspective. The teacher's thinking is as follows: "The students lose too much instructional time when they leave the room each day. Although the therapy might be useful, it is even more important that they learn the curriculum being presented in my classroom. In addition, they lose the possibility of learning from each other when they are isolated in the therapy room. The solution is for them not to receive the proposed therapy."

The speech therapist's thinking is as follows: "These students each have speech and language problems that are significant and severe enough to warrant intensive therapy. The solution is for me to bring them to my therapy room so that I can provide the intense therapy that is required."

At this point conflict is emerging because each educator is presenting only the solutions each has generated independently. To establish initial perspective, it must be kept in mind that it is only these proposed solutions that are in conflict, not the individuals themselves. Each of their proposed solutions is based on the personal needs that each perceives. Although each is sharing with the other the solutions he or she generated, the basic needs of each professional that led to the development of those conflicting solutions in the first place have not been shared. The first (and most critical) step in collaborative problem solving is for each person to share with the other not the solutions each has individually generated but instead the needs that the proposed solutions were designed to address.

Thus the teacher might share with the speech therapist the following: "When students leave the room they miss out on important curricular content, group learning activities, and social interactions that are important. What can we do so that the students don't miss out?" Similarly, the speech therapist might share her need as follows: "These students all have speech and language problems that require intensive intervention. What can we do so that this happens?"

One effective way to discover the needs of another (which leads to the solution he or she proposed) is to find out why the other person wants the particular solution he or she initially proposed. What is the reason the person proposed this particular solution? What advantages does it hold for the individual? In essence, what is necessary is for the cooperative teaching partners to be able to distinguish between means and ends, between solutions and needs. Once the fundamental *why* underlying each of the proposed solutions is understood by the other, the collaborative problem-solving process can begin in earnest.

Perhaps needless to say, the identification of the underlying needs that led to the particular solutions that are in conflict is often easier said than done. Reaching below the surface of a colleague's proposed solution to identify his or her underlying need is not a skill that comes naturally to many people. One way to accomplish this is through reflective communication, where one individual explains his or her underlying needs while the other listens attentively, then the listener repeats the needs as he or she heard and understood them to the first speaker. The first speaker then either affirms that the needs were understood correctly or reexplains them until they are. As each person hears his or her position as perceived and stated by the other, he or she can gain additional perspective and understanding. The use of reflective communication significantly improves the chances of creating a successful problem-solving venture (Knackendoffel, Robinson, Deshler, & Schumaker, 1992).

One can further enhance the effectiveness of the communication through active listening strategies. By assuming a posture of involvement (e.g., leaning the upper torso slightly toward the other person, shoulders and face directly facing the other) one communicates his or her receptiveness to the other person. Eye contact also communicates an interest and desire to listen. Because a too-serious facial expression can inhibit communication, it is helpful for listeners to relax and smile and laugh when appropriate. These nonverbal behaviors serve to facilitate effective communication (Knackendoffel et al., 1992). Walther-Thomas et al. (2000) proposed a four-step self-check for listening. That self-check is included as Figure 8.2.

This first step in collaborative problem solving, defining the problem in terms of the underlying needs rather than the solutions that have been generated to meet those needs, is the most important and most time-consuming step, and its value cannot be overstated. Bolton (1979) noted its importance by quoting the old saying, "A problem well defined is half solved."

▶ **Step 2: Brainstorm possible solutions.**

In brainstorming, problem solvers seek to quickly generate as many ideas and solutions as possible without considering their merit and potential. The idea is to create quickly a large and diverse pool of possibilities. These possibilities will be more carefully considered and evaluated at a later time.

In the early stages of brainstorming it is important not to slow the rush of ideas by being critical in any way; all proposals and ideas are initially equally valued. They will be recorded for later review and discussion regardless of their early apparent feasibility

1. Am I *attending* to the speaker and the message with

☐ open posture?

☐ comfortable eye contact?

☐ avoidance of distracting thoughts and behaviors?

☐ constant monitoring through interaction?

2. Am I *hearing* the messages communicated in terms of

☐ the speaker's point of view?

☐ voice quality, pace, and rhythm?

☐ body language?

☐ the feelings as well as the content?

3. Am I *encouraging* open communication through

☐ subtle verbal and nonverbal cues?

☐ paraphrasing when appropriate?

☐ reflecting the speaker's feeling when appropriate?

☐ asking clarifying questions when appropriate?

☐ monitoring my facial expressions and body language?

4. Am I *processing* the message to respond when appropriate through

☐ identifying key themes and supporting points?

☐ relating information from other relevant sources?

☐ making notes when it seems appropriate?

☐ summarizing when it seems appropriate?

Figure 8.2 A self-check for listening. *Note*. From *Collaboration for Inclusive Education: Developing Successful Programs*, by C. Walter-Thomas, L. Korinek, V. L. McLaughlin, & B. T. Williams, 2000, Boston: Allyn & Bacon. Copyright 2000 by Allyn & Bacon. Reprinted with permission.

or lack thereof. This approach ensures the widest possible beginning pool of ideas that can be further considered and evaluated. The guidelines that follow will help brainstorming to be as productive as possible.

• *Don't evaluate.* If each idea is criticized as soon as it is proposed, people soon will stop contributing. After all, why should they open themselves up for immediate and

repeated criticism? When all ideas are accepted and recorded regardless of how apparently outlandish or unworkable they are, people feel safe in making even the most off-the-wall contributions. Sometimes even the seemingly silliest ideas contain seeds that on further analysis contribute to the final solution. The goal is to generate the widest and most diverse pool of possible solutions.

• *Don't explain.* Contributors should not clarify or go into detail about their proposals. This slows down the rapid flow of possibilities. During this phase the participants are looking for possible starting points, not fully developed blueprints. Participants should simply toss out a single-phrase or sentence contribution, then another, and so on, all as rapidly as possible. Explanations can occur after this early phase is concluded.

Making suggestions without offering clarifying explanations is difficult for many school professionals. Over the years most educators have developed sophisticated skills in explaining ideas to colleagues, parents, and students. This tendency to explain further is difficult to shake off easily. However, for the creative problem-solving process to be most effective, participants must be able to throw out an idea and immediately continue in further creative explorations without feeling compelled to explain or defend each idea immediately.

• *Remove limits.* In brainstorming sessions, participants should understand that there are no constraints whatsoever on their contributions. Likewise, participants also should be willing to accept eagerly even the most foolish proposals at face value. Criticism may well inhibit the subsequent contribution of other, more solid, proposals. Also, even the most apparently foolish proposal may contain a germ of an idea, or may spark someone to think in a different way to come up with a useful contribution.

• *Prompt.* Someone (perhaps the person recording ideas) should periodically cue the others by saying, "Okay, what else?" This encouragement solicits still more suggestions while helping the group focus on the task at hand.

• *Expand on the ideas of others*. Some of the most effective proposals are made by piggybacking on the ideas of others, using those ideas as springboards for other possible solutions.

• *Record all contributions*. The person serving as recorder should list each person's contribution on a blackboard or large easel, using a few key words to capture the idea so the group can see and use the previously offered ideas for further inspiration. All participants must see that each contribution is group property. The solution that is ultimately developed will be one created with input and changes suggested by everyone. The final solution will belong to the group, not to any one individual. As such, the recorder should not list each contributor's name by his or her contribution, which would be counterproductive to the collaborative spirit.

• *Listen for natural break points*. A common mistake in brainstorming sessions is for someone to say something like, "Okay, let's spend 5 minutes brainstorming this situation." The problem here is that often 5 minutes (or any other arbitrary figure) is too long. Often the ideas that ultimately are most useful are proposed early on. The remainder of any arbitrarily established time limit then results in individuals "burning out," getting off task, or becoming otherwise distracted in unproductive sidebar conversations.

It is better to avoid establishing a predetermined time limit on brainstorming. Instead, the group facilitator should listen for lulls. A typical pattern of idea production in these sessions is an initial flurry of suggestions for some short period of time, a pause, a second smaller flurry, pause, and so on. A useful guideline is to wrap up the brainstorming session after this second lull or pause.

In the aforementioned situation with the speech therapist and the teacher, after presenting their positions in terms of needs instead of solutions, they sat down in the school's conference room to brainstorm possible solutions to their problem. After a few minutes, they generated the following possible solutions:

1. provide therapy on a rotating basis after school

2. provide therapy by bringing the students into the therapy room during nonacademic times

3. provide therapy in the classroom

4. provide therapy on a less frequent basis than initially planned

5. embed speech and language activities within the typical classroom tasks and activities

Once the two educators had developed these ideas, they were ready to move on to the next step in collaborative problem solving.

▶ **Step 3: Select the solution (or solutions) that seem to best address the previously identified needs of all concerned.**

At this point any proposals from the brainstorming session that initially were not clear should be further explained. This process in itself may spark new possibilities.

When no more contributions are forthcoming, it is time to begin identifying the most promising solutions. The best way to approach this is for each person to select privately the solutions that appear to meet his or her needs. (It is critical throughout this entire process that the emphasis begin with and stay on the meeting of needs, and not on the initial conflicting solutions that were proposed.)

After each person has privately identified one or more solutions that appear to meet his or her needs, these individually compiled lists are compared to find the choices selected in common. If the preliminary groundwork of defining the problem in terms of needs was done well, usually there will be one (or more) solutions identified by all participants as being good solutions.

For this collaborative problem solving to achieve workable and acceptable solutions, all participants must sense that their needs truly will be met with the selected solution. If not, some sense of compromise will set in and participation will be only half-hearted. The individuals will see themselves as having given in and not having their needs met. This can only result in an ineffective resolution.

Part of this selection process might include some forethought concerning possible outcomes of each possible solution. Although not all outcomes can be predicted, considering possible outcomes can help the ultimate success of the solution.

In the example of the speech therapist and the teacher, as they reviewed their list of proposed solutions they found that they had two solutions in common: (1) provide therapy in the classroom, and (2) embed speech and language activities in the ongoing classroom activities. After some discussion they concluded that both ideas should be incorporated. Each educator believed that, when fully implemented, this arrangement could satisfy their previously identified needs.

▶ **Step 4: Plan who will do what, where, and by when.**

At this point the actual transformation of a theoretical solution into a concrete and practical plan must occur. The proposed solution will have implicit and explicit expectations for each involved party concerning who will do what, and where and when these duties will be carried out. A written record of these determinations and agreements is helpful as a reminder for preventing future questions or problems, because specific details may be overlooked in the excitement of having reached a promising solution. This record also should include a plan for evaluation so that necessary data can be collected throughout implementation. This evaluation plan should be complete enough to provide an effective foundation for evaluation without being so time consuming that it interferes with the actual delivery of instruction.

In the example of the speech therapist and the teacher, their general agreement was that therapy services would be provided in the general classroom. In addition, ongoing classroom activities would contain special language-enriched content embedded within them. They then collaboratively developed the following plan.

Three days a week from 1:00 to 2:00 the speech therapist would come into the classroom. During this 1-hour period the students would be divided into small skill groups. These groupings would be based in part on similarity of speech and language needs of the students.

The teacher, a parent volunteer, and the speech therapist would each work with one group for 20 minutes then switch to another group. Each group's lessons would include specific speech and language goals and objectives for each student, as well as language enrichment curricula common to all group members. During each group's 20 minutes with the therapist, the students with specific speech and language needs would receive intensive therapy in the small group and would benefit from similar therapy being provided to the other students in the group.

The second component of their new plan involved embedding of language enrichment and stimulation into classroom activities to address the linguistic needs of all students in the class. In their previously arranged planning times the speech therapist would work with the teacher to help him identify universal design principles into the typical classroom activities to provide better access to the curriculum for all students, and to highlight speech and language goals within the curriculum.

For example, in the past the teacher had required his students to work on end-of-chapter questions independently. The speech therapist worked with him to help identify ways in which this activity could be adapted to be more linguistically enriched. One way was that these activities could be completed cooperatively, verbally within small groups. If each group had eight students and a chapter ended with nine questions, one question could be discussed and answered by all students. Each student would then choose (in a negotiated fashion) two additional questions to be answered orally in a round-robin format. One student would serve as the recorder, responsible for activating an audiocassette recorder for further speech and language analysis by either the teacher, therapist, or both. Other student roles in each group would include a time watcher (to monitor that the tasks are completed in the allotted times), a noise watcher (to check with the teacher for cues concerning noise levels), and a "gopher" (to leave the group to go for help or materials).

This plan met the basic needs identified by the teacher and speech therapist. First, the students would not be leaving the classroom, and so they would not lose valuable instructional time and the opportunity to learn from their peers. Thus the teacher saw his needs met with those students requiring more intensive speech and language services remaining with their classmates in the room.

In addition, the speech therapist saw that she would be able to provide intensive therapy to the students, which was the primary need she had identified. She also saw the possibility of additional learning occurring as she worked with other students in each group who had similar speech and language needs. Thus, her needs could be met and additional benefits gained. This win–win potential is characteristic of successful collaborative problem solving.

▶ **Step 5: Implement the plan.**

At this point it is time to translate the carefully developed plans into action. Assuming that the collaborative problem solvers have effectively and completely identified all the necessary steps and have agreed on who will do what and when, the next step is to take action.

It is at this stage that any lack of clarity in the developed plan, or any overlooked issues, will come to light. The participants should recognize beforehand that even the most carefully developed plans will contain gaps and oversights, simply because it is impossible to completely anticipate all potential scenarios. This should not cause a fundamentally sound plan to be abandoned. Instead, the involved parties simply should return to the problem-solving system to resolve these issues as they occur. Problem solving should be simpler at this point because the involved parties have harmonious goals and have built the necessary foundation of trust.

For example, in the previously described situation, the speech therapist found that her supervisor had planned a number of Friday afternoon staff development programs that frequently would interfere with her ability to go into the classroom on that day. After meeting with the classroom teacher, she identified a number of possible solutions. These included having her come in on Thursdays instead of Fridays; having her develop a series of lessons on audiocassette or videocassette beforehand that her groups could go through independently; and having the volunteer take over the groups on the days when the speech therapist was out. The two educators reviewed and discussed these options and concluded that the solution that would best meet their needs was simply to shift the Friday sessions to Thursdays.

▶ **Step 6: Evaluate the plan.**

The final stage in the collaborative problem-solving process is evaluation. As noted in Chapter 6, there are at least two dimensions of a plan that can be assessed. These are (1) the processes, or individual components of the plan that is developed, and (2) the outcomes, or the results of those processes.

To begin, school professionals should look at the individual processes of the plan they developed. At this level of evaluation they might check to see if there are any missing components, if each component can be implemented practically, and so forth. (As part of this evaluative process the partners in cooperative teaching might carry out a similar analysis concerning the effectiveness of the overall collaborative problem-solving system.) If no deficits or problems in the individual processes involved in the plan are evident, educators then should move on to the evaluation of outcomes.

Simply put, the question the school professionals must answer at this point is this: Is the plan yielding the successful results that were anticipated? In the ongoing example, the speech therapist and the classroom teacher anticipated that their proposed plan would accomplish two outcomes, or respond to their two needs. First, the students who needed specific speech and language services would have their special needs addressed. Second, these students would maintain adequate academic progress by staying in the classroom rather than being pulled out for specialized therapy services.

Both outcomes should be measured. First, the speech therapist might evaluate the speech and language progress of each student with special needs by using whatever evaluative criteria seem most professionally appropriate. In addition, the teacher would maintain ongoing records of the students' academic progress. These records might include documentation of academic skills acquisition based on such sources as classroom tests, work samples, and standardized schoolwide academic achievement tests.

As noted earlier, in this evaluation phase the collaborative problem solvers might also evaluate their problem-solving strategies. For this purpose it is often useful to adopt a similar dual evaluative strategy. That is, they should assess both the processes and the outcomes of their problem-solving approach. To this end the partners in cooperative teaching might conduct evaluations of all the involved processes periodically to make sure that all six steps in their collaborative problem-solving sessions are occurring. If steps are incomplete or altogether missing, are there problems arising that may be attributable to these missing steps?

Similarly, the involved parties also should evaluate the outcomes or results of their collaborative problem-solving activities. The primary criterion for this evaluation is obviously the effectiveness with which needs are met and conflicts avoided or resolved satisfactorily.

Given the inherently high degree of personal subjectivity and perception present in almost all human interactions, a possible third component to evaluate is how each participant feels about the problem-solving process, how satisfied each is with the overall system of collaborative conflict resolution. Each participant might take time to think independently about what was liked most and least about the process, any regrets about something said or done, and what might be done differently and better next time. After each has contemplated these issues independently, the educators might then come together to discuss the issues. These additional analyses of the process can help ensure that it works as well as possible.

Figure 8.3 graphically illustrates the six steps of collaborative problem solving. The questions associated with each of these steps can help to ensure productive and effective collaborative problem-solving sessions.

☐ **Step 1: Define the problem in terms of needs, not solutions.**
    ✓ Question: What are the basic needs of each of the involved parties that are underlying the fundamental conflict?

☐ **Step 2: Brainstorm possible solutions.**
    ✓ Question: What ideas come to mind immediately as possible solutions?

☐ **Step 3: Select the solution (or solutions) that will best address the previously identified needs of all concerned.**
    ✓ Question: Out of the large pool of all possible solutions initially generated, which ones appear to hold the greatest promise for meeting the basic needs of the involved parties that were identified initially?

☐ **Step 4: Plan who will do what, where, and by when.**
    ✓ Question: Given the agreed-upon resolution, which participant will do what activities in which locations at which times?
    ✓ Question: Are additional resources necessary for this?
    ✓ Question: Are all aspects and dimensions of the agreed-upon resolution adequately covered in these arrangements?
    ✓ Question: How will the effectiveness of the proposed solution be measured?

☐ **Step 5: Implement the plan.**
    ✓ Question: Is each step of the plan defined clearly enough to actually be implemented?
    ✓ Question: Is each step of the plan practical enough to be implemented?
    ✓ Question: Has each step been implemented as outlined?

☐ **Step 6: Evaluate the plan.**
    ✓ Question: What are the individual processes of the plan that might be evaluated, and how will each be evaluated?
    ✓ Question: What are the individual outcomes of the plan that might be evaluated, and how will each be evaluated?

Figure 8.3 Collaborative problem solving.

TROUBLESHOOTING IN COLLABORATIVE PROBLEM SOLVING

Any process that attempts to guide interactions between people will have occasional difficulties. The following suggestions, some of which amplify previously introduced ideas, are ways to resolve the most common problems people experience as they implement collaborative problem solving (Bolton, 1979).

1. *Handle emotions first.* Strong emotions have a tremendous impact on the interactions of people. If strong emotions are present and ignored, any problem-solving efforts will be significantly impaired. Sometimes these emotions are based on unstated but substantial hidden agendas. When it appears that there are emotional obstacles preventing productive problem solving, especially in the early stages of the process, it can be useful for a participant to suggest that there may be some other unstated problem in the relationship and to ask in the most nonthreatening way possible if there are any concerns. Often subtle cues can reveal these hidden agendas. Once out in the open, hidden agendas can be resolved through the six-step collaborative problem-solving process previously described.

2. *Define the problem.* For collaborative problem solving to be effective, each participant must be willing and able to share his or her specific primary needs, not solutions. This perspective is so different from the initial impulse of many that it is easy to overlook. However, if the problem is not first defined in terms of needs, little progress toward collaborative solutions can be made.

3. *Do not interrupt brainstorming.* Brainstorming requires that the persons involved establish an atmosphere of optimism, support, and trust. Even so, putting one's ideas out for public scrutiny is so difficult that even under the best conditions it is difficult for many people to participate actively. When someone in the group begins evaluating, criticizing, laughing or snickering, or even simply objectively commenting on ideas as they initially are offered, many participants will quickly stop generating or submitting ideas. To be effective in generating the largest and most diverse pool of ideas, this initial brainstorming must be free of evaluations and interruptions. All participants involved must be receptive to all contributions, no matter how silly or far-fetched they may seem at first.

4. *Work out the details.* In the excitement and pleasure at having arrived at an apparent solution to a conflict, it is easy to skip over the nuts-and-bolts aspects of implementation. Although perhaps not as rewarding for many as the initial creative generation of the overall plan, the specifics of how the plan will actually be carried out must be given careful consideration or the chances of success are greatly reduced.

5. *Follow-through and follow-up.* The road to hell (and to conflict in the here and now) is paved with good intentions. Human nature being what it is, many well-meaning individuals will commit to certain responsibilities, and then find that follow-

through is more difficult than anticipated. It is important that each participant complete whatever tasks or responsibilities were agreed upon. To do this, the specific duties and responsibilities of each person should be clearly identified, without coercion.

It also may be effective for each person to help the other with the follow-up. The involved parties might prepare a written summary at the end of each meeting that outlines each person's specific tasks. While trying not to appear pushy, the educators might check with each other in a friendly way to determine how progress on each task is going. Unanticipated hurdles should be identified early, before they become insurmountable.

6. *Repeat the process.* In working with personal computers, it is not unusual to enter a command or series of instructions, only to have the machine fail to respond. Frequently all that is necessary is to enter the command again. Although it is possible to go into a detailed, complex, and systematic analysis of why the first attempt failed, it is almost always easier simply to forget it and proceed.

Similarly, often the best way to approach an apparently failed collaborative problem-solving attempt is to repeat the six steps. It is not unusual to find that the second attempt results in a more productive and successful solution. The chances of success increase when the involved parties approach each step fresh and with a new perspective, rather than simply generating the identical (and ultimately unsatisfactory) responses from the first attempt. Participants should make a conscious effort to think about the situation differently or from a different perspective.

CONCLUSIONS

Living in the newly remodeled schoolhouse means adapting to change. It helps to understand that (a) change is a process, not an event; (b) everyone has very personal and individualized responses to change; and (c) adapting to change is easiest when its practical implications are understood. Successful change requires five factors: vision, knowledge and skills, incentives, resources, and an action plan. Absent one of these, successful change is unlikely.

With change comes the potential for conflict. There are many ways in which conflict can be resolved, some more effective than others. A particularly helpful approach to resolving conflict is collaborative problem solving, in which the individuals in conflict identify the problem in terms of needs, not solutions; then brainstorm possible solutions; and finally select, implement, and evaluate a strategy.

The educators have now settled into their newly remodeled and refurbished schoolhouse and have spent some time applying touch-up paint, moving pictures around, rearranging the furniture, lubricating window blinds, and so forth. In short, they have completed their initial adjustments to the changes. In the rush to actually complete the remodeling project, they may have had little opportunity to step back a bit from the project and think about the meaning of change and how it came about. The next chapter further explores the nature of change, using the analogy of educators in cooperative teaching as change agents, who are aided and abetted in their efforts by change facilitators.

CHAPTER 8 ACTIVITY

Interpersonal Style Survey: The Johari Window

This chapter has focused on enhancing the quality and productivity of inter-personal relationships among school professionals. As you move into collabo-rative structures such as cooperative teaching, you will be asked to participate in more intense social interactions with colleagues than in the past. These new demands for social skills will ask of you greater levels of personal insightfulness and self-understanding.

The Johari Window (named after its creators Joseph Luft and Harry Ingham) is a visual aide that allows individuals to better understand themselves (Adler & Towne, 1996). The greater level of self-understanding that can be gained from completing this exercise can enhance your ability to communicate your basic needs to your cooperative teaching partner. If your partner also completes this Johari Window exercise, he or she will be able to reciprocate these communications more effectively, maximizing the effectiveness of your interactions.

To begin, imagine a frame that contains everything about you—all your per-sonal characteristics, likes and dislikes, and so on, as illustrated below.

Everything about yourself

Next, divide this frame with a vertical line, separating everything about you into one of two categories: things that are known to you and things that are not known to you, as shown next.

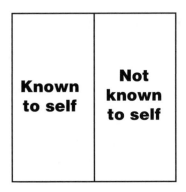

Now go back to the first frame and divide it in two again. However, this time do this in a different way, with a horizontal line. These two top and bottom halves will represent those characteristics of you that are known to others and those characteristics that are not known to others, as follows.

Now the two divided frames can be superimposed on one another to form four quadrants, so that everything about you falls into one of four categories, as follows.

	Known to self	Not known to self
Known to others	**Area 1** **OPEN**	**Area 2** **BLIND**
Not known to others	**Area 3** **HIDDEN**	**Area 4** **UNKNOWN**

Area 1 represents information about yourself that both you and others are aware of (the OPEN area). Area 2 includes information about yourself that others know but that you do not know (the BLIND area). You acquire information in this area primarily through feedback from others. Area 3 represents information about yourself that you know but that others do not know (the HIDDEN area). This includes those unique sets of facts and information that people keep secret from others. Finally, Area 4 is information about yourself that neither you nor others are aware of (the UNKNOWN area). This information must exist because every person frequently learns new things about himself or herself.

The Johari Window can be refined by labeling and conceptualizing the two axes slightly differently. Rather than "Known to self/Not known to self," the horizontal axis might be labeled "Receptivity to feedback." Similarly, the vertical axis might be relabeled from "Known to others/Not known to others" to "Willingness to self-disclose," as illustrated in the following diagram.

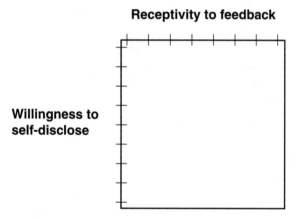

Each of these axes represents a continuum. Some persons will have very high levels of receptivity to feedback from other people and also will be very willing to self-disclose about themselves. Other individuals may be very disinterested in receiving feedback from others and also may be unwilling to share things about themselves. Still other people may have high degrees of one of these two characteristics but low degrees of the other.

Using the points along the continuum of each axis, every person can construct a Johari Window that gives a personalized set of the relative sizes of the four quadrants (OPEN, BLIND, HIDDEN, UNKNOWN). In this reconceptualized Johari Window, the larger Area 1 (the OPEN area) is, the more likely an individual is to both disclose information about herself or himself and solicit feedback and information about himself or herself from others. An example of such an individual's Johari Window follows.

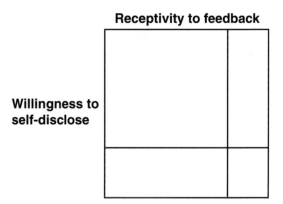

This individual trusts others enough to disclose information about himself or herself, knowing that that confidence will not be abused. That trust in others extends such that this individual also solicits and is receptive to feedback from others. If Area 1 is extremely large it may cause some interaction difficulties, however, especially in the early stages of a relationship. This is because the level of social comfort and trust required for high self-disclosure and high receptivity to feedback from others usually requires some time to be established. Individuals who self-disclose too much too early and who too eagerly solicit and respond to feedback early in a relationship make many people uncomfortable.

Conversely, an individual may have a small Area 1, indicating little self-disclosure and little willingness to solicit or be receptive to feedback from others. Such a person's Johari Window is as follows.

Receptivity to feedback

**Willingness to
self-disclose**

This individual takes few risks and may appear aloof and uncommunicative. It is interesting to note that for this individual the largest quadrant is the UNKNOWN area.

Two other general patterns can emerge in Johari Windows. Some people are very receptive to feedback but engage in little self-disclosure. Their Johari Window pattern is similar to the following example.

Receptivity to feedback

Willingness to self-disclose

These individuals initially may seem highly supportive, because they frequently solicit ideas. Their unwillingness to self-disclose seems at first to be simply unselfishness. However, in the long term these individuals usually will be perceived as distrustful and detached.

Finally, some people will discourage feedback from others but freely self-disclose.

Receptivity to feedback

Willingness to self-disclose

These individuals usually come across as self-centered. Perhaps the major problem for such people is the very large BLIND area. They remain unaware of how they appear to others.

The following questionnaire was developed to help you develop your own personal Johari Window, allowing you to understand your behavior in interpersonal relationships from a novel perspective.* As you go through the questionnaire, keep in mind that there are no right or wrong answers. The best answer is the one that comes closest to representing accurately your probable behaviors in each situation. In each statement, the first sentence or two outlines a situation and is followed by a possible reaction. Rate your reaction according to the following scale:

5 = You always would act this way.
4 = You frequently would act this way.
3 = You sometimes would act this way.
2 = You seldom would act this way.
1 = You never would act this way.

1. You have implemented a successful cooperative teaching relationship with a colleague, but some of her mannerisms and habits are getting on your nerves and irritating you. More and more you avoid interacting with her outside of the classroom.

1	2	3	4	5
never				always

2. In a moment of weakness, you give away a secret shared by a colleague. The colleague finds out and calls you to ask about it. You admit to it and talk with him about how to handle secrets better in the future.

1	2	3	4	5
never				always

3. Your cooperative teaching partner never seems to have time to meet to plan with you. You ask her about it, explaining how you feel.

1	2	3	4	5
never				always

4. A colleague feels you have inconvenienced him and tells you how he feels. You respond that he is too sensitive and is overreacting.

1	2	3	4	5
never				always

*Note. Questionnaire adapted from Reaching Out: Interpersonal Effectiveness and Self-Actualization (7th ed., pp. 41–44), by D. Johnson, 2000, Boston: Allyn & Bacon. Copyright 2000 by Allyn & Bacon. Adapted with permission.

5. You had a disagreement with a colleague, and now she ignores you whenever you are around. You decide to ignore her as well.

1	2	3	4	5
never				always

6. A colleague has pointed out that you never seem to have time to meet with him. You explain why you have been busy and try to reach a mutual understanding.

1	2	3	4	5
never				always

7. At great inconvenience you arrange to take your colleague to a meeting across town. When you arrive to pick up your colleague, you find she has decided not to go. You explain to your colleague how you feel and try to reach an understanding about future favors.

1	2	3	4	5
never				always

8. You have argued with a colleague and are angry with him, ignoring him when you meet. Your colleague tells you how he feels and asks about restoring the relationship. You ignore him and walk away.

1	2	3	4	5
never				always

9. You have a secret that you have told only to one other colleague. The next day another colleague asks you about the secret. You deny the secret and decide to break off the relationship with the person to whom you told the secret.

1	2	3	4	5
never				always

10. A colleague tells you about some of your mannerisms and habits that get on her nerves. You discuss these with her and look for some possible ways of dealing with the problem.

1	2	3	4	5
never				always

11. A colleague is involved in something illegal that you believe will lead to serious trouble. You decide to tell him how you disapprove of his involvement in the situation.

1	2	3	4	5
never				always

12. In a moment of weakness you give away a colleague's secret. She finds out and calls you to ask about it. You deny it firmly.

1	2	3	4	5
never				always

13. You have a partner in cooperative teaching who never seems to have time for you. You decide to forget him and to start looking for a new cooperative teaching partner.

1	2	3	4	5
never				always

14. You are involved in something illegal, and a colleague tells you of her disapproval and fear that you will get in serious trouble. You discuss it with her.

1	2	3	4	5
never				always

15. You work with a colleague and find that some of his mannerisms and habits are getting on your nerves and irritating you. You explain your feelings, looking for a mutual solution to the problem.

1	2	3	4	5
never				always

16. A colleague points out that you never seem to have time to meet with her. You walk away.

1	2	3	4	5
never				always

17. A colleague is involved in something illegal that you believe will lead to serious trouble. You decide to mind your own business.

1	2	3	4	5
never				always

18. A colleague is upset because you have inconvenienced him. He tells you how he feels. You try to understand and agree on a way to keep it from happening again.

1	2	3	4	5
never				always

19. You had a disagreement with a colleague, and now she ignores you whenever you are around. You explain how her actions make you feel and ask about restoring your collegial relationship.

1	2	3	4	5
never				always

20. A colleague tells you about some of your mannerisms and habits that get on his nerves. You listen and then walk away.

1	2	3	4	5
never				always

21. At great inconvenience, you arrange to take a colleague to a meeting. When you arrive to pick your colleague up, you find she has decided not to go. You say nothing but resolve never to do any favors for that person again.

1	2	3	4	5
never				always

22. You have argued with a colleague and are angry with him, ignoring him when you meet. He tells you how he feels and asks about restoring the collegial relationship. You discuss ways of maintaining it, even when you disagree.

1	2	3	4	5
never				always

23. You have a secret that you have told only to one other colleague. The next day, an acquaintance asks you about the secret. You call the colleague and ask her about it, trying to come to an understanding of how to handle secrets better in the future.

1	2	3	4	5
never				always

24. You are involved in something illegal, and a colleague tells you of his disapproval and fear that you will get in serious trouble. You tell him to mind his own business.

1	2	3	4	5
never				always

SCORING

In this survey the 12 even-numbered questions deal with your willingness to self-disclose and the 12 odd-numbered questions target your receptivity to feedback. Transfer your scores from each item to the following answer key, reversing the score for all the questions listed that are followed by an asterisk on the answer key. (That is, for the questions followed by an asterisk, if you answered 5, record a score of 1; if you answered 4, record a score of 2; if you answered 3, record a score of 3; if you answered 2, record a score of 4; and if you answered 1, record a score of 5.) Then add the scores in each of the two columns.

Willingness to Self-Disclose	Receptivity to Feedback
1. ____ *	2. ____
3. ____	4. ____
5. ____ *	6. ____
7. ____	8. ____ *
9. ____ *	10. ____

11. ___	12. ___*
13. ___*	14. ___
15. ___	16. ___*
17. ___*	18. ___
19. ___	20. ___*
21. ___*	22. ___
23. ___	24. ___*
Total ___	Total ___

After your scores in each of the two domains have been totaled, go to the following Johari Window figure and draw horizontal and vertical lines through your totaled scores on willingness to self-disclose and receptivity to feedback, respectively.

Generating your own personalized Johari Window can help to give you some perspective on your basic style of interaction with others. The more honest and accurate your responses to each item are, the more useful this activity will be. Use the results to help you determine how you might better be able to work with other school professionals in the intense professional relationships inherent in cooperative teaching.

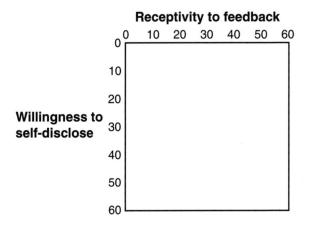

Reflecting on the Changes:
Considering Administrative Implications of Cooperative Teaching

Toto, I don't think we're in Kansas anymore.
—Dorothy in *The Wizard of Oz*

Deciding to remodel a home has significant and long-lasting implications for all who live there. It is rare for two homeowners to be struck simultaneously with the idea to remodel their home. More likely, one person came up with the original idea and then shared it with the other. That individual either quickly accepted the idea or did so only after encouragement and persuasion by the other. The homeowner who first had the idea for the remodeling and then sought the other person's support in essence was a change agent. A change agent is someone who (a) is convinced of the necessity for change, and (b) is willing and able to convince others.

Educators who implement cooperative teaching in the schools also are acting as change agents. Change agents are key people with the expertise to administer the

219

right changes in the proper dosages (Grossman, 1974). They are leaders who are actively committed to making a difference, and are capable of doing so (Fullan, 1993c; O'Hair & Odell, 1995; Pellicer & Anderson, 1995; Walther-Thomas, Korinek, McLaughlin, & Williams, 2000).

PIONEERS

Barker (1993) described individuals who are at the forefront of change as pioneers. Such people possess three critical characteristics: (1) courage to take risks, (2) intuition and insight, and (3) endurance.

First, pioneers are risk takers. The pioneers of the American West blazed a trail to new territories, taking chances and encountering dangers on their journeys. These were risky ventures, fraught with a multitude of dangers. The pioneers were followed by the settlers, who undertook the same journey after it first was made safe by the pioneers. These settlers were low risk takers compared with their pioneering predecessors.

In the schools, educators who develop and implement cooperative teaching are pioneers, high risk takers. These educational pioneers see how their schools might be better and are willing to take actions to back up those beliefs and perceptions. They take chances, putting themselves on the line for possible failure instead of sticking with the status quo.

It is often difficult for people to admit that substantial problems exist when something seems to be running more or less smoothly. In such circumstances one can ignore the problems, which is usually easier than the hard work involved in acknowledging the problems, identifying the specific nature of the problems, and then setting out to correct them.

For example, when a business is not doing well, its executives may refuse to acknowledge any problem and may even put forth impressive arguments to justify the poor showing. This evasion can go on for some time, forestalling any attempt to face the facts (Grossman, 1974). One can substitute the words *school* for *business* and *educators* for *executives* in this analysis. It requires courage to point out problems and then to accept the risks necessary to address the problems.

The second characteristic of pioneers is that they possess insight and intuition. Whether on the frontier in the 1800s or in the schools today, by the very nature of their ventures, pioneers have little data initially. They have no choice but to make judgments based on their professional and personal intuition. Their work is further complicated by the fact that no change that depends on people (such as school restructuring) can ever be completely predictable, because people are never completely predictable (Grossman, 1974). Thus to a large extent these pioneers must rely on little other than their professional intuition.

This is not to say that there is no need for data collection. But in the early stages of any innovation there is a relative dearth of information on which to base judgments. Early decisions must be made using incomplete data. As more experience is gained with the innovation, more data become available for subsequent decisions.

As homeowners go through blueprints before remodeling is underway, they often find it difficult to sense how the project will look when done. At some point they must simply trust their intuition that led to the plans they selected. Similarly, educational pioneers moving into cooperative teaching must realize that they are moving into relatively uncharted territory. When faced with the many questions for which no ready answers yet exist, these pioneers can only trust their professional judgments and instincts.

Finally, pioneers are characterized by endurance, the ability to persevere and continue on through difficult times. They enter into their ventures understanding that any undertaking of substance takes time to complete, with inevitable and unforeseen difficulties along the way. Not all pioneers are successful. In the American West, some gave up and returned, while others died in their efforts. Similarly, when controversies arise, some educators will be tempted to abandon innovative practices and return to the safe and well-known territory of their traditional work in the schools. The ability of pioneers to understand the need for endurance, the need to persevere through difficult periods and then learn from these difficult times for the future, is what makes successful pioneers.

As any homeowner in the midst of an extensive home remodeling project will volunteer, the question, "Is this really worth it?" frequently arises. But if the dust, noise, and general discomfort can be endured, the final results almost always are worthwhile. Remodeling the structure of education is difficult to accomplish, is time and labor intensive, and requires rethinking and relearning on everyone's part (Muncey & McQuillan, 1993). To expect significant reform in the schools without controversy is akin to expecting crops without plowing (Knoster, Villa, & Thousand, 2000). Many educators moving into cooperative teaching will find the inevitable disruption and changes in their routines to be difficult, confusing, and distressing. However, if they endure the initial unstable period, these problems almost always diminish.

It is critical that pioneers in the schools emerge, that professionals engaging in cooperative teaching and other educational innovations serve as agents of change, because fundamental change occurs through a bottom-up approach. Instead of being mandated from those in authority, change must come from practitioners if it is to be effective. It is the collective actions of individuals that create change (Villa & Thousand, 2000).

> *Change is the only thing that has brought progress.*
> —Charles F. Kettering

THE NATURE OF CHANGE IS CHANGING

In their analysis of change, DeBoer and Fister (2001) suggested that change is qualitatively different, and is more difficult to manage, than in the past. The velocity of change in daily life appears to be ever faster and to be coming from all directions. In addition, that change is discontinuous.

In the past, change was incremental and continuous. That is, change was simply more of the same, only better. In this way the past could be used to predict the future. For example, since television's widespread introduction in the 1950s, the television industry has improved its offerings dramatically, but the basic idea of providing shows, movies, and sports remains qualitatively unchanged.

However, many would suggest that contemporary change, especially change in the schools, is abrupt and substantially different from that experienced before. Teachers in general education classrooms today are responsible for the educational success of students who do not speak English and for students who have severe and multiple disabilities. Teachers are being held accountable for their students meeting very specific standards, and in some cases are dismissed when the standards are unmet. These changes have occurred very rapidly, within just the last few years. The result is that schools are being described as turbulent, contradictory, uncertain, and unpredictable (Fullan, 2000). The size and speed of the change in the schools is unprecedented. This requires all concerned to think about successful change strategies.

SIGNIFICANT CHANGE
CANNOT BE MANDATED

One of the consistent findings in business and education is that change is most successful when it is not based on directives from above, but instead evolves from the individuals who are actually responsible for implementing the day-to-day functions associated with the change. The CEOs of some of the world's largest corporations have concluded that change occurs only when all people involved see themselves as owners of that change, rather than simply passive recipients of management-dictated orders (Belasco, 1990).

Top-down mandates can bring about simple changes that do not require skill or thinking to implement and that can be monitored through close and constant surveillance (Fullan, 1993c). However, as educators move into cooperative teaching, they must make substantial changes in values and beliefs, behaviors, use of resources, commitments, motivations, and insights. Such personal change simply cannot be mandated. Personal change must evolve from significant changes in one's perceptions of how things should be.

Administrators cannot force educators to think in substantially different ways. Although an occasional nudge from above can help facilitate professional growth, to be truly effective any innovation such as cooperative teaching must originate from those who ultimately will be responsible for implementing it. As Ferguson (1987) noted, "A belated discovery, one that causes considerable anguish, is that no one can persuade another to change. Each of us guards a gate of change that can only be unlocked from the inside. We cannot open the gate of another, either by argument or by emotional appeal" (p. 112).

To implement cooperative teaching successfully, school professionals must make great changes in the way they go about their daily work. To overcome the inevitable fears and stresses associated with this change, the educators involved must feel that they are responsible for the change and that its success or failure lies directly with them. Administrative mandates alone cannot do this.

Change begins with only one or a few individuals. These pioneers, or change agents, are the people who are cutting the new paths, who are among the earliest at perceiving and understanding the implications of a paradigm shift and developing appropriate responses. If the change is to continue and become institutionalized, a critical mass of change agents must be established. This is the power that brings about change.

> *Don't think that a small group can't change the world.*
> *Indeed, that's the only way it can happen.*
> —Margaret Meade

At any single school, at first there may be only a single pair of educators who are teaching cooperativley. Other educators see the value of that innovation and incorporate it into their own work. As more and more educators follow suit, the critical mass necessary for the change to occur is rapidly achieved—a nonlinear domino effect.

Thus, change agents must actively work for change to be incorporated on a widespread basis. However, widespread implementation of innovation may depend equally on another group of school professionals, the change facilitators.

CHANGE FACILITATORS

Although change cannot be mandated from above, in the absence of administrative support it is unlikely to develop and thrive. If educators moving into cooperative teaching are considered change agents, it may be appropriate to view supportive administrators as change facilitators. Change facilitators are those individuals who are in a position to provide assistance to those who are implementing change. In the public schools, change facilitators are usually school principals or other local, regional, or state-level school administrators. The degree of administrative support is one of the most powerful predictors of the attitudes of educators toward substantial school-change issues (Villa, Thousand, Meyers, & Nevin, 1996), if not the most significant (Fullan & Hargreaves, 1996; Goor, Schwenn, & Boyer, 1997).

Fullan (2000) noted that administrators have learned that to create successful school renewal efforts, they need not take on the greatest possible number of innovations or schedule the greatest number of staff development days. Instead, effective school change occurs when the school staff and administration selects and integrates innovations. Effective school change is characterized by staff who work on "connectedness" with each other, and stay focused on applying what they learn. The main enemies of successful reform are staff overload and fragmentation.

Effective change facilitators perform a variety of functions in helping schools develop, implement, and maintain innovative school restructuring plans such as cooperative teaching. Successful change facilitators practice the following dozen skills and behaviors.

1. *Develop supportive organizational arrangements.* Before a change is implemented, effective change facilitators assist in scheduling and planning, and provide the personnel, equipment, and other resources required. They continue to provide these resources after the change has been implemented. Because requests and demands for resources usually outweigh supply by a heavy margin, change facilitators often must become creative in acquiring resources. An evolving role of administrators as change facilitators is that of resource brokers, that is, networking with their counterparts to maximize the use of local education agency resources (Hord, Rutherford, Huling-Austin, & Hall, 1987).

2. *Build trust.* Effective change facilitators acknowledge concerns of parents and staff, and are flexible enough to preserve significant elements of the school's present programs that parents or staff believe are valuable or believe are at risk when change is imminent. The administrator establishes trust by acknowledging in a meaningful way the concerns of important stakeholders (Udvari-Solner & Keyes, 2000).

3. *Recruit and support capable participants.* One of the best ways an administrator can affect change in a school is to identify and recruit those individuals who are the most capable of bringing it about. The best candidates are those who are (a) interested in the change, (b) willing to risk the possibility of failure, (c) well-respected among the school's staff, and (d) able to effectively communicate about the changes (Walther-Thomas et al., 2000).

4. *Provide for staff development.* Many otherwise competent and motivated school professionals cannot "just do it" when it comes to implementing a significant change (Walther-Thomas et al., 2000). School professionals must receive information and skill training before implementation of any innovation. The training must then continue on an ongoing basis if the change is to be sustained. Training must be tailored to fit the unique needs of the specific individuals and situations involved and must target all involved personnel (Hord et al., 1987).

5. *Encourage risk taking.* There is a risk of failure associated with any change. An administrator who punishes failure will almost certainly minimize any change attempted at the school. Effective change facilitators let staff members know that, when undertaking change, failure is okay and acceptable. Administrators can model this by taking risks themselves (Udvari-Solner & Keyes, 2000).

6. *Consult and reinforce.* This type of support is less structured, less formal, and more individualized than training. Change facilitators must address the present and evolving needs of staff members so that the implemented changes can be sustained. This is typically accomplished by offering individualized follow-up to the formal training (Hord et al., 1987).

7. *Initiate and support early planning.* Effective change facilitators recognize how difficult it is to make substantial change, and how much time it takes to design effective changes. To ensure that they consider all important issues, administrators might facilitate regular planning sessions early in the academic year preceding the year in which the changes are to take place (Walther-Thomas et al., 2000).

8. *Monitor.* Effective change facilitators help develop and support authentic evaluative procedures to advance the changes. The act of gathering information, though critical to success, often is neglected. For example, some administrators stay away from their teachers, believing that their staff is intimidated by administrator visits. Actually, many competent staff members may feel ignored or abandoned in the absence of such visits. Asking open-ended questions and engaging in face-to-face informal conversations are effective ways for administrators to gather useful data and reinforce staff members about the importance of the changes the educators are helping to bring about (Hord et al., 1987).

9. *Promote reflective dialogue and critical questioning.* One of the most important ways a school administrator can support change in a school is to stimulate inquiry, both within himself or herself and among school staff. The change facilitator must ask himself or herself important questions such as, "What are we doing to meet the needs of all students in the school, regardless of their unique characteristics?" In addition, he or she must encourage staff to ask themselves similar questions. Part of this involves the potentially difficult task of helping staff members identify incongruities in practice and philosophy. In other words, does the school "practice what it preaches" (Udvari-Solner & Keyes, 2000). Lambert (1998) extended this, noting that it is necessary to develop a culture of inquiry, a continuous cycle of reflecting, questioning, gathering evidence, and planning for improvement.

10. *Communicate with others.* A significant role of change facilitators is to elicit support from outside individuals and agencies. In the schools, this administrative communication might include public relations campaigns, networking with counterparts elsewhere, presentations to parent–teacher organizations, and so forth (Hord et al., 1987). Effective administrators involve central office administrators in building-level decisions, keeping friends in high places (Udvari-Solner & Keyes, 2000).

11. *Disseminate.* To help other schools adopt an innovation, administrators must provide information to assist those just beginning these efforts. Strategies include mailing descriptive brochures, offering implementation materials or videotapes, establishing Web sites and other electronic communication avenues, and even providing training through program representatives (Hord et al., 1987).

12. *Show courage.* Like the pioneers exploring the American West, administrators must have courage to directly address the difficult, controversial, and sometimes seemingly unanswerable questions that are inherent in substantial change (Udvari-Solner & Keyes, 2000). A courageous school administrator can motivate an entire school staff.

The previous 12 functions are common among all effective change facilitators. But all change facilitators do not approach change in the same way. Extensive research on schools that are actively involved in restructuring efforts has concluded that there are essentially three styles of change facilitators—initiators, managers, and responders (Hall & Hord, 1984).

Initiators are those administrators who have decisive, long-range goals for their schools. They have a clear sense of what their schools should look like and take active steps toward changing their schools to match that vision. They solicit input from their professional staffs and then make decisions based on that input. They push themselves, their staffs, and their students to ensure that everyone continues to move toward the same goals. They energetically and creatively seek and successfully obtain the resources necessary for the furtherance of the goals

Managers are as much reactive as proactive. They support the change agents in their schools without much fanfare. They protect their staffs from what they see as excessive demands and are sensitive to educator needs. They question changes at the beginning. When they see that change is being encouraged from sources such as the district's central office, they will support their staff in bringing those changes about. However, they may not go much past the minimum effort that is required for the change. They also find it difficult to delegate responsibilities and may try to do all the required tasks themselves.

Responders are most concerned with how others will perceive their decisions and the overall direction of their schools. They delegate decisions and solicit as much feedback from all concerned as possible. They are concerned with making school professionals and students content. They may make decisions based more on immediate circumstances than long-range goals, perhaps based on a pervasive and strong desire to please others. Once they make a decision, responders tend to stay with it.

To put it most simply:

- Responders let change happen.
- Managers help change happen.
- Initiators make change happen.

Although it is likely that few change facilitators will fit neatly into only one of these categories, the three types can be seen as points along two lines (see Figures 9.1 and 9.2). Toward one end of the first line (which might be labeled "Receptiveness to Externally Imposed Change") is the responder, who is most receptive to change imposed from outside or above. Conversely, the initiator resists externally imposed change, instead being most sensitive to changes proposed or emerging internally. On a second line (which might be labeled "Level of Personal Involvement in Change"), the responder takes a low profile in helping the change occur (see Figure 9.2). Conversely, the initiator takes the most active role in outlining the directions of the change. The manager adopts a moderate position on both lines.

The success of any school change is highly correlated with the innovation style of the facilitator. Research (Hord et al., 1987) has suggested that the most successful change facilitators were initiators, followed by managers. Responder-led schools were least successful in implementing change. The specific skills of the initiator-style school administrators that were most important in implementing change included their strong vision, push, consistent decision making, and priority setting.

LEADER*SHIFT*

Futurist Joel Barker (1999) coined the term "Leader*shift*" to explain how leadership is evolving in these rapidly changing times. In that work, a leader is defined as an individual whom others would follow to a place they would not go themselves. This definition effectively captures the sense of a school administrator as he or she encourages

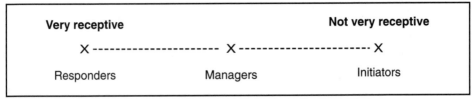

Figure 9.1 Receptiveness to externally imposed change.

Figure 9.2 Level of personal involvement in change.

and supports staff to move into cooperative teaching. Barker made a number of other points relevant to school leaders as they implement change.

1. Effective leaders are like safe bridges: flexible, strong, and able to support others.

2. Effective leaders are future oriented. The future is the place that leaders lead to. According to experts, a leader should spend 90% of his or her time thinking about the future.

3. Effective leaders use excitement and enthusiasm to build support for change. Bully leaders use threats, condemnation, fear, and rejection to obtain compliance. People who work for charismatic leaders are up to 20 times more productive than those who work for bully leaders.

4. Leadership is different today because people are better informed, better educated, and more independent. Thus leaders best lead today by helping a staff create a vision for the future, and then helping to move that vision into reality.

RETHINKING LEADERSHIP

When most people hear the term *school leader*, their first thought is a principal. However, at the risk of oversimplification, a leader is anyone who engages in leadership (Lambert, 1998). School leaders include many who are not involved in the day-to-day management functions, including master teachers, PTA officers, teachers' union representatives, department heads, and local community leaders (Walther-Thomas et al., 2000).

Teachers have long attended to the learning needs of their students. The emerging vision of school leadership now asks that they extend that attention to the learning needs of their colleagues. As partners in cooperative teaching invite others to become involved in their new practice, and help others incorporate changes, they become school leaders. As school professionals perceive this new work as a natural outgrowth of their roles as professional educators, they are less likely to opt out of these guidance roles by insisting that they are not leaders (Lambert, 1998). These shared leadership responsibilities include convening and facilitating dialogue, posing inquiry questions, coaching one another, mentoring new colleagues, and inviting others to become involved with the new ideas (Lambert, 1998). Taking leadership beyond the walls of the principal's office benefits the school in a number of ways. As more staff members share in the leadership of the school, they increasingly demonstrate greater participation, stronger commitment, and more creative problem solving (Adams & Cessna, 1991; Cramer, 1998; Pugach & Johnson, 1995).

CONCLUSIONS

When two homeowners decide to remodel their house, usually the idea initially occurred to one of them, who then convinced the other that it should be done. Similarly, certain individuals in the school serve as change agents, bringing about such innovations as cooperative teaching in their schools by convincing others of the necessity of change. These pioneers have courage, insight and intuition, and endurance. Because no one can force another to change, school administrators are most effective as change agents when they serve as change facilitators, providing support and resources for the school personnel who are most directly involved with change. The role of effective school administrators is changing, from a hierarchical and directive model to a supportive one. Additionally, it is master teachers, not principals, who increasingly are emerging as leaders of school change efforts.

It is now time to show off a bit, to share the excitement of cooperative teaching with others. When homeowners move into their remodeled home, they share the excitement with their friends and neighbors by having a housewarming party, in which guests are invited to come see and enjoy the new structure.

After they have implemented cooperative teaching, educators usually are eager to display their new schoolhouse to others. With school professionals actively involved as significant change agents in remodeling the schoolhouse through cooperative teaching, supported by change facilitators in administrative positions, educators' next step is to help others achieve similar results. This information sharing is critical if the restructuring is to become widespread. The next chapter explains a variety of procedures educators have found effective in spreading the word about cooperative teaching, sharing the information throughout their professional communities.

CHAPTER 9 ACTIVITY

Checklist of Possible Actions of Change Facilitators

As noted earlier, Hord et al. (1987) identified a number of ways in which change facilitators can support change in their schools. In this adaptation of that work, a number of possible actions a change facilitator might take to support innovations in a school are listed. As you read each action, check off in the right-hand column whether the individual serving as change facilitator at your school is taking such actions. Items that are not applicable should be left blank.

This exercise has at least two purposes. First, some change facilitators may want to support an innovation such as cooperative teaching but are unaware of how to do so. The following list of concrete suggestions can yield specific types of assistance that can be requested by the educators serving as change agents at a school.

Second, the overall pattern that emerges from the completed checklist may suggest how enthusiastically a change facilitator actually supports a change. If a change facilitator is providing few of the following types of support, then he or she likely is only nominally a change facilitator.

1. Effective change facilitators develop supportive organizational arrangements

   Is the change facilitator assisting in   Yes   No

   a. developing innovation-related policies?   ____   ____

   b. establishing global rules?   ____   ____

   c. making decisions?   ____   ____

   d. planning?   ____   ____

   e. preparing?   ____   ____

   f. scheduling?   ____   ____

   g. staffing?   ____   ____

   h. restructuring roles?   ____   ____

   i. seeking or providing materials?   ____   ____

   j. providing space?   ____   ____

	Yes	No
k. seeking or acquiring funds?	——	——
l. providing equipment?	——	——

2. Effective change facilitators provide for staff development

   Is the change facilitator

   a. developing positive attitudes? —— ——

   b. increasing knowledge? —— ——

   c. teaching innovation-related skills? —— ——

   d. reviewing information? —— ——

   e. holding workshops? —— ——

   f. observing use of the innovation? —— ——

   g. modeling use of the innovation? —— ——

   h. providing feedback? —— ——

   i. clarifying misconceptions? —— ——

3. Effective change facilitators consult and reinforce

   Is the change facilitator

   a. encouraging people one-on-one? —— ——

   b. promoting innovation use one-on-one? —— ——

   c. assisting in problem solving? —— ——

   d. coaching small groups? —— ——

   e. sharing tips informally? —— ——

   f. providing personalized assistance? —— ——

   g. holding ongoing conversations? —— ——

   h. applauding progress? —— ——

   i. providing small "comforting" sessions? —— ——

   j. reinforcing individuals moving into change? —— ——

   k. celebrating success? —— ——

	Yes	No

4. Effective change facilitators monitor

   Is the change facilitator

   a. gathering information? ____ ____

   b. collecting data? ____ ____

   c. assessing progress informally? ____ ____

   d. assessing progress formally? ____ ____

   e. analyzing data? ____ ____

   f. interpreting data and other information? ____ ____

   g. reporting and sharing outcomes data? ____ ____

   h. providing feedback on collected data? ____ ____

   i. collecting data from all significant parties? ____ ____

5. Effective change facilitators communicate with others

   Is the change facilitator

   a. providing accurate descriptions to others? ____ ____

   b. reporting to appropriate other parties? ____ ____

   c. making presentations at conferences? ____ ____

   d. developing a public relations campaign? ____ ____

   e. gaining the support of important groups? ____ ____

6. Effective change facilitators disseminate

   Is the change facilitator

   a. encouraging others to adopt the program? ____ ____

   b. mailing descriptive brochures? ____ ____

   c. providing start-up materials to others? ____ ____

   d. training visitors to the program? ____ ____

   e. facilitating staff development elsewhere? ____ ____

Having the Open House:
Sharing Cooperative Teaching

And now it's time for you and me to start a revolution.
—Jefferson Airplane, 1969

When a home remodeling project is finally complete, homeowners look forward to showing off the results to friends and neighbors. A house-warming party allows everyone to see how well the project turned out, and how much better the remodeled structure is than the one it replaced.

At the party the homeowners will find their friends and neighbors admiring the new arrangements. Guests contemplating similar changes (and perhaps even those who were not until they saw the results) will ask a variety of questions—recommendations about the best windows to buy, about carpet selection, about decorating consultants, and so on.

As educators restructure the schoolhouse using the architectural blueprints for cooperative teaching, the last step in the process is to share their ideas with colleagues. Educators benefiting from cooperative teaching now can return the favor to those individuals who first shared knowledge and skills with them.

PROFESSIONAL SHARING

All school professionals owe a tremendous debt to previous generations of educators, who spent years identifying effective educational procedures and practices, then passed on their knowledge to their successors today. This tradition of sharing knowledge and skills, common to all professions, allows others to step into roles prepared to take on the work. Much of what professionals do today in schools is based on what their predecessors learned.

One way to think about this is to consider every teacher as a library of knowledge. It has been said that each time an educator dies, a professional library burns. If the books in that library are not read by others, if that information is not shared with others, it is lost forever.

Because it is not possible to directly repay these individuals for sharing their knowledge and skills with their successors, the only way this debt can be repaid is by contemporary educators acquiring and passing on new knowledge to others in the same unselfish tradition. As school professionals move into innovative and effective programs such as cooperative teaching, dissemination is a critical component of their work.

Dissemination is the promotion of thoughtful and appropriate use of effective innovative practices (Allen & Kliot, 1982). This is achieved by promoting awareness of the innovation among potential users, providing information to these individuals to facilitate their ability to make intelligent decisions about the use of the innovation in their work, and giving assistance to help implement an innovation in a given situation. Dissemination activities include the following:

- developing a dissemination plan

- packaging the innovation for dissemination

- training others in the use of the innovation

- establishing awareness activities and communication networks such as newsletters and brochures

ESSENTIAL ELEMENTS IN EFFECTIVE DISSEMINATION

As homeowners consider how to tell others about their newly completed remodeling project, they have a number of options. For example, they might send out letters or cards (with or without pictures); they might send e-mail (with or without image file attachments); they may make and copy a videotape showing the new structure; they might set up a Web site with image files; or they might hold a housewarming party where friends and neighbors can come and see it for themselves. In determining the best way to let others know about the changes, the homeowners would consider who is to be notified and how best to reach them.

Similarly, in planning effective dissemination activities for cooperative teaching, educators first must consider several issues. These include the following:

1. identifying the essential elements of cooperative teaching that make it unique

2. determining the purpose underlying the dissemination

3. determining the target audience to receive the information or training

4. deciding how the dissemination might best be structured to achieve those purposes and reach that target audience

Allen and Kliot (1982) developed a series of questions that can help the potential disseminator become more effective in making these decisions. This information is adapted and provided in Figure 10.1.

Intended Purpose of the Dissemination

The purposes of disseminating information about a program can vary from simply informing others about the program results to providing intensive and extensive training to others to help them develop and implement similar programs on their own. For example, if a state or federal grant was used to assist in the development and implementation of a cooperative teaching program, a typical requirement is that a written report on the program be submitted. This sort of report usually is factual in nature, giving information on such things as personnel involved, time lines along which program development activities took place, and specific outcomes of the program. Numerical data often play a major role in these reports, including information such as number of educators involved and number of students affected, as well as outcomes data such as

1. **Have the essential elements of cooperative teaching been specified adequately (e.g., cooperative planning, cooperative presenting, cooperative processing, cooperative problem solving)?**
   Sources of information to determine this:
   • review of program documents (e.g., the original proposal, progress reports)
   • expert review (e.g., outside consultants) of cooperative teaching in operation
   • observations of cooperative teaching
   • interviews with others who are implementing cooperative teaching

2. **Do the educators follow the essential elements of cooperative teaching as specified?**
   Sources of information to determine this:
   • observation of educators in operation
   • educator and student interviews
   • expert review (e.g., outside consultants) of cooperative teaching in operation

3. **Do the students served through cooperative teaching respond as predicted (i.e., how well are all students succeeding in the cooperatively taught general education classrooms)?**
   Sources of information to determine this:
   • observations of students
   • interviews with students
   • interviews or ratings by parents or school professionals
   • examinations of student work and educator records
   • standardized tests of knowledge and skills
   • curriculum-based or other tests of knowledge and skills
   • scales of attitudes, beliefs, and other similar dimensions
   • behavioral observations and data recording

4. **Have other potential outcomes of cooperative teaching (e.g., collegiality; job turnover and stability; changes in beliefs, knowledge, and skills) developed as expected?**
   Sources of information to determine this:
   • observation of educators
   • interviews with educators

5. **What additional costs are involved in the development and implementation of cooperative teaching (e.g., initial and ongoing staff development costs, travel for visits to exemplary programs, release time, hiring of paraprofessionals)?**
   Sources of information to determine this:
   • budgets
   • expert cost analyses

Figure 10.1 Initial questions in planning dissemination efforts.

achievement test scores and special education referral and participation rates. Although this sort of information dissemination may help others to develop similar programs, it is not the major purpose.

Conversely, if the intention of dissemination is to help others develop similar programs at other schools, then the dissemination takes on a different structure. For example, if a school district becomes convinced that a pioneering cooperative teaching effort at a school was successful in meeting preestablished district goals, then the district may want similar programs established at other schools in the district. In this case, a simple factual summary of the program is unlikely to be effective; other forms of dissemination will be required.

Target Audience

There are a number of individuals who might want information about a school's cooperative teaching program. They include the following:

- parents

- educators at that school involved in cooperative teaching

- educators at that school not involved in cooperative teaching

- educators at other schools involved in cooperative teaching

- educators at other schools who are not presently involved in cooperative teaching but are considering whether to become involved

- principals at other schools

- staff development professionals in school districts

- school district administrators

- local school board members

- state department of education staff and administrators

- professors in teacher preparation programs at universities

- educational researchers

The specific audience identified as a target for the dissemination effort determines its form, structure, and content. For example, educational researchers might be most interested in the theoretical foundations of cooperative teaching (accompanied by extensive lists of references) and statistically based data analyses of the program's effectiveness. Parents, on the other hand, may be more interested in the direct practical implications of cooperative teaching on their children's day-to-day school experiences, whereas administrators might be most interested in overall costs. Yet another possible audience, educators at other schools, instead might need to receive basic awareness information initially, followed by some theoretical background and practical step-by-step implementation strategies. No single dissemination effort can effectively address the diverse needs of all potential consumers of this information. Any dissemination plan must keep the target audience in mind.

Ways To Disseminate Information

Once those conducting the dissemination have determined both its basic purpose and its target audience, the next step is to identify possible ways in which dissemination might take place and determine which of those best fit the purpose and audience. Some of the dissemination options include conducting staff development activities, establishing a Web site, presenting at professional conferences, and writing for professional publication.

Conducting Staff Development Activities for Colleagues

The professional skills of educators are becoming obsolete faster and faster. During the 1940s, without ongoing staff development activities, educators' skills could be expected to be obsolete in 12 years. By the 1980s, that span was reduced to 5 years. It is anticipated that the pace of obsolescence of professional skills in educators will continue to accelerate in the future (Idol, 1993). Thus ongoing staff development and training programs are more critical than ever.

There is no one-size-fits-all approach to getting information out to educators. Different staff members have different needs (Knoster, Villa, & Thousand, 2000). There are perhaps three critical factors for effective staff development procedures (Beninghof, 1996). First, there must be a wide spectrum of professional development activities offered to best meet the diverse needs of all staff and students. Different professional roles require different types of skills.

Second, because the change process is a personalized experience for each person involved, staff development activities plans must acknowledge that attendees likely will be at different levels of readiness to accept the proposed changes. An effective staff development approach provides participants with meaningful opportunities for self-improvement regardless of their level of readiness (Knoster et al., 2000). In disseminating information about cooperative teaching, some have found it useful to develop and administer a short "Readiness for Cooperative Teaching" attitude survey prior to conducting a workshop. This allows the presenters to determine where the attendees are in terms of their background and experience in cooperative teaching.

Third, staff development activities are most likely to be successful when broad input from all major stakeholders has been solicited and incorporated, and when staff members have been involved in the planning process from the early stages. Most important, training priorities should be established by the individuals most directly affected by the proposed changes: the educators at that school. Professional development topics should be based on what a school's staff view as their top priority at the onset of the change process (Knoster et al., 2000). Some workshop presenters have found it useful to informally meet with a school's staff prior to the workshop to fine-tune the content.

Workshops can be an effective way to disseminate knowledge and skills, especially on the local level. It is primarily through on-site staff development activities that many educators update their professional credentials and expertise, and it is on this face-to-face, intensive basis that educational innovators often can have greatest impact.

Effective staff development workshops have several components (Browder, 1983). These include the following:

- identification of goals and objectives for the workshop
- selection of presenters
- determination of incentives for attendance
- decisions about content delivery
- evaluation

Several of these components are particularly relevant for the development of workshops on cooperative teaching.

The *goals and objectives* for a workshop must precede and guide its development. A workshop designed to provide attendees with an introductory awareness of cooperative teaching will be structured very differently and include different content than a skill-based training program designed to result in attendees returning to their schools ready to implement cooperative teaching. The introductary workshop realistically might be done in a single 1- to 3-hour session. The skill-based program likely would require 2 to 3 full days of intensive training, with additional follow-up training sessions scheduled on an ongoing basis. It is a mistake to propose or agree to objectives that are not achievable in the time allotted. Ultimately each goal or objective should lead to the improvement of student learning, especially targeting students who learn in different ways or represent diverse cultural, linguistic, and socioeconomic backgrounds (Renyi, 1996).

The best workshop *presenters* combine skills in adult instruction with a wealth of practically derived information about cooperative teaching in the schools. The most effective workshops are often those presented by practicing educators (Renyi, 1996). Two or three presenters working simultaneously can be especially useful in workshops on cooperative teaching, because the presenters can demonstrate specific cooperative teaching strategies as they conduct the workshop.

Incentives for attendance and subsequent implementation are usually not under the control of workshop presenters. In the absence of incentives, participation may be passive, or there may even be active resistance (Knoster et al., 2000). However, most educators recognize today the changing needs of their student populations, and the need to change the nature of their instruction to better respond to those needs. If the preworkshop publicity emphasizes the advantages for educators in learning about and implementing cooperative teaching, and the potential for ongoing support is noted, most school professionals will be interested in attending.

Such intrinsic motivators as recognition of one's potential for enhanced professional effectiveness and pride in one's professional growth are more effective and more likely to result in durable change (Knoster et al., 2000). Often ongoing administrative support for cooperative teaching is contingent on participants attending and completing training, a potentially powerful incentive.

The initial decisions made about the *delivery of the content* of a workshop on cooperative teaching will have great impact on the workshop's effectiveness. In reviewing the literature on effective staff development programs, Idol (1993) and Renyi (1996) concluded that staff development programs are most effective when they

- emphasize the goal of the enhancement of student learning

- are based in the schools instead of universities

- provide adequate time for inquiry and reflection

- are designed, planned, and presented by practicing teachers

- require school professionals to construct and generate ideas, materials, and behaviors, rather than have the attendees passively receive information from the presenters

- help educators share ideas and provide assistance to each other

- are sustained and part of a long-term professional development plan

- are specific and practical, and provide for hands-on experience

- provide for observation of exemplary programs

These conclusions have practical implications for workshop presenters sharing information on cooperative teaching with their colleagues. To be effective, these programs should include frequent activities in which participants become purposefully involved in small group or partner work, generating and then sharing with others possible solutions to scenarios posed by the presenters. Activities should vary: in some, participants might quietly listen; in others, share ideas in the small group; in others, watch a videotape; in still others, do some sort of physical activity. There should be time, perhaps at a midpoint as well as at the end of the program, for the participants to take a few moments to reflect on what has occurred to that point, and gather their thoughts and questions in writing, either for themselves, the workshop presenters, or both.

In providing staff development for busy and pressed colleagues, the workshop presenter may be tempted simply to provide a practical how-to laundry list of tips for implementing cooperative teaching. However, if participants lack basic understanding about what cooperative teaching is, then they will not understand specific implementation strategies built on the foundation of that knowledge, and subsequent implementation is unlikely to be successful. It is not enough for educators to know *how* to implement cooperative teaching; to be most effective they also must know the *why* underlying the procedures so that they can collaboratively develop their own procedures based on that solid theoretical foundation.

Although conceptual understanding serves as a foundation, the staff development program will be best received if it emphasizes practical strategies that are immediately transferrable to the classroom. The use of real-life examples, of problems encountered and solutions generated, and of mistakes made and corrected, all serve to give the session impact and clarity. In workshop activities where attendees are expected to work together to generate solutions or products based on cooperative teaching (e.g., cooperatively designed lesson plans), the use of practical real-life examples as starting points will elicit higher levels of interaction and better end results.

At a minimum, then, effective staff development in cooperative teaching should include the following:

- basic theoretical information underlying cooperative teaching
- practical suggestions that can help practitioners implement cooperative teaching in their schools
- activities that allow the participants to become directly involved in problem solving by generating options and solutions

In the rush to cover a large amount of information in a short amount of time, presenters may forget that the attention of even the most dedicated professionals in the schools is limited. Few can listen to a near-nonstop, 6-hour lecture with constant rapt attention. A few short breaks with beverages and other light refreshments will enhance the receptiveness of the audience.

Finally, staff development sessions on cooperative teaching are most effective when participants attend as cooperative teaching teams. The commonality of knowledge and skills they receive is invaluable when they return to their schools to begin the planning process.

Figure 10.2 presents a planning checklist (adapted from Browder, 1983) for staff development activities.

An example of a possible outline for a 3-hour awareness workshop on cooperative teaching is provided in Figure 10.3.

In preparing for a staff development session on cooperative teaching, the presenters should organize all materials and content beforehand so that any last-minute problems are minimized. The materials and notes to be used at the workshop should be assembled in their correct order and reviewed before the workshop. Presenting in and of itself is stressful enough. Scrambling at the last minute to find a missing overhead transparency or needed piece of equipment makes the anxiety level unnecessarily higher. Dress and appearance should be comfortable yet professional.

(check boxes when completed)

I. Selection of workshop objectives
- ☐ Have participants been pretested to determine baseline levels of knowledge and skills?
- ☐ Has this information been used to determine workshop objectives?

II. Selection of presenters
- ☐ Are the presenters experienced in adult education and professional presentations?
- ☐ Have presenters been selected to represent diverse backgrounds and perspectives? (check all that apply)
  - ____ teachers
  - ____ support services providers
  - ____ principals
  - ____ other administrators
  - ____ state department of education personnel
  - ____ university teacher educators
  - ____ private consultants
  - ____ other _____

III. Determination of incentives
- ☐ Have incentives for attendees been determined? (check all that apply)
  - ____ released time
  - ____ payment
  - ____ academic credit
  - ____ salary step credit
  - ____ certification renewal
  - ____ personal recognition
  - ____ ongoing support
  - ____ other _____

IV. Delivery of content
- ☐ Has the structure of the workshop been thought out to include the following as appropriate? (check all that apply)
  - ____ active participation
  - ____ self-directed learning
  - ____ fundamental theoretical background
  - ____ practical application
  - ____ live demonstrations
  - ____ overhead transparencies and handouts of graphics
  - ____ videotapes of cooperative teaching
  - ____ opportunities for practice

V. Workshop evaluation
- ☐ Have plans been made to evaluate the effectiveness of the workshop? (check all that apply)
  - ____ evaluation elements determined
    - ____ overall content of workshop
    - ____ the overall process
    - ____ effectiveness of presenter
    - ____ degree to which workshop objectives were met
  - ____ workshop evaluation form developed

Figure 10.2 Planning checklist for cooperative teaching workshop.

I. Introduction
- KWL (Know/Want/Learned)
Find out from participants what they know about cooperative teaching at present, what they want to learn about cooperative teaching, and what they have learned about cooperative teaching (by the end of the workshop).

II. What is cooperative teaching?
    A. Definition (oral presentation and overhead transparencies)
    B. Component parts or elements (oral presentation and overhead transparencies)
        1. cooperative presence
        2. cooperative planning
        3. cooperative presenting
        4. cooperative processing
        5. cooperative problem solving

III. Why is cooperative teaching especially necessary now? (partner activity)
    A. The ongoing restructuring movement in the schools, altering traditional rules, roles, and relationships
    B. Increased movement toward teams and collaboration throughout society

IV. What are the benefits of and barriers to cooperative teaching?
(small group assignment)
    A. Benefits
    B. Barriers
    C. Solutions

V. What is necessary to begin cooperative teaching?
(oral presentation and overhead transparencies)
    A. Identifying the first cooperative teachers
    B. Identifying and soliciting administrative support
    C. Developing training

Figure 10.3 Sample outline for a 3-hour awareness workshop on cooperative teaching.

If possible, it can be enormously helpful to have a copresenter (or at least an assistant who is familiar with the presentation) to aid with distributing handouts, operating video equipment, and turning room lights on and off. Such help allows the presenter to concentrate on keeping the flow of the workshop steady. In addition, two copresenters can demonstrate the very cooperative teaching strategies that they are presenting. Many copresenters have found it effective for one of them to distribute materials while the other displays related materials on an overhead projector or via a PowerPoint presentation. This helps audience members maintain a permanent record of any visual presentation.

Developing and presenting content to adults is a skill that grows with practice. Feedback is critical to this development. Usually workshop presenters ask attendees to complete anonymous workshop evaluations. Although numerical data often are necessary for administrative agency purposes, the most useful bits of feedback are the responses to a set of open-ended questions. Good questions include, "What was the best thing about the workshop?" and "How would you suggest the workshop be changed for future presentations?"

A common mistake presenters make is the premature dissemination of evaluation forms in the preliminary packet that all participants receive before the actual program. This early distribution of evaluation forms often results in evaluations being completed well before the end of the presentation, and results in inaccurate or incomplete data. To prevent this problem, presenters should distribute any evaluation form only after the formal presentation has been completed. A sample evaluation form is presented in Figure 10.4.

Establishing a Web Site

The Internet and the World Wide Web have become symbols of the power of technology to shape people's lives (Roblyer & Edwards, 2000). In the past, when someone needed information about almost any aspect of life (a medical issue, a consumer purchase, a professional question), he or she would go to the library, or call or visit an expert. The World Wide Web has revolutionized the ways in which information is both provided and accessed, putting a universe of information at one's fingertips. In terms of the number of individuals that can be reached, the Web is perhaps the most efficient outlet for professional dissemination of cooperative teaching.

Almost any type of information that can be imagined can be found on the Web, and the amount of that information is nearly limitless. For example, in the summer of

---

Cooperative Teaching Workshop Evaluation Form

For each of the following items, please circle the number that best represents your opinion.

5 = superior   4 = very good   3 = good   2 = improvement is needed   1 = very weak

I. **How well did the presenter(s) describe the following components of cooperative teaching?**

A. Definition	1 2 3 4 5
B. Rationale	1 2 3 4 5
C. Benefits and barriers	1 2 3 4 5
D. Critical elements	1 2 3 4 5
E. Process steps	1 2 3 4 5
F. Other content _____	1 2 3 4 5

II. **How well did the presenter(s):**

A. Pace the instruction	1 2 3 4 5
B. Use a variety of methods and media	1 2 3 4 5
C. Answer questions	1 2 3 4 5
D. Actively involve you in the workshop	1 2 3 4 5

III. **What did you like best about this workshop on cooperative teaching?**

IV. **What suggestions could you make to improve this workshop on cooperative teaching?**

V. **What do you intend to do as a result of attending this workshop?**

VI. **What content should subsequent workshops on cooperative teaching include?**

Figure 10.4 Sample workshop evaluation form.

2001, using the Google search engine (www.google.com), a search on "cooperative teaching" generated almost half a million results.

There are three main reasons why the Internet has so quickly become so popular. First, it is widely available. Anyone who has a computer and a telephone line can access the Internet. Second, it is easy to use, with access based on a simple point-

and-click activity. Anything on a Web page can link to any other Web location throughout the world through a text-based linking system called hypertext. With sites linked to one another this way (hence the term *Web*), Internet users can browse effortlessly, using such Web browsers as Internet Explorer and Netscape Navigator to easily gather tremendous amounts of information. Third, the Web is highly visual and graphic. The original text-based Internet system in the early 1990s was not nearly as popular. It was not until images became a primary means of communication on Web pages that the Internet became so widely accepted (Roblyer & Edwards, 2000).

Information can be provided on a Web site in a variety of formats. Originally Web sites were limited to text only, and text still remains an easy and efficient communication system. However, society increasingly relies on images for the communication of information. To use a Web site most effectively, the site creator should use text and visual presentations.

Images and animation have become near universal on Web sites. Web site creators can buy clip art and clip photo packages with prepared visual images to insert on their Web pages. They also can use digital photographs, either taken with a digital camera or scanned and converted to digital format from a print of a photograph. For example, on a Web site explaining cooperative teaching, actual pictures of educators cooperatively teaching can significantly enhance and expand any text explanations.

Short movies featuring audio and video also can be added to Web sites. Increasingly the digital cameras used to record and store these images in the MPEG ("movie") format are available to schools and individuals. The use of MPEGs to illustrate how cooperative teaching is being implemented at any given school can be a powerful addition to a cooperative teaching Web site.

All that is necessary for a Web site is space on a computer server for the site and skills in Web site design. Most schools already are linked to the Internet via a server that could host a Web site. Until recently, a significant barrier to disseminating information via Web sites was the level of advanced programming skills required to do Web site design and maintenance. By the late 1990s, however, software had advanced to the point where Web sites can be designed by individuals with minimal or no programming knowledge or skills, and today Web site development packages are widely available. These authoring systems allow individuals with basic computer skills to develop Web sites by using a simple point-click-drag approach, much like creating a word-processing document that incorporates images. These programs automatically generate the HTML programming code required for Web pages to be placed on the Internet. Common Web site development software includes Microsoft's FrontPage and Claris' HomePage. Basic Web page authoring software is even incorporated into some word processing software (Microsoft Word), and some browsers (Netscape Navigator).

An educator who wants to disseminate information about cooperative teaching via a Web site should follow several basic design principles to enhance the overall effectiveness of the site. Unfortunately, many Web sites are poorly designed, in part because they are so easy to create (Cafolla & Knee, 1996). The following presents a suggested sequence of steps for developing an effective Web site (Cafolla & Knee, 1996; 1996–1997; 1997).

1. *Plan and storyboard*. This planning can be as simple as using sticky notes with comments on each to represent individual pages. The notes can be moved around on a large piece of poster board to find the best arrangement, either linearly or using a cognitive-map format. The author also might begin thinking about how each page should be linked to the others, and to other, outside pages on the Web. For example, it can be useful on a Web site explaining a school's cooperative teaching program to have a series of links to other Web sites and resources on cooperative teaching. Once planning is complete, the site creator should select an overall name for the site.

2. *Use software to develop pages with text*. In this step, the appropriate number of pages on the site are created and text elements (labels, descriptive text) are inserted.

3. *Insert images and sounds*. At this point the Web site developer adds graphics and sounds. Images and animations are in JPEG or GIF format, whereas movies and sounds are in MPEG format. It may be useful to provide a link for users to a site where any software needed to view the images and sounds may be downloaded at no cost.

4. *Insert links and frames*. After each page is completed with text and images, the appropriate links should be set.

5. *Test by using a browser*. To make sure that the Web site functions as planned, the site creator should exit the Web site authoring program, and access the site with a browser as a user would do. To ensure maximum access by users, try to access the new site, going through all pages and links, with the two most commonly used browsers, Internet Explorer and Netscape Navigator. It is not uncommon to have problems with one of these browsers, but not with the other.

6. *Publish the site*. The Web site must be placed on a server for others to access it. This process is called uploading, and is done by electronically transferring the Web site files from the site creator's computer to the server. (Conversely, downloading refers to users saving information from a Web site to their personal computers.)

7. *Gather comments and revise*. Every Web page is, or should be, in a state of constant revision. Effective ongoing Web site maintenance depends in part on feedback from users. To encourage user feedback, the Web site creator should include a request for comments and suggestions with his or her e-mail address on the home page of the site.

Appropriately, the Web contains a large number of sites devoted to developing effective Web sites. The following basic suggestions for educators developing Web sites to explain their cooperative teaching were taken from http://www.wdvl.com/Authoring/Design/Usability/ (Nielsen, 1999).

1. Site design must be aimed at simplicity above all else, with as few distractions as possible and with very clear information and navigation symbols.

2. Do not tell users what you do not have. It is frustrating to the user. Do not release a partially finished Web site. Keep it under wraps until it has enough functionality to make sense to users. It is fine to have a small article about future plans or upcoming attractions, but the main entry to the site should focus on what a user can do here and now.

3. The home page is the flagship of the site and should therefore be designed differently from the remaining pages. The home page should have a larger logo and a more prominent placement of the school name. The immediate goal of any home page is to answer the questions, "Where am I?" and "What does this site do?" It should be obvious from the design what purpose the site would serve for a first-time visitor. For many site users, the most important function of a home page is to serve as the entry point to the site's navigation scheme. For example, a home page will list the top levels of a hierarchical directory. A home page should offer three features: a directory of the site's main content areas (navigation), a summary of the most important news or promotions, and a search feature.

4. Every page on a Web site should provide a single, consistent link to the home page. This might be placed in the upper-left corner of the page, which is also the preferred placement of the site name and logo. The important point is to make the home page into a landmark that is accessible in one click from any interior pages on the site, no matter how the user entered.

There are many wonderful resources, both in print books and on the Web, for developing Web sites. Before constructing a Web site for disseminating information about their cooperative teaching efforts, educators should access these resources. They then should spend some time browsing the Web, identifying education sites that are either especially good or especially poor, and determining what characteristics make a site effective. This practical perspective is invaluable as they develop their own Web site.

Presenting at Professional Meetings

Professional conferences range from small districtwide professional educator meetings to state, regional, national, and international conferences of such large groups as the International Reading Association, the National Council of Social Studies, the National Science Teachers Association, the International Council for Exceptional Children, the International Association for Cooperation in Education, the Association for Supervision and Curriculum Development, and so forth. Especially at the state or regional levels, these meetings can be effective outlets for information about cooperative teaching.

Typically professional organizations announce a "call for papers" several months to a year before the actual meeting. At the national and international level these announcements often are carried in the back of professional journals. State and regional conferences may send announcement fliers to universities and school districts, and even to all members in that state or region. A call for papers usually explains clearly what information is required for the presentation proposal to be considered. Sometimes professional meetings at the state level do not receive enough quality proposals, making these meetings an especially attractive option for those educators just moving into the professional dissemination phase of their programs. State and regional conferences often attract a prime audience of school practitioners in similar situations and thus can be useful in helping others implement innovative programs such as cooperative teaching.

In submitting a proposal, educators should remember the primary guideline proposal reviewers use: How appealing will this presentation be for the typical attendee at the meeting? For the most part, proposals that have catchy and timely titles and emphasize practical applications are best received.

At the presentation, the presenter should distribute a single-page outline of the content of the presentation. This handout enables audience members to follow along with the presentation without being overwhelmed by a multipage handout. Also, sometimes audience members who receive detailed multipage handouts simply read the handouts without listening to the presentation itself or take the extensive handout and leave. The single-page outline should contain the presenters' names, addresses, phone and fax numbers, and e-mail addresses, so that later they can be contacted for additional information.

One effective structure for educators making presentations about cooperative teaching is for them to first give a concise overview of the theory underlying cooperative teaching, explain some basic procedures for implementing cooperative teaching, and then show a videotape of cooperative teaching in action. Videotapes can illustrate the concepts and make the ideas come alive for audience members; it is often the images from a videotape that will stay with attendees as they return to their schools.

For maximum effectiveness, a 27-inch video display should be provided for every 18 to 20 participants. Alternatively, a large projection display could be used. If the video is longer than 10 to 12 minutes, the presenter should periodically take breaks or pauses to help the participants think through what they have seen up to that point.

Finally, conference participants will grasp the idea of cooperative teaching most completely if two presenters conduct the session on cooperative teaching. For example, one presenter might maintain primary responsibility for the major content delivery, while the second presenter organizes activities to support the learning of the content. Seeing the presenters practice cooperative teaching themselves helps the participants understand the principles. In addition, graphics, even those as simple as colored overhead transparencies, can add tremendously to the effectiveness of the presentation.

Writing for Professional Publication

Many educators have never given serious consideration to writing for publication in the professional journals in their fields. In colleges of education such professional activities are seen as part of the job of professors and serve as a partial basis for determinations such as tenure, promotion, and salary increases. Practicing educators in the schools, however, traditionally have received minimal support or encouragement for professional writing. This is unfortunate because these professionals possess a wealth of invaluable knowledge and information that goes untapped.

A number of professional journals in the field of education are aware of this situation and are actively seeking manuscripts from practitioners. As an example, the journal *TEACHING Exceptional Children* (TEC) published by the Council for Exceptional Children (Reston, VA) features articles about practical methods and materials for classroom use. TEC specifically has identified papers submitted from educators in the field as its highest priority. Upon request, TEC will help link practitioners in the field with university teacher educators who can help the practitioners prepare a manuscript. Similarly, the journal *Intervention in School and Clinic* published by PRO-ED (Austin, TX) has been most receptive to papers written by practitioners.

Unfortunately, these programs have had only limited success at eliciting professional writing from practitioners. The majority of articles in most professional education journals continue to be prepared by university professors in teacher education programs, even though the people who know best how schools function are those educators involved in public school operations on a full-time daily basis. Teachers, counselors, principals, and other school professionals all have an abundance of ideas and methods that could be shared productively with colleagues elsewhere. The school affiliation of an author of a journal article might even elicit an immediately receptive audience among other practitioners reading the journal because such readers would be likely to assume that the article is practical, not "ivory tower." Nevertheless, relatively few teachers write for professional journals.

When asked why this is the case, educators offer a variety of obstacles to professional writing that they either anticipate or have actually encountered. Some of the more common of these include time constraints, the complexity of the subject, and fear of writing (Barth, 1990).

In the discussion in Chapter 4 on time management, we identified many of the problems associated with the busy schedules of educators. Good professional writing is time consuming; many who do write discover that is difficult to find the time that writing requires. (Chapter 4 offered a number of practical suggestions for identifying blocks of usable time.)

Another obstacle for educators to professional writing is the increasing complexity of schools and their innovative practices. Interactions of professionals with each other and with students in effective innovative schools are complex and multileveled, and do not lend themselves easily to the logical analysis professional writing requires. The gap between the daily "illogical" reality of human interactions in the schools and the cold logic of the professional writing found in most journals is difficult for even the best writers to overcome.

A third reason many school practitioners hesitate to write for professional dissemination is that many perceive writing as an onerous and demanding task, one likely to result in criticism and rejection. This perception often is based on the experience of years of education in the schools during which most attempts at writing were returned covered in red ink. Such histories of criticism inevitably lead to people avoiding writing whenever possible and approaching it only with the greatest trepidation and reluctance.

Even given these realities, some educators are committed to professional writing. There are a number of reasons for this commitment. We have already discussed the idea that all contemporary educators carry professional debt due to their predecessors' teaching innovations. The only way in which that debt can be repaid is for educators to share their knowledge with others.

Most educators teach because they want to help students learn and grow. An innovative and creative educator might significantly affect a few dozen students directly over the course of a school year. However, if that same educator prepares a manuscript describing an innovative program that is published in a national journal, several thousand colleagues across the country may see it. Many of them might then use those strategies to better serve their students. Thus the educator's professional contributions can be magnified a thousandfold through dissemination via professional journals.

Another reason educators should write for professional publication is that writing helps educators to better understand their own work (Barth, 1990). To prepare a manuscript for publication, one must think through the entire program being described. In writing a paper describing cooperative teaching efforts, the author must analyze his or her program from beginning to end, from the initial establishment of agreed-upon philosophies of education to the final evaluation methods. Writing about one's educational efforts enhances the development of the educator as reflective practitioner. In one sense, whether the paper is ever published is irrelevant. The primary value of writing can come in helping authors think more clearly about their work.

Whether overtly acknowledged or not, publishing a paper describing one's program yields professional recognition. Most educators find it rewarding to have a paper that describes their program appear in a professional journal under their names. Once a paper is published, readers will call, e-mail or write to ask questions, give comments, and so forth. It is not unusual for an educator who has published a paper explaining some innovative program to find himself or herself identified as an expert and asked to present a staff development session on the topic. For most educators the idea of leaving one's mark on the professional landscape is appealing.

One of the early decisions an author must make is to determine an outlet. There are so many professional journals available that the choices can seem overwhelming. Perhaps the best way to begin is to start deliberately small. Smaller local and regional journals usually accept proportionately more of the manuscripts they receive than the national journals, so an author submitting to one of these starts off with a better chance of acceptance.

There are a number of excellent starting points for local and regional publishing opportunities about cooperative teaching (Criscuolo, 1987). For example, many school districts or state departments of education have a monthly bulletin that contains routine district announcements and so forth. Often the editors of these bulletins are receptive to a proposal for a column along the lines of an "Educator Exchange," wherein a guest author describes an exciting program such as cooperative teaching that is being implemented. Educators are usually interested in what their colleagues have to say, especially if it helps address practical problems they face daily. Local newspapers often are interested in the idea of a school-related column in the education section of the paper, written by local educators with a parent audience in mind. Such an outlet is a perfect vehicle to let parents (as well as colleagues) throughout the region learn about cooperative teaching. Such an article also can serve as a wonderful public relations tool for the schools.

Similarly, educators might submit a paper describing their cooperative teaching to a state education journal or newsletter. Many of these publications are eager to receive and publish papers that will be useful for their readerships. If the paper is not accepted, most editors will explain their analysis of the manuscript and even offer a second review upon revision.

Journals

After an author gains writing success in these ways, he or she may want to submit a paper to a more prestigious journal, perhaps one published by a professional organization on the regional or national level. Although these journals (especially at the national level) typically accept only a minority of submitted manuscripts, they can provide a high profile for dissemination. Outlets such as *Learning* magazine, published by Springhouse Corp. (Springhouse, PA), *Instructor* magazine by Scholastic Inc. (New York, NY), and the journals *Preventing School Failure* by Heldref Publications (Washington, DC), *Intervention in School and Clinic* by PRO-ED (Austin, TX), *Cooperative Learning* by International Association for Cooperation in Education (Santa Cruz, CA), and *TEACHING Exceptional Children* by the Council of Exceptional Children (Reston, VA), are especially interested in publishing how-to manuscripts submitted by practitioners. As suggested earlier, it can be useful for the author to link up with a university professor in teacher education, as many of these professors have experience in preparing manuscripts for national journals.

Both authors of this book have published in a variety of professional journals and currently are serving as journal editors or reviewers. As such, we have identified a number of ways practitioners can increase the likelihood of a paper describing a cooperative teaching effort being accepted by a journal.

First, manuscript size is a significant consideration. Papers approximately 10 double-spaced pages in length are optimal for many journals. Bigger usually is not better here. Some journals offer special theme issues, and themes targeting collaboration or collegiality are excellent opportunities to disseminate information about cooperative teaching. For some journals, including photographs increases the chance for acceptance. (A phone call or e-mail to the journal editor asking this and other questions before sending the manuscript is usually a good idea.)

It also is useful to read several recent issues of the journal being considered to learn about typical content and styles of papers published there. The paper should be directed toward the readers, not the editors. The use of jargon should be minimized, as should the excessive use of whatever buzzword is currently fashionable.

In addition, it is helpful to have an outside reader go through the paper before it is submitted. This reader should be one who will be very systematic. In fact, the reader who concludes the paper is "just perfect as is" probably has not read it very critically, and will not be of much help. One should deliberately seek out an honest appraisal from someone who will read it skeptically. Such colleagues can be hard to find and should be treasured. The prospective author should ask the reader to be especially attentive to the overall clarity, logic, organization, and presentation of the paper. It is easier to receive criticism from a friend than from the journal editors.

A useful strategy for authors is to keep a manuscript folder close at hand. Whenever the authors observe something potentially interesting in their cooperative teaching, they can jot it down and drop it in the folder. At some point a significant amount of information will have accumulated there. Then the cooperative educators (who have now become cooperative writers) can pull out the folder, shuffle the various papers into related groups or topics, arrange the topics in a logical order appropriate for the paper, and start writing, with much of the hard preliminary work already well underway.

For most writers the most difficult part is getting started. One strategy for many successful writers is to simply write something down and come back to it later, using it as a starting point, then repeatedly reviewing and revising it. The first draft of a paper should not be thought of as necessarily anything near the final version. Writing is a process, not a one-time event. When the writer accepts this, the writing becomes easier. In this process, the writer watches thoughts grow and become refined.

Finally, the prospective author should keep one inarguable point in mind. A paper that is never submitted will never be published. Simply by submitting a paper, one is automatically far ahead of most colleagues who will never reach that stage. Every professional in education who has been successful in publishing also has had many papers rejected. This is especially true in an author's first few attempts, when he or she is still learning how to publish his or her work.

Some of the most productive writers in education do not allow a manuscript to stay on their desk for more than 48 hours. When a manuscript is rejected, the author revises it in accordance with the editorial comments and resubmits it within 1 to 2 days of its receipt from the first journal. Persistence and endurance here truly do pay off, as success breeds success. After an author has had a first paper accepted, the second usually is easier, the third easier still, and so on. (For a more extensive discussion of professional dissemination through publication, see Hourcade and Anderson [1998].)

RESISTANCE TO CHANGE

Any educator engaged in dissemination activities as part of the role as change agent routinely will encounter individuals who are resistant to change. In their review of the literature, Knoster et al. (2000) noted that many have concluded that the individuals who are affected by the changes most directly will almost inevitably resist change in the schools. Most school professionals are invested in the status quo (as any other equivalent group would be). When first approached about cooperative teaching, many educators will deny any potential value, express reservations, or demonstrate passive resistance in other ways.

Such responses are understandable. At least at first, any change will result in additional work and effort for educators. Functions that have long been automatic for educators will require more consciousness, time, and energy. What individuals may be resisting is not the change per se but the inevitable uncertainty that accompanies change (Richardson & Margulis, 1981). Thus some resistance to change in the schools, especially to change that is as fundamental as cooperative teaching, is reasonable.

Resistance to change can be seen as a sign that those individuals are actively involved in and committed to the school and its programs. A passive educator who is willing to do anything and everything suggested to him or her, with no evidence of question or concern, is likely uncommitted to or cares little about anything, including the quality of educational services he or she delivers to students. Such individuals may be going through the motions to collect a paycheck. Educators evidencing resistance to cooperative teaching are at least involved in and thinking about how schools should function and are anticipating the possible impact of proposed innovations.

The following predictors can identify professionals in the schools who are most likely to resist cooperative teaching:

- educators who see no problems in the status quo

- educators who see individuals from outside his or her school as "know-nothing outsiders" who "don't know our situation here"

- educators who have been exposed to trendy innovation after trendy innovation over the past few years, none of which seemed to last

- educators who see the imposition of cooperative teaching as a top-down mandate

- educators who do not see themselves as active participants in the planning and development process

- educators who perceive no payoffs for changing

- educators who simply prefer working alone

As educators move into cooperative teaching, they often become eager to help their colleagues develop along similar lines. Sometimes in the process these educators serving as change agents will be hurt, confused, irritated, or rejected by the unexpected depth of the resistance to change they encounter from their colleagues. They then may respond in a number of unproductive ways, including becoming impatient and angry, proceeding only in a half-hearted way, getting into power struggles with their colleagues, or simply giving up. However, there are better ways of reacting to resistance.

RESPONDING TO RESISTANCE

Professionals in the areas of counseling (Egan, 1982; Richardson & Margulis, 1981) and business management (Grossman, 1974) have identified a number of ways that individuals can respond effectively to resistance to change. Several of these may be especially useful for educators who are successful in cooperative teaching seeking to disseminate this information to skeptical colleagues.

Recognize that some resistance is normal. It is important that resistors not be made to feel defensive about their concerns or objections about radical innovation in the schools. It is often useful for an educator to begin a workshop or presentation by explaining that it is likely that many attendees have concerns or reservations about the proposal and then soliciting comments that will allow these concerns to emerge. Alternatively, the workshop presenter may ask participants early on to identify possible barriers that their colleagues are likely to offer to the implementation of cooperative teaching. This allows participants to list the barriers and concerns they themselves feel without personally exposing themselves to risk and criticism. After the workshop presenter has listed these barriers on a large pad or overhead transparency, the attendees then might participate in a generalized, solution-focused problem-solving session in which responses to each barrier can be generated.

Personal anecdotes describing how the presenter felt similar objections at first can help to establish a sense of unity, a feeling that, "We all feel this way at first."

WORKSHOP PRESENTER: "When I first heard of cooperative teaching, my first thought was how impractical and unworkable it would be. Two educators present at the same time in the same classroom? How could that ever work? Wouldn't students be confused and distracted with two teachers talking at the same time? I also questioned . . . ." (goes on to list one or two other typical initial concerns)

Look for and find an area of agreement to start with. It is not unusual in the course of conducting a staff development session on cooperative teaching to have someone offer a strongly worded argument against its adoption. A useful perspective to keep in mind at this point is that people want to be right and will do almost anything to sustain this. One of the most effective ways of dealing with resistance is to find a point on which to initially agree with the resistor. After validating the individual on that point, one can then use that as a launching point for further discussion. Consider the following scenario (adapted from Richardson & Margulis, 1981).

WORKSHOP PRESENTER: "It is important to plan for cooperative teaching beforehand so that each educator knows his or her role, at least in general. This also will allow . . ."

WORKSHOP ATTENDEE (INTERRUPTING): "Excuse me, but my day is already packed and hectic from the moment I get to school until I leave late in the afternoon. There just is no time available for this planning you're talking about, at least not at my school."

At this point the presenter has several options. She can say that the issue of finding time will be covered later. However, this may sound as if the presenter is dodging the issue. The objector as well as other attendees are then likely to tune out everything until the time issue is finally addressed. The presenter also could say something along the lines of, "Everyone has time, you just have to look for it." However, this response denigrates and devalues both the objector and his point, as well as everyone else in the audience who heard the objector's comment and thought, "Yeah, me too."

The presenter knows from the experience of thousands of educators who are involved daily in cooperative teaching that time can be found to do the necessary planning. However, at this moment the objector cherishes his belief to the contrary. To respond effectively the presenter must find a way to agree with and support him.

PRESENTER: "You're right, many educators feel exactly the same way. The work-day for educators always seems to go from one task to another without a break. No good teacher I know seems to have much free time. So any changes we make cannot take away from the important work all of us are already doing."

Here the presenter is ensuring that the objector sees the two of them as being on the same side, agreeing on a very basic issue. She clearly is in agreement with the objector and his point, putting the two of them psychologically on the same side. This is further emphasized by the deliberate use of the word "we." Once that agreement is established, the presenter can then continue explaining how the issue of time can be approached.

Often when objections emerge they are rooted in problems from the past. This can form the basis for the next avenue the presenter might explore with the objector.

PRESENTER (CONTINUING): "I understand your school tried using collaborative consultation last year. Some of you may have felt you were in meetings all the time."

OBJECTOR: "That's exactly right! Meetings every day after school, it seemed like! Plus I ended up with the same problems and really no more help than before."

By establishing early agreement, the workshop presenter made it safe for the objector to open up a bit and explain why he felt as he did. She can now begin to understand some of the reasons underlying his objections and can avoid stepping on any psychological land mines. Although it may not fit her previously established workshop schedule, this might be a good time for the presenter to note the differences between cooperative teaching and other approaches. The presenter might use the objector's analysis of the previous approach to make the point even more directly, while simultaneously drawing him in almost as a temporary copresenter.

The presenter then should suggest a couple of the easier ways planning time for cooperative teaching can be arranged and might even offer specifically to sit down and help that individual conduct an analysis of time usage. A direct offer of help is difficult to turn down when in essence it already has been requested.

In initially establishing how she agrees with him, the presenter made it easier for the objector to open up to her, which then gave her a better idea of the underlying issues. Had she instead immediately suggested that there was plenty of time for planning if he just looked for it or managed his time better, she would have established an adversarial relationship, implying that he was lying, incompetent, or both. Instead, the two of them were established psychologically as working side by side. It is absolutely critical for presenters to keep in mind that dissemination efforts cannot become a contest with winners or losers, with some who are right and others who are wrong. Although one's natural reaction might be otherwise, the best way to deal with resistance is by first getting in agreement with resistors, rather than fighting them (Richardson & Margulis, 1981).

Accentuate the positives, and highlight any drawbacks in the most constructive way. People are attracted to things that seem beneficial. In disseminating information about cooperative teaching, presenters should highlight those aspects that are most appealing. For example, the characteristics of cooperative teaching that most educators find most desirable are the potential for working with another adult in the classroom and the sort of professional collaboration and assistance this provides. Dissemination efforts should highlight the inherent advantages of having a colleague simultaneously present to "bounce ideas off of."

Conversely, some educators fear that they will be asked to assume professional responsibilities in the context of cooperative teaching that they find difficult or impossible. Consider the following example.

PRESENTER: "Cooperative teaching takes place at the high school level in much the same way. One common arrangement is to have the high school content-area teacher, for example a biology teacher, paired with a special educator."

ATTENDEE: "I don't see how that could work, at least for me. By training I am a special educator and know very little about advanced biological concepts. I don't want to go home and study this stuff every night."

At this point the workshop presenter might be tempted to say something like, "Oh, you could learn that material." However, that does little to allay these concerns. At a recent workshop conducted by the senior author, just such a concern was raised. The presenter responded to the point as follows.

PRESENTER: "Let's remember the basic idea behind cooperative teaching. The idea is to have two educators who bring complementary sets of skills to the room. The biology teacher's skills are in the mastery of the content being taught. What sort of skills might a special educator bring to that or any other classroom?" (This last question was directed toward the workshop attendees at large.)

FIRST RESPONDENT: "The ability to alter materials?"

SECOND RESPONDENT: "Knowledge of academic survival or study skills?"

THIRD RESPONDENT: "Small group instructional strategies?"

PRESENTER (RECORDING THESE RESPONSES ON A CHART OR TRANSPARENCY): "Sure, all of these and many more. The idea is not for both educators to have all the same skills, because that is impossible. Cooperative teaching does not involve identical twin educators, because having the same set of skills twice does little good. Instead we're looking for a package of two different but complementary sets of skills. So the special educator would not be expected to come in with the same knowledge of biology that the biology teacher possesses, though she may well learn much of that over time. Instead, she must bring to that situation the specific unique instructional skills she possesses that can help all students succeed in that biology class."

This discussion was then immediately followed by a videotape of a similar arrangement at a high school. In that tape the educators involved noted that the strength of their cooperative teaching program is that it combines the knowledge the science teacher has with the knowledge of curricular alterations and instructional strategies that the special educator brings to the class. Rather than requiring twice the skills of either of the involved educators, cooperative teaching effectively combines and synthesizes the two discrete sets of teaching strengths into one comprehensive and powerful instructional package. In this way, what the special educator perceived as a shortcoming of cooperative teaching was recast as an advantage.

Express curiosity or interest. By expressing interest in a point raised in an objection, the presenter can learn more about the objection. Sometimes in verbalizing an objection, the individual will begin to withdraw parts of it, making a response easier to develop and structure. In any case, when the presenter shows interest in hearing more about the objection, the potential for the development of an adversarial relationship is minimized. In addition, the more information the presenter has about the objection, the more effectively she can then respond to it.

ATTENDEE: "I don't see how cooperative teaching could work at our school. Most of the teachers I've talked with don't seem to like the idea of another teacher in the classroom."

PRESENTER: "That's interesting. Tell me more about the kinds of things they said."

ATTENDEE: "Well, one teacher said she . . ."

Paraphrase the objection. Similarly to expressing curiosity or interest, when the presenter paraphrases the objection, the objector usually will go on to elaborate or modify the objection. This gives the presenter additional information from which to respond and ensures that the presenter clearly understands the concerns. The objector then also has the opportunity to either confirm that the objections were heard and understood correctly or, if not, to make the appropriate corrections or clarifications.

> ATTENDEE: "I think the parents of our students with special needs would object if they heard that we were no longer going to bring those kids to the resource room."
>
> PRESENTER: "So it's your sense that these parents would think that their children would no longer be receiving intensive intervention if the special educator instead came to the students' general education classroom."
>
> ATTENDEE: "Yes, that's exactly what they would say. They want the intensive services."

At this point the workshop presenter clearly understands the concern. With this understanding in place, the presenter can then respond appropriately.

Ask what it would take to convince the objector. A classic line from a car salesman is to ask a prospective buyer, "So what would it take to get you into this car today?" The reason it is a classic is that it is effective, and has resulted in many a car sale. It gives the salesman the information he needs to develop a response.

In talking with educators about cooperative teaching, it is sometimes useful to ask the equivalent question early in the workshop to get an initial idea of the directions in which the presentation might be redirected. This also is a useful question to ask when some sort of impasse apparently has been reached. Often the objector will explain exactly what is required to convince him or her. This gives the presenter the additional information to continue problem solving. Asking the question also takes the pressure off the presenter and puts some burden on the objector while keeping the discussion moving.

> ATTENDEE: "I'm sorry, but I just can't see cooperative teaching being accepted at our school."
>
> PRESENTER: "I understand that you have some reservations about this. What would it take to convince you that it might work?"
>
> ATTENDEE: "Well, at a minimum I would have to see some written assurance that there would be administrative support. Also, . . ."

Suggest the opposite. In presenting information about cooperative teaching, it is sometimes useful to argue for the opposite position. It can be an eye opener for attendees at a workshop to hear a presenter on cooperative teaching come out strongly advocating the status quo (albeit subtly exaggerating its problems). Such an approach almost automatically has the audience members quietly disagreeing with the idea that the status quo is good and instead coming to see that change is necessary. This receptive mindset then becomes fertile ground for quickly switching gears and advocating cooperative teaching.

PRESENTER (AT THE BEGINNING "I think it's clear to all of us that our present system
OF THE WORKSHOP):   of teachers working alone in their classrooms is
the ideal educational system. It allows us to best
meet the needs of every single student in our
schools and uses the unique skills each of us has
for the best advantage of all students."

CONCLUSIONS

Change is not so much about programs and materials as it is about individuals and their beliefs and actions. Change is lived in the first person (i.e., emotionally), and rationalized in the third person (i.e., intellectually). It is not effective to plan for change at a systems level. Instead, change facilitators must focus on the *people* affected by the change.

As Fullan (1993c) noted, most educators choose their profession from a sense of moral purpose. When student teachers were asked why they had chosen careers in education, the reported reason most frequently given was to make a difference in the lives of their students (Stiegelbauer, 1992). Unfortunately, the initial sense of moral purpose these educators bring to their work becomes lost in the day-to-day, mind-numbing repetition of most educational programs.

A promising solution to this sense of being professionally inconsequential (Farber, 1991) is a change in the role of school professionals, from maintainers of the educational status quo to that of change agents (Fullan, 1993c). This evolution in roles is inherent in the development and implementation of cooperative teaching. As educators come to see themselves as agents of change, they simultaneously will address two issues that are critical for many school professionals: the ability to have significant and substantive impact on student lives and the opportunity to overcome the sense of powerlessness that many experience in the present system.

The ability to have greater impact on student lives appeals directly to educators, who want to make a difference for students. For increasing numbers of students, the status quo is ineffective in helping them acquire the skills that are needed in a rapidly changing world. Educators who seek to change their educational programs through cooperative teaching typically report that by doing so they are able to respond more effectively to the diverse needs of students. Through cooperative teaching educators are able to bring to the classroom a combined instructional package more potent than that which a single educator possesses alone. This combination offers the potential for dramatic and substantial impact on the lives of students.

The second issue cooperative teaching addresses is that of overcoming the sense of powerlessness school professionals often experience. By facing the same experiences year after year, many educators come to see themselves as isolated components in a nonresponsive system. Through cooperative teaching educators have the opportunity to renew themselves and their instructional programs, using individualized feedback from another professional in the classroom to guide and facilitate their professional growth.

There are few occasions as exciting as moving into a newly remodeled home. Homeowners look around their new structure, bask in the glow of the obvious improvements, and compare it with their previous dingy and inadequate structure. Their excitement grows as they anticipate the substantial enhancements they will enjoy in their daily lives.

Cooperative teaching offers every educator the chance to reignite the initial spark of excitement felt when first beginning a career in education. That excitement will be contagious, spreading to students and colleagues alike. To paraphrase Barker (1993), the world (and the schools that reflect that world) is changing rapidly and dramatically. The educator frightened of and resistant to the inevitability of change will perceive only threats. The educator who is flexible, who welcomes change for the growth possibilities it presents, and who is eager to share with others instead will perceive opportunity.

> *When you give away some of the light from a candle by lighting*
> *another person's flame, there isn't any less light because you've given*
> *some away. There's more. When everybody grows, there isn't less*
> *of anybody. There's more of, and for, everybody.*
>
> —Kaleel Jamison

CHAPTER 10 ACTIVITY

Go Do It!

Together educators can ignite the spark that enlightens the environment for all. Now go do it!

Appendix: Sample Time Log

In constructing a time log to meet the unique needs of any educator, the first step is the identification of all the activities one engages in throughout the professional day. These obviously will vary from individual to individual. The following possibilities, though far from exhaustive, can serve as a starting point for the generation of one's own individualized list of typical daily activities in the school.

- individual professional planning

- directly teaching or working with students

- miscellaneous school duties (e.g., lunchroom duty, playground duty, bus duty)

- athletic coaching or club/activity advisement

- meetings with other school professionals

- meetings with parents

- student advisement and counseling

- miscellaneous paperwork (e.g., filling out report cards, attendance forms)

- monitoring students as they work independently (e.g., in cooperative learning activities, at independent seatwork assignments)

- evaluation of students (e.g., grading tests, calculating report card grades)

- changing the classroom's physical environment (e.g., changing bulletin boards, rearranging student desks or tables and chairs)

This list should be added to as appropriate to reflect the specific activities one typically engages in at the school. Each activity should be recorded in one of the activity columns in the Time Log at the end of the appendix.

The next step is to informally estimate how much time one spends in each activity. This might be done on an approximate percentage basis or in terms of hours or minutes per day.

After this initial estimate is completed, the next step is to record one's typical daily usage of time in the first column of the time log. For a period of 3 to 5 days, one should account for each 15-minute period of time throughout the school day. At the end of each day the total time spent in each activity should be calculated and perhaps converted to a percentage of the entire time available during the school day.

After 3 to 5 days of data collection, the educators should compare that data with the initial estimates. Typically there are significant discrepancies between how one perceives one's time is being spent at school and how it really is being spent. In such cases, is the situation a satisfactory one? Are changes necessary?

The reality for many educators is that additional time for cooperative teaching may not be able to be gained through lightened professional duties elsewhere. In such cases, the time necessary to plan and implement effective cooperative teaching must be secured from presently inefficiently used blocks of time.

Time Log

	Estimate	Day 1	Day 2	Day 3	Day 4	Day 5			Notes
8:00–8:15									
8:15–8:30									
8:30–8:45									
8:45–9:00									
9:00–9:15									
9:15–9:30									
9:30–9:45									
9:45–10:00									
10:00–10:15									
10:15–10:30									
10:30–10:45									
10:45–11:00									
11:00–11:15									
11:15–11:30									
11:30–11:45									
11:45–12:00									
12:00–12:15									
12:15–12:30									
12:30–12:45									
12:45–1:00									
1:00–1:15									
1:15–1:30									
1:30–1:45									
1:45–2:00									
2:00–2:15									
2:15–2:30									
2:30–2:45									
2:45–3:00									
3:00–3:15									
3:15–3:30									
3:30–3:45									
3:45–4:00									
4:00–4:15									
4:15–4:30									
4:30–4:45									
4:45–5:00									
Total									

References

Adams, G. R., & Schvaneveldt, J. S. (1985). *Understanding research methods*. New York: Longman.

Adams, L., & Cessna, K. (1991). Designing systems to facilitate collaboration: Collective wisdom from Colorado. *Preventing School Failure, 35*(4), 37–42.

Adams, L., & Cessna, K. (1993). Metaphors of the co-taught classroom. *Preventing School Failure, 37*(4), 28–31.

Adler, R. B., & Towne, N. (1996). *Looking out/looking in: Interpersonal communication*. Fort Worth, TX: Harcourt Brace.

Allen, C., & Kliot, L. A. (1982). Some guidance for the evaluation of dissemination activities. In G. Harrison & D. Z. Mirkes (Eds.), *Process to product* (pp. 131–158). Monmouth, OR: Western States Technical Assistance Resource.

Altman, I., & Taylor, D. A. (1973). *Social penetration: The development of interpersonal relationships*. New York: Holt, Rinehart & Winston.

Ambrose, D. (1987). *Managing complex change*. Pittsburgh, PA: Enterprise Group.

Arends, R. I. (1982). The meaning of administrative support. *Educational Administration Quarterly, 18*, 79–92.

Barker, J. A. (1992). *Future edge: Discovering the new paradigms of success*. New York: Morrow.

Barker, J. (1993). *Paradigm pioneers* [Videotape]. Burnsville, MN: Charthouse International Learning.

Barker, J. (1999). *Leadershift: Five lessons for leaders in the 21st century*. St. Paul, MN: Star Thrower.

Barr, R. D., & Parrett, W. H. (2001). *Hope fulfilled for at-risk and violent youth: K–12 programs that work*. Boston: Allyn & Bacon.

Barth, R. S. (1990). *Improving schools from within: Teachers, parents, and principals can make the difference*. San Francisco: Jossey-Bass.

Bartholomew, B., & Gardner, S. (1982). *Status of the American public school, 1980–1981*. Washington, DC: National Education Association.

Batten, M. (1991). *Recently recruited teachers: Their views and experiences of preservice education, professional development, and teaching*. Canberra, Australia: Department of Employment Education and Training.

Bauwens, J., & Hourcade, J. (1995). *Cooperative teaching: Rebuilding the schoolhouse for all students*. Austin, TX: PRO-ED.

Bauwens, J., & Hourcade, J. J. (1997). Cooperative teaching: Picture of possibilities. *Intervention in School and Clinic, 33*, 81–85, 89.

Bauwens, J., Hourcade, J., & Friend, M. (1989). Cooperative teaching: A model for general and special education integration. *Remedial and Special Education, 35*(4), 19–24.

Belasco, J. A. (1990). *Teaching the elephant to dance: The manager's guide to empowering change*. New York: Penguin Books.

Beninghof, A. M. (1996). Using a spectrum of staff development activities to support inclusion. *Journal of Staff Development, 17*(3), 12–15.

Bennis, W., & Biederman, P. W. (1997). *Organizing genius: The secrets of creative collaboration*. Reading, MA: Addison-Wesley.

Bloom, B. S., Engelhart, M. D., Frost, E. J., Hill, W. H., & Krathwohl, D. R. (1956). *Taxonomy of educational objectives. Handbook 1: Cognitive domain*. New York: McKay.

Bolton, R. (1979). *People skills: How to assert yourself, listen to others, and resolve conflicts*. Englewood Cliffs, NJ: Prentice Hall.

Brant, R. (1993). How restructuring applies to me. *Educational Leadership, 51*(2), 7.

Browder, D. (1983). Guidelines for inservice planning. *Exceptional Children, 49,* 300–307.

Bunch, G. (1997). From here to there: The passage of inclusion education. In G. Bunch & A. Valeo (Eds.), *Inclusion: Recent research* (pp. 9–20). Toronto, Ontario, Canada: Inclusion Press.

Cafolla, R., & Knee, R. (1996). Creating World Wide Web sites. *Learning and Leading with Technology, 24*(3), 6–9.

Cafolla, R., & Knee, R. (1996–1997). Creating World Wide Web sites: Part II—Implementing your site. *Learning and Leading with Technology, 24*(4), 36–39.

Cafolla, R., & Knee, R. (1997). Creating World Wide Web sites: Part III—Refining and maintaining the site. *Learning and Leading with Technology, 24*(5), 13–16.

California Department of Education. (1997). *Language census report for California public schools.* Sacramento: Educational Demographics Unit, California Department of Education.

Carnine, D. (1994). Introduction to the mini-series: Educational tools for diverse learners. *School Psychology Review, 32,* 341–350.

Case, A. D. (1992). The special education rescue: A case for systems thinking. *Educational Leadership, 50*(2), 32–34.

Chalfant, J. C., Pysh, M. V. D., & Moultrie, R. (1979). Teacher assistance teams: A model for within-building problem solving. *Learning Disability Quarterly, 2,* 85–96.

Conner, D. (1989). *Managing organizational change: Dangers and opportunities.* Atlanta, GA: Resources.

Coombs, C. (1987). The structure of conflict. *American Psychologist, 42,* 355–363.

Costa, A. L., & Garmston, R. J. (1985). Supervision for intelligent teaching. *Educational Leadership, 42,* 40–50.

Costa, A. L., & Garmston, R. J. (1999). *Cognitive coaching: A foundation for renaissance schools* (4th ed.). Highlands Ranch, CO: Center for Cognitive Coaching.

Covey, S. R. (1989). *The 7 habits of highly effective people.* New York: Simon & Schuster.

Cramer, F. (1998). *Collaboration: A success strategy for special educators.* Boston: Allyn & Bacon.

Criscuolo, N. P. (1987). Encouraging teachers to write for publication. *Teacher Education Quarterly, 14,* 102–107.

de Bono, E. (1986). *CORT thinking teacher's notes: Breadth* (2nd ed.). New York: Pergamon.

DeBoer, A. L., & Fister, S. L. (2001). *Working together through the seasons of change.* Salt Lake City, UT: DeBoer-Haller.

Dettmer, P., Thurston, L. P., & Dyck, N. (2002). *Consultation, collaboration, and teamwork for students with special needs* (4th ed.). Boston: Allyn & Bacon.

Dewey, J. (1916). *Essays in experimental logic.* New York: Macmillan.

Dixon, R., Carnine, D. W., & Kame'enui, E. J. (1992). *Curriculum guidelines for diverse learners* (Monograph). Eugene: University of Oregon, National Center to Improve the Tools of Educators.

Donaldson, G. (1993). Working smarter together. *Educational Leadership, 51*(2), 12–16.

Drawbaugh, C. C. (1984). *Time and its use: A self-management guide for teachers.* New York: Teachers College Press.

Education for All Handicapped Children Act of 1975, 20 U.S.C. § 1400 *et seq.*

Egan, G. (1982). *The skilled helper.* Belmont, CA: Wadsworth.

Elam, S., Rose, L., & Gallup, A. (1996, September). The 28th annual Phi Delta Kappa/Gallup poll. *Phi Delta Kappan, 78*(1), 41–59.

Elmore, R. F., Peterson, P. L., & McCarthey, S. J. (1996). *Restructuring the classroom: Teaching, learning, and school organization.* San Francisco: Jossey-Bass.

Farber, B. (1991). *Crisis in education.* San Francisco: Jossey-Bass.

Federal Register. (1977, August). (Vol. 42, pp. 42474–42515). Washington, DC: U.S. Government Printing Office.

Feiler, R., Heritage, M., & Gallimore, R. (2000). Teachers leading teachers. *Educational Leadership, 57*(7), 66–69.

Ferguson, M. (1987). *The Aquarian conspiracy*. Los Angeles: Tarcher.

Force-field analysis. (2000). [On-line]. Available: http://www.mindtools.com/forcefld.html

Friend, M. (2000). Myths and misunderstandings about professional collaboration. *Remedial and Special Education, 21*, 130–132.

Friend, M., & Bursuck, W. (1996). *Including students with special needs: A practical guide for classroom teachers*. Boston: Allyn & Bacon.

Friend, M., & Cook, L. (1992). *Interactions: Collaboration skills for school professionals*. New York: Longman.

Friend, M., Reising, M., & Cook, L. (1993). Co-teaching: An overview of the past, a glimpse at the present, and considerations for the future. *Preventing School Failure, 37*(4), 6–10.

Fullan, M. G. (1993a). *Change forces: Probing the depths of educational reform*. Bristol, PA: Falmer Press.

Fullan, M. G. (1993b). Innovation, reform, and restructuring strategies. In G. Cawelti (Ed.), *Challenges and achievements of American education: The 1993 ASCD yearbook* (pp. 116–133). Alexandria, VA: The Association for Supervision and Curriculum Development.

Fullan, M. G. (1993c). Why teachers must become change agents. *Educational Leadership, 51*, 12–17.

Fullan, M. G. (1997). Complexity of the change process. In M. Fullan (Ed.), *The challenge of school change* (pp. 33–56). Arlington Heights, IL: SkyLight.

Fullan, M. G. (2000). The three stories of educational reform. *Phi Delta Kappan, 81*, 8.

Fullan, M., & Hargreaves, A. (1991). *What's worth fighting for? Working together for your school*. Andover, MA: The Regional Laboratory for Educational Improvement of the Northeast and Islands.

Fullan, M. G., & Hargreaves, A. (1996). *What's worth fighting for in your school?* New York: Teachers College Press.

Garnett, K. (1996). *Thinking about inclusion and learning disabilities: A teacher's guide*. Reston, VA: Council for Exceptional Children.

Gates, W. (1999). *Business at the speed of thought*. New York: Warner.

Gay, G., & Lentini, M. (1994, April). *Communication resource use in a networked collaborative design environment*. Paper presented at the American Educational Research Association Conference, San Francisco. (ERIC Document Reproduction Service No. ED385226)

Geisert, P. G., & Futrell, K. (1995). *Teachers, computers, and curriculum: Microcomputers in the classroom* (2nd ed.). Boston: Allyn & Bacon.

Gibb, G. S., Ingram, C. F., Dyches, T. T., Allred, K. W., Egan, M. W., & Young, J. R. (1998). Developing and evaluating an inclusion program for junior high students with disabilities: A collaborative team approach. *B. C. Journal of Special Education, 21*(3), 33–44.

Goodlad, J. I., & Lovitt, T. C. (Eds.). (1993). *Integrating general and special education*. New York: Macmillan.

Goor, M. B., Schwenn, J. O., & Boyer, L. (1997). Preparing principals for leadership in special education. *Intervention in School and Clinic, 32*, 133–141.

Grossman, L. (1974). *The change agent*. New York: Amacom.

Hall, G. E., & Hord, S. M. (1984). *Change in the schools: Facilitating the process*. Albany: State University of New York Press.

Harris, K. C., Harvey, P., Garcia, L., Innes, D., Lynn, P., Munoz, D., Sexton, K., & Stoica, R. (1987). Meeting the needs of special high school students in regular education classrooms. *Teacher Education and Special Education, 10*, 143–152.

High poverty among young makes schools' job harder. (2000, September 27). *Education Week*, pp. 40–41.

Hord, S. M., Rutherford, W. L., Huling-Austin, L., & Hall, G. E. (1987). *Taking charge of change*. Alexandria, VA: Association for Supervision and Curriculum Development.

Hourcade, J., & Anderson, H. (1998). Writing for publication. In J. A. Malone, B. Atweh, & J. R. Northfield (Eds.), *Research and supervision in mathematics and science education* (pp. 277–298). Mahwah, NJ: Erlbaum.

Hourcade, J. J., & Bauwens, J. (1996). Cooperative teaching: Levels of involvement. *The Special Education Leadership Review, 33*(1), 57–64.

Idol, L. (1993). *Special educator's consultation handbook* (2nd ed.). Austin, TX: PRO-ED.

Idol, L., Paolucci-Whitcomb, P., & Nevin, A. (1986). *Collaborative consultation.* Austin, TX: PRO-ED.

Individuals with Disabilities Education Act Amendments of 1997, 20 U.S.C. § 1400 *et seq.*

International math and science study finds U.S. covers more in less depth. (1994, June 24). *Education Week,* p. 10.

Johnson, D. (1981). *Reaching out: Interpersonal effectiveness and self-actualization.* Englewood Cliffs, NJ: Prentice Hall.

Johnson, D. W. (1990). *Reaching out: Interpersonal effectiveness and self-actualization* (4th ed.). Englewood Cliffs, NJ: Prentice Hall.

Johnson, D. W. (2000). *Reaching out: Interpersonal effectiveness and self-actualization* (7th ed.). Boston: Allyn & Bacon.

Jonassen, D. H. (2000). *Computers as mindtools for schools: Engaging critical thinking* (2nd ed.). Upper Saddle River, NJ: Merrill.

Joyce, B. (1988). *Student achievement through staff development.* White Plains, NY: Longman.

Joyce, B., & Showers, B. (1995). *Student achievement through staff development: Fundamentals of school renewal* (2nd ed.). White Plains, NY: Longman.

Kagan, S. (1996). *Cooperative learning: Resources for teachers.* San Juan Capistrano, CA: Kagan.

Kame'enui, E. J., & Simmons, D. C. (1999). *Toward successful inclusion of students with disabilities: The architecture of instruction.* Reston, VA: Council for Exceptional Children.

Knackendoffel, E. A., Robinson, S. M., Deshler, D. D., & Schumaker, J. B. (1992). *Collaborative problem-solving.* Lawrence, KS: Edge Enterprises.

Knoster, T. (1993). *Reflections on inclusion at school and beyond.* Lewisburg, PA: Central Susquehanna Intermediate Unit.

Knoster, T. P., Villa, R. A., & Thousand, J. S. (2000). A framework for thinking about systems change. In R. A. Villa & J. S. Thousand (Eds.), *Restructuring for caring and effective education: Piecing the puzzle together* (2nd ed., pp. 93–128). Baltimore: Brookes.

Kochhar, C. A., West, L. L., & Taymans, J. M. (2000). *Successful inclusion.* Upper Saddle River, NJ: Merrill.

Kohn, A. (1999). *The schools our children deserve.* Boston: Houghton Mifflin.

Krug, S. E. (1992). Instructional leadership: A constructivist perspective. *Educational Administrative Quarterly, 28,* 430–433.

Kugelmass, J. W. (2000). Not made for defeat. *Educational Leadership, 57*(7), 25–28.

Lambert, L. (1998). How to build leadership capacity. *Educational Leadership, 55,* 17–19.

Larson, C. E., & LaFasto, F. M. (1989). *Team work: What must go right/what can go wrong.* Newbury Park, CA: Sage.

Leiner, B. M., Cerf, U. G., Clark, D. D., Kahn, R. E., Kleinrock, L., Lynch, D. L., et al. (2000). *A brief history of the Internet.* Retrieved April 23, 2002, from http://www.isoc.org/internet/history/brief.shtml Authors.

Little, J. W. (1981). *School success and staff development in urban desegregated schools: A summary of recently completed research.* Boulder, CO: Center for Action Research.

Longstreet, W. S., & Shane, H. G. (1993). *Curriculum for a new millennium.* Boston: Allyn & Bacon.

Lortie, D. (1975). *School teacher: A sociological study.* Chicago: University of Chicago Press.

Los Angeles County Office of Education. (n.d.). *Patti's teacher's corner: What is reciprocal teaching?* Retrieved February 12, 2002, from http://teams.lacoe.edu/documentation/classrooms/patti/2-3/teacher/resources/reciprocal.html

Louis, K., & Miles, M. (1990). *Improving the urban high school: What works and why.* New York: Teachers College Press.

Lovitt, T. C. (1993). Recurring issues in general and special education. In J. I. Goodlad & T. C. Lovitt (Eds.), *Integrating general and special education* (pp. 49–72). New York: Macmillan.

Mackenzie, R. A. (1972). *The time trap: How to get more done in less time.* New York: McGraw-Hill.

Maurer, R. (1991). *Managing conflict: Tactics for school administrators.* Boston: Allyn & Bacon.

McLaughlin, J. A., & McLaughlin, V. L. (1993). Program evaluation. In B. Billingsley (Ed.), *Program leadership for serving students with disabilities* (pp. 343–370). Richmond: Virginia Department of Education.

Meese, R. L. (2001). *Teaching learners with mild disabilities.* Stamford, CT: Wadsworth.

Mercer, William M., Inc. (n.d.). *Readiness quiz.* Retrieved January 22, 2002, from http://www.mercerweb.com/readiness_quiz/readiness_quiz.htm

Meyer, A., & Rose, D. H. (1998). *Learning to read in the computer age.* Cambridge, MA: Brookline.

Meyer, A., & Rose, D. H. (2000). Universal design for individual differences. *Educational Leadership, 58*(3), 39–44.

Minority groups to emerge as a majority in U.S. schools. (2000, September 27). *Education Week,* pp. 34–35.

Mixed needs of immigrants pose challenges for schools. (2000, September 27). *Education Week,* pp. 38–39.

Montgomery, J. K. (1990). Building administrative support for collaboration. In W. A. Secord (Ed.), *Best practices in school speech–language pathology* (pp. 75–79). San Antonio, TX: Psychological Corp.

Morimoto, K. (1973). Notes on the context for learning. *Harvard Educational Review, 10*(4), 245–257.

Morrison, G. R., Lowther, D. L., & DeMeulle, L. (1999). *Integrating computer technology into the classroom.* Upper Saddle River, NJ: Merrill.

Mueller, P. (1997). *A study of the roles, training needs, and support needs of Vermont's paraeducators.* Unpublished doctoral dissertation, University of Vermont.

Muncey, D. E., & McQuillan, P. J. (1993). Preliminary findings from a five-year study of the coalition of essential schools. *Phi Delta Kappan, 74,* 486–489.

Murphy, C. (1997). Finding time for faculties to study together. *Journal of Staff Development, 18*(3), 29–32.

National Board of Employment, Education and Training Schools Council. (1992). *Developing flexible strategies in the early years of schooling: Purposes and possibilities* (Project Paper No. 5). Canberra: Australian Government Publishing Service.

National Commission on Excellence in Education. (1983). *A nation at risk.* Washington, DC: U.S. Government Printing Office.

National Staff Development Council. (2000, December). *Learning to lead, leading to learn.* Retrieved February 14, 2002, from http://www.nsdc.org/library/leadstaff.html

Nielsen, J. (1999). Site design. In J. Nielsen, *Designing Web usability* (chap. 4). Indianapolis, IN: New Riders. Retrieved May 18, 2001, from http://wdvl.internet.com/Authoring/Design/Usability/

Newmann, F. M., & Wehlage, G. G. (1995). *Successful school restructuring.* Madison: Wisconsin Center for Educational Research.

Nias, J., Southworth, G., & Campbell, P. (1992). *Whole school curriculum development in the primary school.* Philadelphia: Falmer Press.

O'Hair, M. J., & Odell, S. J. (Eds.). (1995). *Educating teachers for leadership and change: Teacher education yearbook III.* Thousand Oaks, CA: Corwin.

O'Neil, J. (2000). Fads and fireflies: The difficulties of sustaining change. *Educational Leadership, 57*(7), 6–9.

O'Neill, J. (2000). Capturing an organization's oral history. *Educational Leadership, 57*(7), 63–65.

Orfield, G., Bachmeier, M., James, D. R., & Eitle, T. (1997). *Deepening segregation in American public schools.* Cambridge, MA: Harvard University.

Orkwis, R., & McLane, K. (1998). A curriculum every student can use: Design principles for student access. Reston, VA: ERIC Clearinghouse on Disabilities and Education/The Council for Exceptional Children.

Paulsen, M. F. (1995). An overview of CMC and the online classroom in distance education. In Z. L. Berge & M. Collins (Eds.), Computer-mediated communication and the online classroom in distance education (pp. 31–58). Cresskill, NJ: Hampton Press.

Pellicer, L. O., & Anderson, L. W. (1995). A handbook for teacher leaders. Thousand Oaks, CA: Corwin.

Project Forum. (1999, February). Issue: Linkage of the IEP to the general education curriculum. Quick Turn Around. Washington, DC: National Association of State Directors of Special Education.

Pugach, M. C., & Johnson, L. J. (1988). Peer collaboration. Teaching Exceptional Children, 20(3), 75–77.

Pugach, M. C., & Johnson, L. J. (1995). Collaborative practitioners, collaborative schools. Denver, CO: Love.

Pugach, M. C., & Johnson, L. J. (2002). Collaborative practitioners, collaborative schools (2nd ed.). Denver, CO: Love.

Rainforth, B., & England, J. (1997). Collaborations for inclusion. Education and Treatment of Children, 20, 85–104.

Raudsepp, E. (1990). Are you flexible enough to succeed? Working Woman, 15(10), 106–107.

Ray, T. M. (1998). Implementing the NCTM's standards through cognitive coaching. Teaching Children Mathematics, 4, 480–483.

Raywid, M. A. (1993). Finding time for collaboration. Educational Leadership, 51(1), 31–34.

Rehabilitation Act of 1973, 29 U.S.C. § 701 et seq.

Renyi, J. (1996). Teachers take charge of their learning: Transforming professional development for student success. Washington, DC: National Foundation for the Improvement of Education.

Richardson, J., & Margulis, J. (1981). The magic of rapport: How you can gain personal power in any situation. San Francisco: Harbor Putnam.

Robbins, P. (1991). How to plan and implement a peer coaching program. Alexandria, VA: Association for Supervision and Curriculum Development.

Roblyer, M. D., & Edwards, J. (2000). Integrating educational technology into teaching (2nd ed.). Upper Saddle River, NJ: Merrill.

Rosenholtz, S. (1989). Teachers' workplace: The social organization of schools. New York: Longman.

Rudduck, J. (1991). Innovation and change. Bristol, PA: Open University Press.

Sack, J. L. (2000, October 25). CEC report tracks "crisis" conditions in special education. Education Week, p. 15.

Sarason, S., Levine, M., Goldenberg, I. I., Cherlin, D., & Bennet, E. (1966). Psychology in community settings: Clinical, educational, vocational, and social aspects. New York: Wiley.

Scruggs, T. E., & Mastropieri, M. A. (1996). Teacher perceptions of mainstreaming/inclusion, 1958–1995: A research synthesis. Exceptional Children, 63, 59–74.

Shanker, A. (1989). Equity and excellence [Videotape]. Elmhurst, IL: North Central Regional Educational Laboratory.

Shulman, L. S. (1986). Paradigms and research programs in the study of teaching: A contemporary perspective. In M. C. Wittrock (Ed.), Handbook of research on teaching (3rd ed., pp. 3–36). New York: Macmillan.

Smith, D. D. (2001). Introduction to special education. Boston: Allyn & Bacon.

Smith, T. E. C., Polloway, E. A., Patton, J. R., & Dowdy, C. A. (2001). Teaching students with special needs in inclusive settings (3rd ed.). Boston: Allyn & Bacon.

Stainback, S., Stainback, W., & Ayres, B. (1996). Schools as inclusive communities. In W. Stainback & S. Stainback (Eds.), Controversial issues confronting special education: Divergent perspectives (2nd ed., pp. 29–43). Boston: Allyn & Bacon.

Stiegelbauer, S. (1992, March). Why we want to be teachers. Paper presented at the Annual Meeting of the American Educational Research Association, San Francisco.

Thorsen, C. (2003). Technology-based instructional models for classroom teachers. Boston: Allyn & Bacon.

Tindall, E. (1996). *Principal's role in fostering collaboration for students with special needs.* Unpublished doctoral dissertation, College of William and Mary, Williamsburg, VA.

Turnbull, H. R., & Turnbull, A. P. (2000). *Free appropriate public education.* Denver, CO: Love.

Udvari-Solner, A., & Keyes, M. W. (2000). Chronicles of administrative leadership toward inclusive reform. In R. A. Villa & J. S. Thousand (Eds.), *Restructuring for caring and effective education* (2nd ed., pp. 428–452). Baltimore: Brookes.

U.S. Census Bureau. (1998). *Poverty in the United States: 1998.* Washington, DC: Author

U.S. Department of Education. (1996). *Digest of education statistics, 1996.* Washington, DC: U.S. Government Printing Office.

U.S. Department of Education. (1998). *Twentieth annual report to Congress on the implementation of the Individuals with Disabilities Education Act.* Washington, DC: Author.

Vaughn, S., Moody, S. W., & Schumm, J. S. (1998). Broken promises: Reading instruction in the resource room. *Exceptional Children, 64,* 211–225.

Villa, R. A., & Thousand, J. S. (2000). Reflection: Closing the circle. In R. A. Villa & J. S. Thousand (Eds.), *Restructuring for caring and effective education* (2nd ed., p. 626). Baltimore: Brookes.

Villa, R. A., Thousand, J. S., Meyers, H., & Nevin, A. I. (1996). Teacher and administrator perceptions of heterogeneous education. *Exceptional Children, 63,* 29–45.

Walther-Thomas, C. S. (1997). Inclusion and teaming: Including all students in the mainstream. In T. S. Dickinson & T. O. Erb (Eds.), *We gain more than we give: Teaming in middle schools* (pp. 487–522). Columbus, OH: National Middle School Association.

Walther-Thomas, C., Korinek, L., McLaughlin, V. L., & Williams, B. T. (2000). *Collaboration for inclusive education: Developing successful programs.* Boston: Allyn & Bacon.

Watson, A., Buchanan, M., Huyman, H., & Seal, K. (1992). A laboratory school explores self-governance. *Educational Leadership, 49*(5), 57–60.

Weiderhold, C. (1991). *Cooperative learning and critical thinking: The question matrix.* San Juan Capistrano, CA: Resources for Teachers.

Weinstein, C. F., & Mayer, R. F. (1986). The teaching of learning strategies. In M. C. Wittrock (Ed.), *Handbook of research on teaching* (3rd ed., pp. 315–329). New York: Macmillan.

White, A. E., & White, L. L. (1992). A collaborative model for students with mild disabilities in middle schools. *Focus on Exceptional Children, 24*(9), 1–10.

Wiggins, G., & McTigue, J. (1998). *Understanding by design.* Alexandria, VA: Association for Supervision and Curriculum Development.

Young, K. (1994). *Constructing buildings, bridges, and minds.* Portsmouth, NH: Heinemann.

Zemelman, S., Daniels, H., & Hyde, A. (1998). *New standards for teaching and learning in America's schools* (2nd ed.). Portsmouth, NH: Heinemann.

Zionts, P. (1997). Inclusion: Chasing the impossible dream? Maybe. In P. Zionts (Ed.), *Inclusion strategies for students with learning and behavior disorders* (pp. 3–26). Austin, TX: PRO-ED.

Index

About the Authors

Jack J. Hourcade is a professor in the College of Education at Boise State University. He has published extensively regarding students with special needs and is an associate editor of the journal *TEACHING Exceptional Children*. In his free time he plays guitar and bass in several Boise bands.

Jeanne Bauwens is a private educational consultant and conducts school staff development programs in cooperative learning and cooperative teaching. In this work, she works with thousands of educators each year throughout the United States, Canada, and Australia, helping schools integrate collaboration in teaching and learning. When not professionally engaged she combs the beaches near her home on the Oregon coast.